THE BRIDE, THE SERPENT & THE SEED

THE BRIDE, THE SERPENT & THE SEED

BY
DENISE MOUNTENAY

Table of Contents

Dedication & Going Forward

This book is dedicated to The Bride of Christ so she will be knowledgeable and equipped to be a voice for the voiceless, now and in generations to come. This book is also dedicated to the Holy Spirit who inspired me, and also to my children in heaven. Much gratitude to Brett, the most generous man I know, for helping to send me to go to the nations with this message. Many thanks for Missionary/Teacher, Mr. Roy Wallace, the most angelic man I ever met; along with special thanks to Rev. Canon Ivor Ottrey, Charity, Pastor Greg, Sue, Kathy Fraser and Lisa Dodman too for all their help and input. Thank you to Shannon Moody of British Columbia, for her anointed drawings showing the spiritual pain of abortion to women. A big thank you to my wonderful husband Paul, and our remarkable son Shawn, and especially for all those Facebook and email friends who pray and support my work and Mission-**I could not have accomplished all this without your ongoing prayers and support!**

I love you, and Thank GOD for you!

Endorsements

I *have known Denise Mountenay, author and pro-life leader, since 1999. We met at a Pro-life Conference in Edmonton where she was among the distinguished speakers, and who boldly told us her story of rape, abortions and God's amazing grace and healing power. She has dedicated her life to this great cause.*

Furthermore, she was the first to create and register an organization called, "Canada Silent No More" collecting testimony declarations, encouraging women to speak out on the pain of abortion. She brings education and insight to the forefront of this controversial issue.

Her first book "Forgiven of Murder" a true story, was a national best seller and superb book. Now after 27 years of experience, research, public speaking around the world, as well as giving presentations to medical students and at the UN, she is an expert on this subject of abortion. I highly endorse this book to you, it is fantastic. Denise is an honest, courageous, compassionate, Christian woman who is a great leader in seeking protection for the unborn and their mothers. I commend her to you, trusting you will come to admire and support her, as I do.

Sincerely,
The Rev. Canon Ivor Ottrey Medicine Hat, Alberta, Canada
Monday, November 23, 2015 9:12 AM

Subject: Presentation at Central Alberta Christian High School
To Whom it Concerns:

Central Alberta Christian High School had the privilege of listening to Denise Mountenay recently. She came to speak to our students about the impact abortions have had on her life. She was an engaging speaker who was able to connect with our students. Denise opened up and told us all about her life and the challenges she faced through adolescence and beyond. Her personal experiences held our students' attention, and Denise was able to demonstrate the impact that family and societal influences played in her decision making process. We learned about the harm caused by abortions not only to the mother, but to the world around us.

Denise Mountenay is a dynamic speaker who has an important story to tell. Her message is clear, and her ability to communicate enables high school students to better understand the harm caused by abortions.

Veronica Den Oudsten
Central Alberta Christian High School
Career Counselor

Email "Thanks for the excellent presentation Denise. As one of the staff suggested
"That was the best pro-life presentation we've had ever". I too felt you made a strong connection to our students and your message was impactful."

Mr. Brandsma
Principal at Central Alberta Christian High School

Regarding Denise Mountenay:

I had the privilege of meeting Denise sometime in late 2015, as she approached me about sharing her story with the young people of our church. As I listened to God's grace in her life, I realized that this story needed to be told, not only among our young people, but also to our entire church family.

In January of 2016, I invited Denise to be our Sanctity of life speaker in all three of our worship services. Her presentation was compelling as she talked about a topic that most people are silent and indifferent to; the issue of the unborn child who is unable to speak on their own behalf and therefore are destroyed. As Denise herself shares her story, she has had three abortions and eventually experienced God's saving grace and forgiveness. Since then Denise has explored the huge ramifications that abortion has had, not only on the unborn, but also on the health of women; spiritually, emotionally, psychologically and physically.

Denise is an excellent communicator and she shares with wisdom, grace, tact and without condemnation. Her presentation in our church was positively received and many men and women responded to God's invitation regarding forgiveness and healing.

I would certainly recommend Denise as a speaker on this vital topic that is being dismissed as a society. I realized that 18% of all abortions are committed by evangelicals, and many of them are either ill-informed or live in silent shame.

I certainly share Denise's concern to make this message of God's grace known to our generation who are suffering in a culture espousing death. I believe that God has raised her up to challenge our generation with the compelling facts of what abortion is really all about.

Pastor Paul Vallee
Living Stones Church
Red Deer, Alberta, Canada

INTRODUCTION

My prayer:

*F*ather God, Creator of the heaven and earth, and every-thing in it, I pray that You will anoint these many words with Your wisdom, knowledge and understanding. I pray that eyes that have been blinded, will see what You see; and ears that are deaf, will be opened to hear what You are saying to Your Bride, the church today.

I pray Holy Spirit that You will prepare the hearts of the people who read this book to receive Your Word, to know Your Truth and follow Your Ways in regards to these issues so close to Your heart. I pray that the serpent and his lies, and evil schemes will be exposed for all to plainly see. I pray that in the Spirit we will cut off the dragon's head. For we wrestle not against flesh and blood, but against dark powers, principalities and spiritual wickedness in high places. Change minds, hearts and lives according to Your will, Lord.

May Your Seed Father God, no longer be crushed, poisoned, dismembered, exterminated or eliminated; but according to Your will, Father, May Your Seed, Your children, be fruitful and multiply For Your Kingdom on this earth.

Ultimately, I pray that You Father will be Glorified, Yeshua (Jesus) will be Blessed, Your Bride awakened, and children saved from the deceitfulness of the immoral, and rescued from the spirit of death so rampant in the earth today. As I blow my shofar, and sound this alarm, I pray that hearts would be stirred to make a difference, while there is still time for us to do so, in Yeshua's Holy Name. Amen.

My hope and prayer is that this book will uncover the false-hoods of the evil one, as well as teach you to know the truth about the greatest crime against humanity in our generation. Hoping that God will set you free to accomplish everything He has for your life on this planet earth. Ultimately, I believe that women and children will be saved as a result of this reality being told. May you be stirred up to be a voice, for those whose voice cannot be heard?

Chapter 1

The clock is ticking...

From the ancient book of *Genesis*, written over 3,500 years ago, to the last book in the New Testament Bible written over 2,000 years ago, the book of *Revelation*, we see the continuing saga of the seed of the serpent, and the seed of the woman engaged in a war.

According to the Word of God; the serpent, evolved from a fallen angel, Lucifer, who rebelled against God, creator of heaven and earth, better known as 'Satan'. An evil spiritual being who works to destroy the people, who are created in the image of God.

This book is not just about my journey and the revelations our Father in Heaven has given me. It is a message about discovering the truth, God's truth. It is correspondingly about being alerted to another father, the father of lies, and a murderer from the beginning-Satan. It is exposing his evil lies and strategies. We will examine the roots of horrible malicious deeds and spiritual deception.

This report will reveal some notable demonic connections, as well as certain events whereas we will survey their outcomes in our world today. I want to encourage you to arise to a new level of courage, boldness and justice as time is short.

This message is about our loving and Holy God, Creator of all things, and His heart on the most important gifts He gives to us. The gift of life, including eternal life through the sacrificial death and resurrection of His Son, Yeshua (Jesus), His love, mercy, grace, forgiveness of sins, purpose, provision and for most people, children. Children are a blessing and a hope for the future; they are the inheritance of the Lord. Children are the seed of life, generations to come to take dominion over the earth hopefully for God's Kingdom and His Glory. The things of this world, money, material goods, metal and wood will rust and fade away, but our children are left to go on, and their children and so on, until God's Judgment Day.

There are no accidents with God. He knew you before you were born. He knows us now, and He has a destiny, plan and purpose for every human being conceived in His image. We are a reflection of God. Your parents may not have 'planned' you being here, but God, the creator of the universe, did! Thank God your mother chose to let you live, when she could have had your life snuffed out on a whim, by a doctor, without any questions asked. In many nations this is condoned, tolerated and paid for by the government.

God gave us a free will; He did not create us as robots. We can choose to believe in His word, and obey Him, or we can choose to do things our way (be our own god) or we can worship other gods. However, remember that there are consequences to every choice we make. Sometimes consequences are passed down from generation to generation. It is up to us to choose life, to follow God, or to follow our own self-centered desires. The book of Deuteronomy talks about this in the Bible.

Yeshua/Jesus is a historical figure, He was conceived of the Holy Spirit, born of the virgin Mary, did many miracles, died on the cross and rose from the dead...He is alive. He talked about the divine law of sowing and reaping. We can sow seeds of love and kindness, self-control, forgiveness and life, and we can also sow seeds of anger, bitterness, resentments, greed, un-forgiveness and destruction as well as many things in between. *"No one can serve two masters; for either he will hate the one and love the other, or he will stand by and be devoted to the one and despise and be against the other. You cannot serve God and mammon (deceitful riches, money, possessions, or whatever is trusted in)."* Matt. 6:24 So, who is your boss, your spiritual father, what is your motive in life?

As Jesus/Yeshua said, *"Do not gather and heap up and store up for yourselves treasures on earth, where moth and rust and worm consume and destroy, and where thieves break through and steal. But gather and heap up and store for yourselves treasures in heaven, where neither moth nor rust nor worm consume and destroy, and where thieves do not break through and steal; For where your treasure is, there will your heart be also."* Matt. 6:19-21 What kind of treasures are you heaping up for eternity?

"But seek (aim at and strive after) first of all, His kingdom and His righteousness (His way of doing and being right), and then all these things taken together will be given you besides." Matt. 6:33

What do we reap when we are lethargic, apathetic/indifferent, complacent, self-centered and disobedient? The answer is in this book. The solution is unmistakable.

For some of us, this book will bring to light areas where we have missed the mark, where we have believed the lies, where we put our fears and our independent will, above God's ways and His will. My prayer is that the Holy Spirit will convict us of our shortcomings so we can change, turn around and begin to show others His way, truth and life. Know there is hope, and a new way of living.

There is a war raging on this planet every day, and in our hearts. It is a war between the forces of God's light, life and truth, and the forces of spiritual darkness, disobedience, rebellion and deception. God's mature soldiers are equipped to wipe out the enemy in the spiritual realm... wearing the full armour of God. God's armour consists of the helmet of salvation, the breastplate of righteousness, and the belt of truth. To complete this armour one must carry the offensive weapon and use it too, the sword of the Spirit, which is the Word of God. Know what the Bible says. Our feet are ready and prepared to go where He commands us to go, whether we feel like it, or not. We hear His voice; we obey His commands. He supplies all of our needs according to His riches and Glory sometimes it is through His Church, His people. If we see our brother or sister in need, God wants us to help them.

Can you recognize the times, that the days are evil?

Just watch the news. Uprisings of Muslim jihadists, globally who are randomly shooting unarmed, innocent people in train stations, hotels, concerts, stadiums and restaurants. They are suicide bombers who pray, kill and die because they are taught and believe that their god, "Allah" wants them to do this.

There are identity crisis problems in this age. Men having surgeries and taking hormones to try and look and act like women. Women taking steroids to look and act like men, same-sex marriages, abortions as a method of birth control, millions of baby girls aborted just because they are girls, and radical Islamist Muslims now beheading Christians and non-Muslims…Are we brave enough, ready and willing enough to proclaim God's word; His truth and His way in love, to a lost and corrupt world?

Truth is, God's mature militias wage war in the spirit praying against those forces of darkness who deceive this generation into believing many lies.

Know this, *"But the [Holy] Spirit distinctly and expressly declares that in latter times some will turn away from the faith, giving attention to deluding and seducing spirits and doctrines that demons teach, Through the hypocrisy and pretensions of liars whose consciences are seared (cauterized),"* 1Tim. 4:1, 2

Recently, a young "Christian" man posted on Facebook, that he was gay, a homosexual, and that was that. It was interesting how so many people praised him and shared how happy they were for him. However, I felt so sad to hear this. The same would apply if I knew a Christian who was committing adultery on his wife, or if I knew a Christian was addicted to pornography or drugs or dabbling in the occult or whatever. We can choose to repent, stop it, turn away and go the narrow road, God's way, or we can choose to go the worldly, sinful way. Sure, sin might feel good for a season, but in the end destruction comes. Read Romans chapter one, verses 26 to 32!

"But understand this, that in the last days will come (set in) perilous times of great stress and trouble [hard to deal with and hard to bear]. For people will be lovers of self and [utterly] self-centered, lovers of money and aroused by an inordinate [greedy] desire for wealth, proud and arrogant and contemptuous boasters. They will be abusive (blasphemous, scoffing), disobedient to parents, ungrateful, unholy and profane. [They will be] without natural [human] affection (callous and inhuman), relentless (admitting of no truce or appeasement); [they will be] slanderers (false accusers, troublemakers), intemperate and loose in morals and conduct, uncontrolled and fierce, haters of good. [They will be] treacherous [betrayers], rash, [and] inflated with self-conceit. [They will be] lovers of sensual pleasures and vain amusements more than and rather than lovers of God. For [although] they hold a form of piety (true religion), they deny and reject and are strangers to the power of it [their conduct belies the genuineness of their profession]. Avoid [all] such people [turn away from them]." 2Tim. 3:1-5

These six things the Lord hates, indeed, seven are an abomination to Him: "A proud look [the spirit that makes one overestimate himself and underestimate others], a lying tongue, and hands that shed innocent blood..." Ps. 120:2, 3. *"He who justifies the wicked and he who condemns the righteous (innocent) are both an abomination [exceedingly disgusting and hateful] to the Lord."* Prov. 17:15 This means that God hates those who are haughty, those who lie, and those abortion doctors who shed innocent blood. Also, those who justify abortion He sees as atrocious.

"And they have built the high places of Tophet, which is in the valley of the son of Hinnom, to burn their sons and

their daughters in the fire; which I commanded them not, neither came it into my heart." Jer. 7:31 Whether they burn children with chemicals, or dismember them in the womb, it is revolting to God.

"So when you see the appalling sacrilege [the abomination that astonishes and makes desolate], spoken of by the prophet Daniel, standing in the Holy Place-let the reader take notice and ponder and consider and heed" [*this*]-[*Dan. 9:27; 11:31; 12:11.*] Mat. 24:15

As we read above, an abomination includes the shedding of innocent blood; God hates it. They used to sacrifice children to the gods of Molech and Baal. Today children are still being sacrificed, but in a different way, to different gods. Today, pregnant women have the right to sacrifice their children's lives, without question. Many are pressured into it, but some are more concerned about losing their figure, missing out on some classes, or having to change careers. So they choose abortion as a violent form of birth control. Sadly, we tolerate, condone and even pay for the destruction of these children with our tax dollars and silence while in the sanctuary of their mother's womb.

God was not kidding, when He said, "My people perish for lack of knowledge." Hosea 4:6

Some babies die by chance, but no babies should die by choice. Many people today have been deceived by the refuge of lies. They say, "Well, 'it's her body, she can do what she wants with it." However, when a woman gets pregnant, she does not grow another head, and two sets of arms and legs, no, there is another unique person there from conception with his or her own DNA, and body. Some call themselves "pro-choice". Yes, we can choose what to wear, what to eat, who to hang out with and who to have sex with, however when it comes to the choice of having another human being killed, it should be unthinkable! The right to have your innocent child killed before birth is an abomination to God. It is more of a wrong, than a right! They also try to dehumanize the child in utero by calling him or her a "zygote, fetus or product of conception". Did you know the word "fetus" is Latin for "little one"?

However, these are only the first stages of human development, and we continue as children, adolescents, adults and seniors in the cycle of life.

For the last 40+ years, innocent children are being systematically killed by "doctors" for millions of dollars in profit. Chemical and invasive abortions abound. Surgically induced abortion forces the cervix open, then sharp instruments are pushed through the cervix and into the womb to crush and dismember the growing baby, while alive. A suction tube with curette is attached to cut, crush and suction out the child's body parts.

Even children know abortion is wrong, so why do so many adults think it is ok? Just recently, Planned Parenthood, ironically the largest abortion provider in the USA and probably globally was just exposed in the business of human trafficking! Yes, as about a dozen or so separately interviewed and secretly videotaped abortion doctors and clinic managers confessed and talked about the sale of aborted baby's corpses and body parts.

They are all over social media now, and some politicians are pushing to take away the funding of millions to these death camps. I really hope and pray that as this evil is brought to light that people will see the humanity of these aborted cadavers and be outraged enough to say and do something to stop the carnage. The tapes reveal how they carefully dismembered so as not to damage the body parts for sale, and how they sell the body parts, such as legs, heart, liver and brains for experiments and to cosmetic companies.

A Missouri Pathologist stated in a hidden camera interview on the documentary show 20/20, that he gets the fetus's for about $50.00 each, and sales them for a huge profit. *20/20* said that Jones told them he paid "just $50 plus overhead" for an average "specimen," but that "he charges an average of $250." In fact, by selling different body organs, Jones told *20/20* that he can make up to $2,500 on a single fetus.

Abortion causes the womb, (a perfect incubator where every human life grows and develops) to become a desolate, empty, desecrated place. Tragically, the uterine wall often gets ripped and scarred by fragments of tiny bones from the developing baby which get lodged into the uterine lining, often becoming painful scar tissue, causing a need for hysterectomies in young women, or infertility. The womb becomes a tomb. It becomes a death chamber for a defenseless little child. In God's eyes, it is murder, it is a crime scene.

I believe that this is the abomination that causes desolation that the prophet Daniel spoke about for us to really take notice and ponder in this generation.

Do you know that God also talks about children of the devil, in the Bible? Every day "children of the devil" are lying, stealing, destroying people and getting away with it. *"By this it is made clear who take their nature from God and are His children; and who take their nature from the devil and are His children: no one who does not practice righteousness [who does not conform to God's will in purpose, thought, and action] is of God; neither is anyone who does not love his brother (his fellow believer in Christ).* 1John 3:10

> *Jesus said that many will come in His name, but not be of Him. He warned us, "But take heed to yourselves and be on your guard, lest your hearts be overburdened and depressed (weighed down) with the giddiness and head-ache and nausea of self-indulgence, drunkenness, and worldly worries and cares pertaining to [the business of] this life, and [lest] that day come upon you suddenly like a trap or a noose; For it will come upon all who live upon the face of the entire earth. Keep awake then and watch at all times [be discreet, attentive, and ready], praying that you may have the full strength and ability and be accounted worthy to escape all these things [taken together] that will take place, and to stand in the presence of the Son of Man."* Luke 21:7-36

The notorious German Nazis spent lots of money and manpower to plot and fulfill the "final solution" in order to get rid of the "unwanted" Jews; in much of the same way abortion proponents and population controllers do it today. In many nations the enemy has, and continues to spend millions of dollars annually scheming to kill and annihilate "unwanted" children through birth control and legalizing abortions especially targeting Africa and South and Central America now, where abortions are still restrictive and illegal. They are working tirelessly to promote their lies, rhetoric, deception and agenda on websites, TV, radio, movies, literature and through UN agencies and programs.

Moreover, we are letting the enemy distort minds, with our money and our silence! Legal abortion is advertised and promoted as "safe" (without harm) and a woman's right to have her baby killed before birth. Horribly, abortion has become a socially acceptable form of birth control that is endorsed and encouraged by media, politicians, movie stars and teachers to teenagers and young women as a right...when it is actually a wrong.

Jesus told some people;

> *"If God were your Father, you would love Me and respect Me and welcome Me gladly, for I proceeded (came forth) from God [out of His very presence]. I did not even come on My own authority or of My own accord (as self-appointed); but He sent Me. Why do you misunderstand what I say? It is because you are unable to hear what I am saying. [You cannot bear to listen to My message; your ears are shut to My teaching.] You are of your father, the devil, and it is your will to practice the lusts and gratify the desires [which are characteristic] of your father. He was a murderer from the beginning and does not stand in the truth, because there is no truth in him. When he speaks a falsehood, he speaks*

*what is natural to him, for he is a liar [himself]
and the father of lies and of all that is false."*
John 8: 42-44

The good news is that if you were involved in an abortion(s), or were complacent or apathetic about it, or for whatever sins you have committed, you can simply with a genuine heart, ask God to forgive you. Stop trying to justify it, or deny it was a baby. Humble yourself, and submit to God. He wants to adopt us from the kingdom of darkness, into the Kingdom of Light. He loves you! Yeshua/Jesus Christ paid the penalty for all of our sins, even abortion. He became the sacrificial lamb for all those who believe, confess, turn from their wicked ways and follow Him. He gave His Life for you, so you could be free from the penalty of sin and live for Him, and have eternal life in Heaven. Have faith in God and His goodness and love towards you.

God wants to take our mess and turn it into a MESSAGE! His mercy and grace is amazing. He forgives all of our sins, IF we believe and change, along with the victory we have through our Lord and Saviour, Yeshua (Jesus' name in Hebrew). This is my journey.

Chapter 2

Life on Planet Earth

Sometimes our family heritage, upbringing, genetic make-up, traumatic events and where we've been, will influence and determine what we do and where we will go in life…Letting God take control, takes you on an adventure of a lifetime. Here is my personal story.

I grew up being indoctrinated on the theory of evolution in the public schools I attended as a child and young teenager. My Dad grew up in Nazi Germany and must have witnessed some horrible atrocities. He was indoctrinated to believe that we evolved from apes, and told there was no God. He was a hard core atheist. He told me that the Bible was full of fairy tales. My Mom believed there was a God, but never went to church or talked about Him, until near her end of life.

In my late twenties, I began to seek God. Wondering, if there really was a God? Who is God, which way to God?

So where did we come from? I remember saying out loud one day, while driving, "God, if you are real, prove it, come into my life and show me." And He began to open my eyes.

Looking at the big picture of the world, I realized that there has got to be a God, a reason and a purpose as to why we are all here on this little blue/green planet called 'Earth' out in the middle of a humungous universe.

When seriously contemplating the wonders of nature, plants, flowers, insects, animals and life, I realized that we could not have evolved from apes, as the secular/atheist books, artists and teachers taught us in school.

First of all, it is a scientific fact that only life begets life, and every living creature reproduces naturally after its own kind. Apple trees reproduce apple trees, elephants have baby elephants, giraffes, giraffes, monkeys, monkeys, whales, whales, ants, ants, birds, birds etc. and we people of all races, have beautiful baby human beings... Do you see what I mean?

There is not one fossil to demonstrate evolution from one kind of species to another kind. There is no evidence of any pre-human evolving into a human. As well, there are huge missing links between non-living things like sand and dirt as well as big missing links between plants and animals, and animals and people. More on debunking the theory of evolution later.

Watching the Discovery Channel and the Hubble Canvas on high definition is incredible...It is a vast universe, with zillions of stars and other planets, including unknown black holes, and matter and meteors and all kinds of gases and components...but not one ounce of life that they can discover.

It is peculiar that if one living cell was found on Mars... the media would exclaim LIFE on Mars...as big news, however, they totally deny the life and humanity of children in the womb. Selah.

The colours in the universe are brilliant and the artwork in the heavens are so spectacular to say the least. Yet, as far as scientists can tell, there is no other life, on any planet, no life around this galaxy, no signals from outer space, and no intelligent communications. Only the spiritual beings created by God, such as angels. Perhaps God does have life on other planets, but this I do not know.

For certain we know that there is this one amazing, radiant planet, we call 'earth' so full of life, and spinning miraculously, in our universe. It is just the perfect distance from the sun, the perfect gravity pull from the moon, the perfect amount of rains and water, oxygen and food to sustain animal, insect and human life.

Before I became a follower in Christ, I was seeking the supernatural. I dabbled with new age stuff like horoscopes, astrology, Tarot Cards and Ouija Boards…always flipping the cards, until I got the answers I wanted to see. I was seeking the supernatural, seeking GOD, seeking truth.

On checking out all the major world religions…I grasped the basics on what they taught and believed.

In time, I discovered that most religions have some good teachings, be kind and good to one another, be at peace, respect the environment etc. But, there were gaps and some pretty bizarre beliefs too. For example, I could not imagine that I was reincarnated from say a kangaroo or some other animal into me…or after I die I would mysteriously turn into a mouse or a cow or some other creature. I sure do not recall being anything or anyone else before now. Besides, we inherit our entire DNA from our parents, making each of us a unique individual.

Some say this religion is the way to God, some say that religion is the way to God. However, they all have different beliefs to get to heaven and the hereafter.

Mohammed started the Islamic religion about 600+ years **after** Jesus Christ/Yeshua was crucified and raised from the dead. Yet, Muslims teach their children and converts so many false dogmas that veer far from what the original Jewish Prophets and teachings of Jesus Christ. They have twisted and distorted most of the Old Testament and New Testament writings to their own imaginations, far from the truth.

Like they believe that it was Ishmael who was the favourite and chosen son of Abraham, and almost sacrificed on the altar, instead of Isaac, the promised son. They deny that Yeshua/Jesus Christ was crucified, and raised from the dead. They do not believe that He was the Son of God, or God in the flesh. Nonetheless, they say they believe He was a mighty Prophet of God, but sadly, they don't believe what He said.

Sure, many Muslims are wonderful, peaceful people. Muslims are taught it is ok for a man to have more than one wife...Mohammed himself thought it suitable to have 9 wives; but his followers are only permitted to have a maximum of 4 wives. Mohammed's first wife was a much older, rich woman, who helped to fund his new religious crusade.

He also thought it was ok for himself to marry a little girl when she was a meager six-year-old child, her name was Aisha. However, it is reported he didn't have intercourse with her, until she was nine years old! To me only a pedophile would do that to a little girl. What kind of man has a six-year-old WIFE? This is abhorrent and disgusting to me as a victim of child rape, myself. This is why I would never become a Muslim.

Many Muslim women are oppressed, and if caught in adultery only the woman gets stoned to death, not the man. In the docu-drama called, "The Stoning of Soraya," based on a true story, you see how she was framed by her abusive husband who wanted another younger wife, and by falsely accusing his wife of adultery, and having another man also lie for him, she had no defense. Soraya was buried in the hard earth with only her head protruding above the ground. Then her husband, two sons, and people in the community callously threw rocks and stones at her face and head, until she went unconscious, and was eventually stoned to death.

In Islam, Sharia law, it is the victim of rape who gets punished, if she reports it.

Sharia Law Punishes Raped Women, not the rapists!

On October 30, 2008, the United Nations condemned the stoning to death of Aisha Duhulowa, a 13-year-old girl who had been gang-raped and then sentenced to death by a Sharia court for fornication (Zina). She was screaming and begging for mercy, but when some family members attempted to intervene, shots were fired by the Islamic militia, and a baby was killed.

Local Sharia courts in Bangladesh regularly punish raped minor girls and women by flogging and beating them with shoes. Similar cases of punishing raped women are Mina v. the State, Bibi v. the State and Bahadur v. the State. Sharia courts in Pakistan have punished thousands of raped women by long term imprisonment. While the rapists go free to rape other girls and women!

This is outrageous! Plus, she needs at least four witnesses to prove he/they raped her. How ludicrous. This same Imam leader who many call a prophet of God, is followed by 1.6 billion Muslims today. He also killed and beheaded many people. It is a religion of violence according to the Quran and other books they adhere to. Go to: www.prophetofdoom.net for quotes and resources.

Not all Muslims are terrorists, thank God, but most terrorists are Muslims. They want to convert all the world into Islam, as they force people to convert in Africa and the Middle East. They are pushing their way down through Africa and into Europe at an alarming speed and some are maiming and killing thousands of Christians on the way. More on this later.

When I first read the book of Revelation, on the part about Christian martyrs, I wondered, who would want to kill Christians? We are the good guys, we feed the hungry, visit people in prisons, we build and run hospitals, we build schools and orphanages, we try to go after the bullies and keep the peace. We usually go where no others would dare go.

In the year 2015-16, several news reports on how radical, Muslims are torturing and beheading Christians in Nigeria, Kenya, Iraq, Iran and Syria etc. Hundreds, perhaps thousands of them? They are called, ISIS, and they are burning churches in Iraq, Syria, all over the Middle East. Notably, Israelis are targeted by suicide bombers, and Communists are tearing down crosses and persecuting Christians in North Korea, Cambodia and in China too.

Pray for boldness and courage to witness to Muslims so they can know the one true God, and be set free. I have led a few Muslim taxi drivers in New York City to the Lord. Guess I am really an evangelist at heart. The Muslims are multiplying and want to subdue the earth for Allah…and if current population trends continue, it is predicted that Muslims will outnumber Christians worldwide by 2070.

Most religions teach that if you are a "good person" and do good things or offer food to little statues/idols you will get to heaven. But, I have come to discover that we are not that good after all, and we also do and say many bad things during our lifetime on earth. You might be a really nice person, most of the time...but have you ever lied? Ever? Well, that would make you a liar. Have you ever stolen anything? Even something small, or more than once, cheated on your taxes, took something that wasn't yours? That would make you a thief. Have you ever used the Lord's name in vain? Have you ever looked at a man or woman with lust in your eyes? Then you have committed adultery in your heart. Did you have sex before marriage? That sin is called fornication. Have you ever hated anyone? Jesus said, if you hate someone, you are a murderer in your heart. Big or small it is our sins that separate us from a Holy God.

Truth is, we are all sinners. Or do you think you are a god?

One day at the age of 30, a Bell Telephone repairman in Toronto came to fix the phone in my little apartment. He was a 'born again' Christian. A friendly black man who gave me profound answers to my questions and comments about God.

When I learned that Jesus was a real historical figure, that He gave His life, a living sacrifice, was brutally beaten beyond human recognition and truly suffered and died to pay the penalty for all of my sins...that got my attention.

Sure, I was a nice person, always loved people, did good things, but was such a huge sinner! I was a drunkard, fornicator, adulteress and murderer just to name a few. I was headed for hell on a fast train; fortunately, I had not died in one of the three separate car accidents in my youth. I was kidnapped once by a biker when I was a teenager; thank God, no harm was done. Many times I could not remember how I drove home, drunk. Once I almost drowned in the ocean in Puerto Rico, so stoned on valium I could barely stand up as the waves kept knocking me down...and by the grace of God I survived many calamities; some people do not.

We all sin, and make mistakes…I don't care how nice you are, or what a great giving, loving person you are, you are a sinner too! We have all broken God's commandments; some of us struggle with stealing, lying, pride, gluttony, pornography, shame, anger, bitterness or gossip etc.

When I sincerely asked God to forgive me, for the sin of having my own children murdered by doctors, through abortion, I felt a huge release of guilt and shame! The difficult thing has been to forgive myself. Over time I have. When we do not forgive ourselves, then what we are really saying, is that what He did on the cross was not good enough for us.

When I surrendered my life to God in January of 1987, an amazing, phenomenal adventure began as I was adopted into the Kingdom of GOD, as His child, a daughter of the King of Kings. I was transformed from the kingdom of darkness into the Kingdom of Light. It is similar to a caterpillar, who was eating the food and lies of the world, then going into a cocoon with God's word and truth then marvelously changing into a butterfly. I became heaven bound, instead of earth bound. His mercy and grace are astounding. My favourite song is *Amazing Grace.*

By faith, I cried out to GOD to forgive me for all of my sins. By faith, I know He did. I believe in the Bible. I love the Torah, the Old Testament, where the Jewish prophets like Daniel, Zechariah, King David, Isaiah, Jeremiah and others prophesied about the Messiah to come. They said He would be born in Bethlehem, He would suffer and die too. "Who hath believed our report? and to whom is the arm of the LORD revealed? For he shall grow up before him as a tender plant, and as a root out of a dry ground: he hath no form nor comeliness; and when we shall see him, *there is* no beauty that we should desire him.

He is despised and rejected of men; a man of sorrows, and acquainted with grief: and we hid as it were *our* faces from him; he was despised, and we esteemed him not. Surely he hath borne our griefs, and carried our sorrows: yet we did esteem him stricken, smitten of God, and afflicted. But he *was* wounded for our transgressions, *he was* bruised for our iniquities: the chastisement of our peace *was* upon him; and with his stripes we are healed.

All we like sheep have gone astray; we have turned every one to his own way; and the LORD hath laid on him the iniquity of us all. He was oppressed, and he was afflicted, yet he opened not his mouth: he is brought as a lamb to the slaughter, and as a sheep before her shearers is dumb, so he opens not his mouth. He was taken from prison and from judgment: and who shall declare his generation? for he was cut off out of the land of the living: for the transgression of my people was he stricken.

And he made his grave with the wicked, and with the rich in his death; because he had done no violence, neither *was any* deceit in his mouth. Yet it pleased the LORD to bruise him; he hath put *him* to grief: when thou shalt make his soul an offering for sin, he shall see *his* seed, he shall prolong *his* days, and the pleasure of the LORD shall prosper in his hand. He shall see of the travail of his soul, *and* shall be satisfied: by his knowledge shall my righteous servant justify many; for he shall bear their iniquities. Therefore, will I divide him *a portion* with the great, and he shall divide the spoil with the strong; because he hath poured out his soul unto death: and he was numbered with the transgressors; and he bare the sin of many, and made intercession for the transgressors." Isaiah 53:1-12

The prophet Isaiah totally describes Jesus Christ beaten and crucified for the sins of mankind. Yes, but most Jewish people are still waiting for this to happen and for Him to come. As it is written, He was born of the Virgin Mary, died on the cross for our sins, was raised from the dead and is alive. He sent us believers the Holy Spirit to teach and guide us into all truth. As I began to read the Bible and learn of Him, His ways, truth and life, I determined to submit to God, resist temptation and follow Jesus.

God altered my life radically; I now wanted to please GOD more than myself. At first, I tried to justify smoking…Well, God made the tobacco, so I should be able to smoke it…then I heard the Holy Spirit say, "God also created mushrooms that can kill you, it doesn't mean you are to eat them." Then I read that scripture in 1 Corinthians 6:19 that says our body is the temple of the Holy Spirit, and we are not to pollute it. Well, smoking definitely was polluting my lungs…I had been a chain smoker for over 15 years, so I knew that God wanted me to quit smoking…and I'd rather please Him, more than me. With His help, I quit drinking, quit doing drugs, stopped fooling around and even quit smoking. Praise God, I have been clean and drug/smoke free since 1987!

My Dad had a rough life growing up in war torn Nazi Germany, (the town today is in Poland). He had an older brother, Ernst, and a twin sister, Gretel. Their father, a carpenter by trade and father of three, was forced to enlist in the German army and was never heard of or seen again. His body was never recovered.

While a young teen my dad hastily joined the Navy, so he wouldn't be forced into the SS Nazi Youth regime. The SS had a very bad reputation, he did not want to be mixed up with them. His older brother was a mechanic and enlisted to repair the big German tanks.

My father had spent some time in France, after the war, but the Germans were much disliked, especially in Europe. So he immigrated to this great nation of Canada, with hope for a better life. He was a hardworking man, a diesel mechanic. He had been wounded by shrapnel in his legs, during the Second World War. He had witnessed a lot of brutality and faced starvation several times. He also rescued one of his colleagues carrying him a long way to get medical attention. Yet, whenever I asked him, my father never wanted to talk about the war, his experiences as a teenager or young man.

His mother, brother and twin sister ran for their lives from the Russians and Poles. Their family lost everything, all their furniture, personal belongings, and their home to the Polish.

In about 1954 my dad travelled by ship across the huge Atlantic and arrived in Montreal, Quebec, Canada. He could not speak a word of English. He immigrated to Toronto, where he met my mother in a crowded Swiss/German Restaurant. They quickly fell in love. My father was an intelligent hard working and very handsome man who loved to read the Encyclopedia Britannica for hours, daily. He also had a mean temper which I witnessed now and then over the years.

My Mom arrived in Canada around 1956, as I recall. She was born in a very authentic traditional Swiss village in Switzerland called, Appenzell. Despite her rough childhood and teen years, my mom was a fun loving Swiss yodeler and entrepreneur. My mother was conceived and born out of wedlock on March 12, 1932. It was a miracle she survived as she only weighed a mere pound. My grandmother gave her up to be raised by her parents, strict Roman Catholics. Her grandparents lovingly nurtured and pampered my Mom, and they were very close. However, they would not allow her mother to marry her birth father, and she was forbidden to meet or know him either. Her birth father was heartbroken at the loss, and never married anyone. My great grandparents died when my mother was only 13 years old.

By then, my grandmother had married another man, and they had four daughters together. So my mom had to go live with her birth mother, step-father and 4 step-sisters who were very mean to her for a long time, she told me. Although difficult, my dearly beloved mom recounted her pain as an illegitimate child, being mocked and ridiculed. For years she had felt like an outcast, abandoned by her mother.

My mother once told me that she had a very bad experience at the age of about 13 or 14, when a Catholic Priest boldly initiated a sexual encounter with her...frightened and confused, she ran out of the church never to go back.

Back in the day, young couples would not be permitted to be alone together and would have chaperons. However, on her first date without a chaperon, and under the influence of a few glasses of wine, my mother gave in to the affectionate advances of a man. Soon she was pregnant with my half-sister.

There was much shame, guilt and condemnation as now my mom was pregnant out of wedlock herself. The guy who took advantage of her drove her to visit an abortionist/baby killer in 1953 who instructed her to come back when she began to go into labour, and he would take care of this unplanned pregnancy. He had a big oven in his kitchen and she understood that he would deliver the baby, and then throw her/him into the fire. He scared the kejeebies out of her. She was in her second or third trimester by then and she bolted out of there so fast, never to return.

Nevertheless, due to the shame, guilt, and condemnation of the local villagers and family, my mom decided to leave her firstborn daughter with her parents and siblings for a while and travel to Canada to start a new life. She tried to get my aunts to release my sister and have her come and live with us, but they were so attached to her, they refused to let her come. I thank God for my sister, who eventually moved to Canada to join us at the age of 16. She married an amazing hard working man, and has three beautiful children of her own. She is now the proud loving grandmother of eight grandchildren, so far. She was not planned, but she was never a mistake!

My mom had a gift for singing and yodeling. She became quite liberal in her thinking. Looking back, I can see her influence in my life, and how it took many turns and changes through the many dangers and trials I endured.

My parents were drawn to each other because they both spoke German and were lonely in this foreign country. My dad was very bright, handsome, and hardworking diesel mechanic. My mom was a woman with passion and personality exuberating lots of joy. My mother was beautiful and full of life. She informed me that I was conceived on Toronto Island, one hot spring day in April…and I was born on January 17th to Ruth and Johannes. They were new European immigrants, full of hope for a better life here in Canada, and quickly got jobs. They worked hard and began to integrate into the Canadian society and way of life. My mom was on the board for Children's Aid, she also had a heart for seniors and owned a nursing home for many years. One year she ran in local politics as a town counsellor.

My awesome little brother John was born when I was two years old. Boy was I jealous of this new babe in the family. However, it was great to have someone younger than me to tease, play and wrestle with. Today he is married with two beautiful daughters and two gorgeous grand-daughters, so far. He grew up to become an amazing police officer. My hat goes off to those people who go after the bad guys and who risk their lives for us and our communities.

Cops and Robbers: One night my brother and a fellow officer were pursuing two young guys that were doing 'home invasions' and driving around in a stolen jeep. There was a Canada wide warrant out for their arrest. It was after 3AM and my brother and the other officer boxed the jeep into a cul de sac and demanded they put their hands up and get out of the vehicle. They refused to surrender. The driver first tried to back out, but couldn't go anywhere as the police car was there, then he put the SUV into drive and hit my brother standing in front of the vehicle with his gun out. The jeep hit my brother on the corner of the driver's side and the gun immediately went off on impact. Only one shot was fired and it hit the driver in the neck and he died instantly.

My brother felt terrible that this young man died, but his conscience was clear that under the circumstances he had to protect himself. The mother of the teenager began suing everyone including my brother. They ended up charging my brother with manslaughter. He was an upstanding officer going after the bad guys, and now his whole life and career were on hold. John is such a kind, wonderful man, husband and father, we supported him 100%.

It was a beautiful sunny day when I drove my parents to the court to support my dearly loved brother. On the first day of the preliminary hearing, during the first recess, we were standing outside the courtroom in the hallway. My brother was standing right beside me, and in front of our mom; when suddenly a guy in black clothes and a bandana jumped my brother from behind and began thumping him on the back. It was like in slow motion...I remember thinking, 'what a jerk, what is he doing'. Then someone grabbed this guy and was also stabbed in the arm. My brother, began to fall to the floor in slow motion. It was surreal, he was dressed in a suit and tie, now covered in blood. Blood was squirting out of his neck in a stream...I kneeled beside him and said, "John you're going to be okay." Another man came beside me and I told him to put pressure on his neck...he did. I then ran down the halls screaming for someone to call 911, get an ambulance, he's bleeding. It seemed like forever for the paramedics to get there. When I ran back to John, his wife had his head in her lap on the floor...a huge pool of blood everywhere, and his eyes were closed, his face was white as a sheet and swollen. I ran over to my mom, who was across the hall, frantically she was calling out, "please don't hurt him, he is my only son." I grabbed her hands and said, "Mom, Lets Pray!" And with all of the authority I could muster, I prayed a declaration that John would live and not die. I rebuked that spirit of death and murder and commanded it off of him right then in Jesus Holy Name.

While waiting for the ambulance my mom began having shortness of breath and started to have chest pains so we had to call another ambulance for her. John's oldest daughter was there also, and due to the entire ordeal she started to have an asthma attack...our family occupied three rooms at the hospital that morning. I thank God that he survived that vicious attack, it was a miracle. They all did. Soon my brother and his family had 24-7 security as their lives were in danger. We were dealing with Muslims who had vengeance in their hearts and wanted him dead.

The next time we had to go back to court, a couple of months later to continue with the manslaughter trial, they assigned armed guards to protect us. They would not allow us to mix with the public. We had to spend recesses in another area. I prayed for mercy, favour and justice. John had dedicated his life to this work, and he was a nice guy, and a good clean cop. He didn't drink or smoke, he played hockey and was a great husband and father. After hearing all of the forensic and other evidence in court it was clear that John was indeed hit by the vehicle and he did nothing malicious or criminal in this incident. The judge dismissed the case…and I just cried. We went through this entire trauma; the shock of the death of the teenage lad, the vicious attempted murder on my brother's life, the effects on our whole family and it almost killed my Mom and Dad too. These people nearly killed John twice and all because he was trying to protect our communities from robbers and thieves. He continued working as a police officer until his retirement last year.

Chapter 3

My Childhood & Teen Pregnancy

From the age of nine to eleven, I was continually fighting high grade fevers and was losing a lot of weight fast...I remember the frequent times my dad would wrap me up in a bundle of blankets, the cold shivers and chills would race

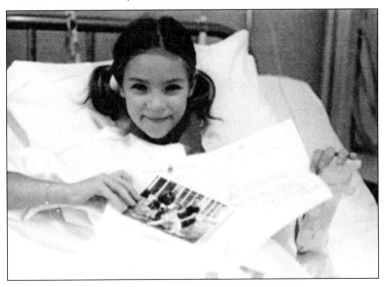

through my bones. He would then pick me up in his strong arms and carry me out to the car for another trip to the doctor's office or hospital in the middle of the night. They would pump me full of antibiotics and aspirins to bring down the fever, but it was only temporary. After weeks of these high fevers, they needed answers and whisked me off to The Princess Margaret Hospital in Toronto, a cancer hospital and they did a myriad of tests on my tiny, underweight body. After several weeks and more tests, they transferred me to The Sick Children's Hospital where I was poked and prodded for months. High doses of penicillin and intravenous needles along with tubes and more needles were taking their toll on my little fragile arms and hands. They were so swollen from the IV and needles; I could hardly bear it any longer-when would this end?

Doctors concluded that I was dying, they didn't know exactly why, and told my parents I only had about six months to live. There was nothing else they could do.

I recall feeling some pain, the chills of fever, but I was a pretty happy and content child, very independent and had no fear. My Mom brought me the cutest dolls and even my own radio. I just loved listening and singing to music. In the middle of the night I would get these hunger pangs and sneak into the hospital kitchen on my floor and fix myself some delicious toast with honey. Years later, my mom-not a religious woman, confided to me that she had prayed to God for my life.

There was a female doctor who would not give up, she kept trying different tests and procedures and ultimately they discovered a tumor in my lung as big as a tennis ball. They 'accidentally' ruptured it while doing a bronchial scope down my throat and into my lungs. It eventually drained, the tumor disappeared, the fevers stopped. I was healed!

At the age of eleven, I wrote an essay called, "My Dream" and it was about how I wanted to be a lady lawyer when I grew up and I remember using the word, "jurisprudence" and how important that is in law. While I was in hospital, my mom sent a copy of my speech to Rt. Hon. John Diefenbaker, former Prime Minister of Canada. We became pen pals, and soon he invited us to come and visit him in our capital city of Ottawa. He called me his friend, gave us a personal tour of the Parliament Buildings, and invited the media to come and do a story. Well, that was the first door God opened for this little girl to meet a dignitary. It was such an honour to meet him and so special to see our nation's capital with him.

One horrifying night, when I was only 13 years old, I was having a sleep over at a girlfriend's house, which changed my life; I was defiled. Her parents owned a gas station and it was fun pumping gas and cleaning the windshields; we laughed and giggled for hours. Later that night her older brother, who was in his twenties, entered the bedroom and he put one hand over my mouth, and then forcibly raped me. I was shocked and paralyzed. He robbed my purity, self-esteem and dignity! I wept quietly, terrified that he would come back into the room if he heard me. I never told anyone about this tragedy until many years later. Like many young children, I had been violated; my innocence and virginity were stolen.

Immediately after the rape, at the age of 13, I began to smoke, drink and take drugs. It was a way to escape the disgrace of rape. Another thing that influenced my life negatively was the 60's and 70's sexual revolution. It was quite acceptable in those days to do these things, and with a very broad-minded European mother who never chastised me for it either. When I was about 30, I finally told my mom about the rape. She warned me not to report it to police, as the rapist was probably married with children now, and this could ruin his reputation. So I let it go, not really thinking about it. Sad that it didn't seem to matter to her as to how badly it had affected my life, and future.

Later, in my forties and living in another province I was getting obscene phone calls, and reported that to police. Talking to the officer, and in conversation, I confided that I had been raped at the age of 13. He asked if I ever reported it, and I told him "No". He said this is the reason why these guys keep raping children and young teenagers and getting away with it. Because very few people ever report it, due to fear, shame and often the perpetrators are relatives or friends of family. As well, many times the people they confide in, do not believe them. So the majority of pedophiles and rapists are never made accountable for their terrible degrading deeds against women and children, and they do it over and over again sexually abusing more young people.

Many years after the incident, I found the courage to give a video-taped statement of this rape to police. It was very upsetting as I cried in anguish recalling that awful event and reliving the shame and defilement I felt. As expected, the rapist lied and denied his actions, when interrogated by police; otherwise he would have gone to jail. The officer doing the investigation said that his sister, my friend was so upset during his questioning with her that she just cried and could barely talk. He thought that perhaps Tim had violated her also, she seemed too terrified to say anything. It became Tim's word against mine, and with no physical evidence after all these years the case was dropped. I am glad that I finally reported it to police, now the pervert knew that I did not forget, and that I tried to make him accountable. I wanted this on record, just in case he has done this to other girls, or ever attempted to again in the future. It is now between him and God. I have forgiven him and pray he has changed.

When I speak in high schools, I encourage youth and young adults to report any inappropriate touching or sexual abuse by others. Please tell someone if anyone has ever raped or touched you too. Whatsoever is hidden, shall be revealed. Perpetrators and pedophiles need to be exposed and stopped. They always seem to go after the young and the weak. Do you realize that my story is quite typical? Studies show that about one in five girls are sexually assaulted, and many never tell anyone because of the shame, guilt and fear that the predator will come back to attack them again.

Pregnant at 16, with Jennifer

Jerry was the first love of my life. He was an incredibly good looking man in his early twenties, I adored him and was totally infatuated with him. We drank and laughed and he carried me up into his bedroom more than once where he had an old double bed and lots of blankets. A few months later he broke my heart when he told me he wanted to break off with me and go back with his former girlfriend. I was devastated, crushed.

My mom thought it would be good for me to get away, and fly to Switzerland and stay with my Aunt Maria, her husband and my grandfather who owned a restaurant there. I could work, make a few Swiss Francs as a waitress, and learn how to speak German. My aunt was about seven months pregnant with her first child, Markus at the time.

Soon after I arrived, I started to feel nauseous in the mornings and was vomiting. My aunt insisted I go to the doctor for a checkup. He took some tests and then told me I was going to have a "baby". My first reaction was shock, and fear as I took a lonely walk up the mountain, followed by awe. After a good cry, I thought, "hey, I can do this!" I am fairly intelligent, independent and young.

I began to make secret plans to keep my baby, work as long as I could work and be a mom. I even began to steal a few baby outfits from my aunt, thinking she would not notice this little hat, that little outfit, or those cute adorable tiny booties missing.

Then one day I was riding my grandfather's moped, and came around a very sharp curve and hit a van, head on. I flew up into the windshield and right down to the ground. The moped was a right off. Yet, without a helmet, I did not even have a scratch! In the back of my mind, I wondered if I would have a miscarriage. No, I and the baby were fine.

Feeling horrible that I had ruined my grandfathers moped, and he had no insurance on it, I called my mom back home crying hysterically. I told her I was fine, but my hormones were going 100 miles an hour. She flew over the next day.

Eventually, I got the courage to tell my Mom that I was pregnant…I knew she would be disappointed. Mom's advice to me was, "Denise, love, you are so young, why don't you come back to Canada with me and you can just have this 'operation' and forget about all this, and go on with your life," she exhorted.

So I rationalized that since it was okay to get 'un-pregnant' with my mom, my boyfriend, the doctor and the government, then it must be okay. Nothing was ever explained to me about fetal development, or what an abortion really is, or what it would do to my baby. There were no questions asked, it was far too easy. Jerry, the father of this child, went into total denial when I told him he got me pregnant. Suddenly, he had a "prostate" problem…I wondered, what's a prostate? He didn't want anything to do with me anymore. The appointment was made by my mom, where I went into our local hospital and a Jewish Obstetrician/Gynecologist abruptly ended the life of my first child. I just tried to forget about this pregnancy, and this first love, and go get on with my life as my mother urged.

Resembling many young, disillusioned women, I began looking for love in all the wrong places like in bars and at parties. You see, deep down I thought that no 'nice guy' would ever want to marry me now, because I was not a virgin anymore, and had an abortion too. I felt dirty and used, I felt like I deserved the bad guys. I went on the birth control pill…but soon I started to bloat, eat like a horse and gained weight… the pill was not agreeing with me. I had bad side effects, so I stopped popping those synthetic steroids. I began to drink heavily and do more drugs. I was not a Christian, did not know God or grow up in a Christian family… but was I much different from most teenagers in the seventies or today? I cannot think of one person I knew back then, who went to church, or called themselves a Christian.

Pregnant with Daniel

The doctor suggested I have an Inter-Uterine Device (IUD) a copper T, which he inserted deep into my womb…, but it was so painful, I almost fell off the table. My body began to naturally reject this foreign object. After some time, I got an infection, and landed in a hospital with terrible abdominal pains and had to have the IUD removed. The Pill gave me bad side effects.

Fast forward ten years, I was still looking for love in all the wrong places. By now I had worked for a lawyer, sold cars and even got my license and sold Real Estate for a couple of years until interest rates went sky high. Then I landed a great job, selling multiple lines of insurance (auto, home, commercial, travel and life), a new career, where I was making good money. I loved my job, loved meeting people, and was doing very well in this field. I even won several awards too...Yahoo!

I had been dating Jim, a computer expert/entrepreneur for some time. We had a good time together. He had his own house, was very successful, but he only wanted an intimate, casual relationship, nothing serious. I really wanted more, to get married and settle down. We broke up.

Soon after this break up, I met a really nice, handsome doctor at a Tennis Camp in northern Ontario, and we had a whirlwind romance. I thought this was it. My parents were so proud and happy I was seeing this Medical Doctor, (an ear, nose and throat specialist). Within three weeks, he asked me to come and live with him in his beautiful home, in St. Catherine's, so I quickly gave notice to move out of my apartment. I took a leave of absence from my successful insurance career and moved right in with him. He got me a beautiful big diamond ring, and as soon as his divorce came through he wanted to marry me.

I was so thrilled and happy; finally, a man to love forever! He was everything any woman would ever want in a man, in a husband, in a father for her children.

Then suddenly, I realized that I had missed two periods, so I went for a check-up. The doctor took a urine sample and told me I was pregnant. Now I was 26, still single, and it was a little complicated. When I got the calendar out, I realized that Glen, the doctor, could not have been the father. So, I went to see Jim (computer guy-changing names to protect the guilty) to tell him I was pregnant, and give him the news that he was the father.

Well, he immediately went into a fit of rage. He shouted that I "better have an abortion!" He said that I better leave and he never wanted to see me again. He began yelling and screaming at me to get out of his house. I was crying just broken, and left in tears.

45

I called my Mom to explain the dilemma, and she said, "Denise, you better have an abortion, or Glen will never see you again." She warned that I could not fool him as he was a doctor and I better just go and get this done quick.

My Jewish doctor in Toronto informed me that I was about 8-9 weeks pregnant. So I asked him, "What is developed, what is there?" He took a pen and blank piece of paper and put a dot on the page, and said, "It's just a clump of tissue, nothing…" Of course I believed him, he was the doctor! But years later I learned that he totally lied to me! Is it ok for doctors to lie and misinform their patients? Mine did, and many do according to dozens of women I have talked to over the years. More on this later.

Unfortunately, I believed my doctor, and was deceived again. Like most young women, I too was pressured to abort my children by my parents and/or the boyfriend/husband. There was never a medical necessity-these were healthy children and I was a healthy pregnant woman. And for the record, if abortion was illegal, I would never have had an abortion, and my children would have the pleasure of being alive today.

This time I was told to go to an abortion clinic, as it would be done faster this way. They made an appointment for me to go to a Buffalo, New York abortion clinic. I was still never given any information about what an abortion really is, or ever given any other options like parenting or adoption choices. Never told what an abortion would do to my baby. Abortion staff told me it was a "safe" procedure and no big deal. In reality I was just another number. The reception area was full of young women delving into secular-humanist feminist magazines, not making eye contact with one another, no talking, or thinking about why we were really there. I was asked to fill out some medical questions on a clip board, asking if I had any allergies, and the receptionist asked if I knew why I was there...that was it. No information, and no informed consent! Then I was told to put on a gown, and was led down a long corridor. It was like being on a conveyor belt. I was then led to another waiting room where I was offered two Tylenols. I asked the nurse for "two bottles".

I now know why they had us go down a very long corridor… they sure would not want the women in the reception area hearing the screams of pain coming from the women going through the procedure. It was the most horrifying experience in my life. Feet in stirrups, I was unable to move. It actually felt like I was being raped again. Searing pain, like a knife ripping through my abdomen I cried, and begged him to stop… he would not. I was wide awake. The pain was excruciating! A nurse squeezed my hand and held me down, while I pleaded with the abortionist to stop, telling them I changed my mind… the abortion doctor would not stop… I was trapped.

Immediately after he was done, I curled up into a fetal position and went into some kind of shock. This may have been legal, but it was no "safe" procedure. Soon afterward, I got an infection, and had to go to the hospital for treatment.

Of course I never told my dreamy new fiancé doctor about the ordeal. I began drinking more. Not long after the abortion, he broke up with me, as if he knew. I ended up with a damaged cervix and badly scarred uterus/womb from the abortions. For months I went into a deep depression, and isolated myself from family and friends. I couldn't even work. I just wanted to die. I began to self-destruct by medicating myself with more drugs and alcohol.

Pregnant with Rebecca*:*

Months later an old girlfriend convinced me to go out bar hopping with her again. Wanting affection, I met a handsome young man, and had a one-night stand. He did not want to wear a condom, and he took advantage of my inebriation, and I got pregnant a third time.

However, because I did not even know the father's last name, and because I was so filled with shame, and still unawares of the truth, I rationalized that I had to have another abortion, but never in an abortion mill again, as that was so traumatic. So I quickly made an appointment to have this pregnancy (baby's life) terminated in a hospital, under general anesthesia. It was too easy, it was totally legal, and like most abortions, had become a form of birth control. There was never a "medical necessity". These were all fully paid for by your tax dollars! No other options, or alternatives were given to me, ever, no questions asked and no information on the humanity of my babies.

Where else can you book an appointment with a Surgeon and tell him what you want, because it's your body? But with the abortion operations, just a phone call and in days you can go through the motions uninformed and ignorant, and make the biggest mistakes of your life.

It wasn't until many years later while reading my sister-in-law's book on *Pregnancy & Childbirth*, that I learned about fetal development, discovering the realities of our DNA, and how my children actually had beating hearts, by three weeks, arms, legs, fingers and toes by 8 weeks! Abortion killed my children.

I sure miss my girls and my other sons. I really should have born five children, instead of one. I should be a grandmother by now! My heart breaks for the losses and the brutal deaths of Jennifer, Daniel and Rebecca. I also believe that as a result of the internal injuries to my cervix and uterus, I had a miscarriage at the age of 35, whom I named Tyler. Who would these children of mine, have become? What would they be doing to bless our world today? How much love I could have given to them? Satan had my children killed, by blood thirsty butchers, who make millions in profit doing it, and I let it happen, their father's let it happen, society let it happen too, albeit ignorantly. Sadly, even the church is letting it happen. This is why I must speak for them!

Like millions of other women, abortion had become a violent form of birth control for me! How awful, how selfish, how destructive, how ignorant. Abortion killed my three children! They never got the chance to be loved, to laugh, to be hugged, to feel the warmth of a blanket, or eat ice cream. There will never be another Jennifer, Daniel or Rebecca, my aborted children who never got a chance.

We can choose what to wear, what music to listen to, what university to go to, who to go out with, who to have sex with… but the choice to have one's baby killed, should be unthinkable! I was dead wrong, and have paid the price of unbearable regret, grief, sorrow and pain, knowing I had my own innocent children murdered at the hands of paid assassins (doctors).

Our governments not only condone this great crime against the tiniest, and most innocent human beings, but they also pay them to do it with our tax dollars. I hold the abortion doctors most accountable because they know that these are children with the potential to live for 70+ years! Not only that, but legal abortion hurt me, and thousands of other women physically, psychologically, and spiritually. The scars remain to this day.

Can you imagine going to your doctor and telling him you want your right arm cut off? No, nothing wrong with it, but it's your body, your choice, and you demand he cuts it off just because you are left handed and you think it might be a burden to you. What doctor would really do that?

Do you know that 64% of post abortive women confessed that they didn't really want an abortion, but were pressured by their boyfriend/husband or parents? Birth control does not always work. Young women get pregnant on the Pill, IUD and sometimes condoms break too. If you don't want a baby right now…don't make one. Hang on to your hormones. Wait, you can do it! God's way is always better in the long run, not your way.

I came to learn the hard way, that abortion really did not liberate women, it only 'liberated' the men, and exploited vulnerable pregnant women. Abortion gives the guys the freedom to have all the sex they want, without the responsibility of parenthood. They want sex, but no commitments. They want the intimacy, but not the consequences. Most men, it seems, are very apathetic in addition to being cowards. Usually going into shock at the news she is pregnant, but often in anger and fear, letting her know he just wanted sex, not a baby. Then blames her, rarely offering help or support for her or for the child.

Many men are complacent, and say, "It's up to you. Do what you think, but remember, this wasn't planned, it was an accident." However, she is hearing, 'You don't really care about me, or this baby...If you loved me, you would want to have this baby of ours and be a Daddy'. Deep down she may feel that he should be ecstatic and fighting for the life of his son or daughter to live. Never to come into an agreement with death for this child who is naturally growing inside of her. Abortion opens the door to a spirit of death, and kills their opportunity and blessing to be parents to this child. It kills years of joy of loving a son or daughter and watching him or her grow into an amazing person.

Then again, there are those exceptional fathers who want their baby to live. These courageous men try to persuade her to let their baby live, to stay together, they offer support and comfort and a life together. Yet, some women will still go and abort that baby despite his efforts and desires as the father for his child. These men are most devastated. Especially, since they are helpless to protect their child from being executed. They soon begin to distrust women and hold deep seated anger, resentments, and feelings of betrayal, along with fear of getting involved with another woman, unless they can truly forgive and get on with their lives after the mourning, the grieving and healing. Then there are men out there who had sex with women and never knew they got that woman pregnant, never had the opportunity to appeal for that child's life, and she aborted the child without his knowledge or input.

Every pregnancy ends in a delivery, either the delivery of a beautiful baby, or the delivery of a dead baby.

Truth is, once conception takes place, the entire DNA is there, and the creation of a new LIFE begins...making the couple parents, whether they acknowledge it or not. Abortion then makes the man and woman, parents of a dead child. For years many will try to justify their abortion(s) and deny it was a baby, but one day this revelation will strike them.

Abortion is the shedding of innocent blood. It hurts women, men, nations and rips the heart of God. How would you feel about your children being torn apart, dismembered and poisoned while alive? Children that you had a hope and a future for. Children that were destined to lead nations, to minister to the sick, to feed the poor, share the gospel, and to be a blessing in this world.

But, I thank God for HIS amazing mercy, forgiveness and grace, even towards the vilest sinner. If we confess our faults and sins, have Godly sorrow, repent/change and overcome evil with good by faith, we can have eternal life. It is a gift from God.

Born Again

Finally, after seeking God in my late 20's, I found Him at the age of 30. Sure, I had checked out the Tarot Cards, Buddha, Mohamed, Hindu and many world religions...but there was always something missing, something was off. How could I worship a god that was in the form of a statue made by men? Or like some religions that allow men to have more than one wife-that is just wrong; that is just not right or fair...or having hundreds of idols? One day I said, "God, if you are really there, please show me, and come into my life."

Then, God sent a Born Again Christian to come and repair the phone in my Toronto apartment. We talked, and I found him so wise and knowledgeable about spiritual things. He asked if I had read the Bible...I hadn't read it, and told him it was just a bunch of fairytales, written by people. He challenged me to start reading it slowly, and ask the Holy Spirit to help me understand it. He invited and encouraged me to start going to church...and this is when I asked God to forgive me for ALL of my sins. When I realized that Jesus/Yeshua, died on the cross for all of my iniquities, and paid the penalty, that I deserved, I was so intrigued. I broke down, crying a lot, and surrendered my life to GOD.

My favourite song became "Amazing Grace". While devouring the Bible, and going to church about three or four times a week to meetings, and talking to people about God; I discovered that there was no mention of baptizing babies in the Bible. John the Baptist preached, "Repent, and be baptized for the remission of sins." Besides, how could a baby sin, let alone repent? My mom had my brother and I baptized in a United Church as infants, of which I have absolutely no recollection. Today I would not want to be a part of that denomination, because they think abortion is ok, as well as same-sex marriages…and neither of these things line up with scripture. I knew I needed to get water baptized as a Believer, according to the Word of God. My total immersion in water baptism as a young adult was awesome! I felt so clean, so renewed… soon I quit smoking, drinking and drugs…and quickly started praying for a husband. I was a new woman; the old Denise had died. I was already 30 years old now and had always wanted to meet a great guy, get married and have a family. My clock was ticking.

Jesus appeared to me

One night in my Toronto apartment, I was about to get into the bathtub full of bubbles, when I heard a voice say, "Jesus is coming with your three children". What? Up to this point, I had asked God to forgive me for those abortions, wailed and grieved the loss of my children and totally surrendered my life to Christ. I knew that I had been forgiven by God, but had never thought if they were boys or girls, or what their names were.

As I was sitting down in the water, I thought that He would come with three little fetuses cupped in His hands. Then suddenly, I looked over, and there was Jesus standing behind my three aborted children, with His arms extended out. They were as old as they would have been at that time! When I looked at Him, my first inclination was; *Wow, you really look like how you look.* I had been skeptical of those artists who drew or painted pictures of Him. How would they know what He looked like? Yet, He really did look like that man depicted on the cross and in paintings and books.

Then, tears began to flow down my cheeks as I beheld my eldest child, a beautiful teenage girl, with long brown hair, she would have been about 16 or 17 years old at that time, and I

52

just somehow knew that her name is "Jennifer". She looked so much like me, but slimmer and with long hair! Crying, I said, "Jennifer, I'm so sorry, please forgive me", and with love in her voice, she said, "I forgive you Mom." Then, I looked at Daniel in the middle, he would have been 6 or 7 years old at that time, and he was so adorable, with darker blonde, wavy hair, and I told him I was so sorry, and to please forgive me. He replied, "I forgive you, Mom". Really weeping now, I looked at Rebecca, who would have only been about 5 or 6 years old. She was so cute, she had long, dark hair and beautiful eyes, and they were all so gorgeous. I asked her to forgive me too. She responded with, "I forgive you Mommy, don't cry, we're with Jesus."

Then as I was wiping some tears from my eyes, they suddenly disappeared! Wow, isn't that amazing? I sure miss them. Yes, Jesus/Yeshua is alive, He is real, and He appeared to me. No one can ever take that away from me, or try to convince me otherwise. Every aborted child, is in heaven, with our Lord, nonetheless they never got to fulfill their destinies on the earth.

THE GATES OF HELL OPEN WIDE: I will never forget the night, Jan. 28, 1988. I was watching The CBC, National News, and listened to the dreadful broadcast wherein the Supreme Court of Canada, had struck down the abortion law, in Canada, in the Morgentaler case.

It is interesting to note that Henry Morgentaler was the father of the abortion industry in Canada, and he broke the laws, to change the laws to bring in lawlessness in our nation. He was a survivor of Dachau and Auschwitz Nazi concentration camps, and perhaps legal abortion was his way to get back at the Gentiles, by methodically and legally killing their babies before birth; in the hundreds of thousands? Also becoming rich in the process.

Alone in my Toronto apartment, while sitting on my couch, I cried aloud, in anguish knowing that the floodgates of hell where now opened wide for children to be killed before they were born. My heart made a determination, and I just knew God wanted me to be a voice for my aborted children who had no voice. Soon I was compelled to speak out about this great evil, this great injustice against children and pregnant women. God began to give me strength to share my pain, my story in public. In hopes that women and children would be saved from death and destruction.

The first time, I stood up in a Young Adults Bible Study to share…I could not even talk, I just cried... eventually with deep remorse and pain, I began to get the story out on how I believed the lies, of what the doctor told me. How I was pressured to abort my children and ignorant of the truth on fetal development. I began to talk about the horrible experiences and share the humanity of children in the womb. It was really hard, really tough…but someone had to start speaking out about these atrocities, as a former abortion patient. My new friend Bev Hadland, of Straight Talk, was the only other woman I knew who was publicly sharing her abortion pain and regret, back then, as well Bev gave a power packed teaching on abstinence too.

The barbaric practice of abortion has been rampant and become common in the last 40 years. The Holy Spirit was drawing me and confirming in His Word, the Bible that God wanted me to work full time as a voice for the voiceless. Gradually, my desire to sell insurance began to dwindle, and my desire to walk by faith and obey God completely increased. From 1982 until 1989 I worked as a multi-line insurance agent, and was very successful in my career, often winning contests and awards. My parents thought I went over the deep end, when I left my lucrative job, and was not getting any income. However, I just knew that God would supply all of my needs.

The very first time I went to share my pain of abortion publicly in a Young Adults Bible Study, two of my friends stood up with me, one on each side, holding my arms. As I began to speak, I could only cry. It was several attempts before I got the courage and tenacity to speak. I still shed tears most times, but God knows there are hard hearts who need to hear the truth about what an abortion really is and what it does to women. God began to open doors for me to share my testimony on Christian Television and in churches.

I became the Founder/President of "Christians for Life-Toronto". We helped organize the largest pro-life rally in Canada on Parliament Hill, in Ottawa, where over 25,000 Christians of all denominations, mostly Catholics attended. Nobel Peace Prize winner, Mother Theresa was our honored speaker at the Rally for Life. A copy of her talk ended up on one side of the cassette, and my testimony on the other side. Soon I was getting invited to also speak on Radio and in High Schools, Universities, Conferences and Prisons. This issue I discovered, is very big on God's heart.

Getting together with other single women to pray, I led out in prayer for our future husbands to be. When I started praying for my husband, I did not know him at all. By faith I just started praying for this guy, who was going to be my husband. Asking God to send people across his path that were born again believers, that he would be a mighty man of God, etc. Sometimes I would pray that if there were any other women in his life that they must "Get out" in Jesus Holy Name. Well, as it turns out...prayers in faith, are powerful! When I started praying for Paul, whom I did not know, he was not even a Christian. While I prayed, it turns out a fellow worker was a born again, spirit filled Christian who gave him a gospel tract to read, and invited him to church. Paul soon surrendered his life to God, he quit all the bad stuff he was into, he quit drinking and smoking, and he quit doing drugs too. Yet, he was still living common law with some other woman. Then one day he asked God if he was supposed to marry her, and the Holy Spirit said, "No, I have someone else for you". Tada...that would be me.

In the meantime, God was using me to share my testimony on the pain of rape, teen pregnancy, legal abortion, and exposing the lies on this horrific procedure. I often thought and said, "Lord, how am I ever going to get a husband sharing my horrible past?" But, I knew I had to be obedient to do God's will, not my will, and just trust Him.

Then one day, the Lord had me share in Paul's church. We did not meet then, but he heard my whole story. We actually met in another church, where we were both visiting to hear Gerry Savelle, an anointed preacher, and then Paul began to pursue me. He was a strong Christian man, and so full of joy. We wanted to do things God's way, so we waited until our wedding night for sexual intimacy. Yes, it is possible, you can do it too. We set boundaries, and made all these rules...to keep ourselves in check. And we were faithful! We had an amazing wedding and went to beautiful Cartagena, Columbia for our honeymoon.

Soon after being married, and praying for a child. God BLESSED us with a wonderful, amazing son. I cannot describe the amazing love a Mother has for her child. However, my cervix was so damaged from past abortions that it would not dilate, he started going into distress, and I had to have an emergency C-Section after 21 hours in labour. Shawn was born at 9.5 pounds! He is the greatest blessing of our lives.

I just LOVE being a mother! The love and joy is incredible! We wanted more children, but due to the cervical damage and scarring in my uterus from those abortions, I had a miscarriage after Shawn, and was never able to have any more children. He is the only survivor of my womb.

Doctors could not believe I had him. He is a miracle! A precious gift from GOD! We are so proud of him. I love him so much. Please pray for him, I am sure it must have been difficult growing up as an only child, knowing your mom had your siblings killed by doctors. This grieves my heart so.

The years fly by, and the next thing you know our children are grown up, and gone to begin their own journey of making some good, and some bad choices, that will forever affect their own lives and families. I want to protect him from all evil and harm...but our children have to experience their own spiritual journey on earth. Please pray for Shawn.

We are not perfect, but with God in the center, all things are possible. We have been blessed with 25 years of a pretty good marriage so far. Paul is a wonderful husband and father. I could not do all my ministry, if it wasn't for my husband being such a hard worker and providing for our home and needs, as well as prayerfully supporting me in this great cause for life.

For many years I had prayed for my parents, my family and old friends to believe in God and to know that Jesus died on the cross for their sins too, and that by faith, they could have eternal life in heaven.

My parents had come to live with us the last year and a half of their lives. I was so thrilled to have them here, as we were very close. My dad was a hardened atheist all of his life... until on his deathbed that is, at the age of 76.

They were both quite ill; my dad had several by-passes, and still had heart blockages. My mom had congestive heart failure, emphysema, COPD, was obese and also diabetic, dependent on insulin needles.

About six months before my mom died, while she was in the hospital, one day she told me a couple of Philippino ladies prayed with her, and she wanted to get water baptized as an adult. She had been baptized Catholic as a baby, but felt that didn't really count, according to the Bible. All the references in the Bible share about how we are to repent and be baptized for the remission of sins. How can a baby sin, or feel bad about sinning? Jesus and John the Baptist preached and practiced adult baptism, even Jesus was baptized when he was about 30 years old. Nowhere does it say to baptize babies.

My mom insisted that I bring a nice black forest cake for the nurses and others and bring my friends Ray and Margo who play the guitar. By this point my mom had suffered a stroke and couldn't walk anymore, although she really, really tried. So we had her body lifted into a giant hospital sling, and brought her down the long corridor to the bathing room where we prayed and she got dunked into the warm water, total emersion and baptized in the name of Jesus Christ. It was so wonderful! I was ecstatic. She called out to my dad to let us pray for him too…but he refused. The nurses and patients loved the music and told me it was their very first water baptism in that hospital.

The last time my dad was rushed by ambulance to the hospital, he was in critical condition. After several hours with him, I was exhausted and went home around 1 am.

At around 4 am a nurse called me and said, "Your dad wants to see you." I quickly got dressed and drove back to the hospital. One look at him in intensive care and I just knew he was dying. He had oxygen tubes going into his nose and mouth; he was sitting up in his bed, struggling to breathe and he was afraid. I could see fear on his face. First, I called my brother, and had Dad talk to him, then I called our sister and had him talk to her also.

I began to cry, "Dad, please let me pray with you…this is your last chance…they cannot help you anymore…please let me pray with you?" He nodded his head and said, "Ok". I quickly told him to repeat after me, as I led him in a sinner's prayer! This was incredible, my dad, the atheist, finally humbling himself, and asking God to forgive him for all of his sins! This was a huge miracle. He confessed that Jesus was born of the virgin Mary, died on the cross for his sins, was raised from the dead and is alive. He asked God to come into his heart. Wow, I was thrilled, this was amazing!

Crying all the time, and knowing his time was short, I asked if I could read him something from the Bible, and he nodded again. I read him Psalm 23…The Lord is my shepherd, and also Psalm 91, another one of my favourites. I prayed for the Holy Spirit to comfort my dad and to give him peace. I said, "Dad look to the angels, look to Jesus." Then suddenly he began to focus on something in the room and slowly he began to tilt his head upward towards the ceiling... and then he was gone. I began to wail and grieve the loss of my dad, but so delighted that he finally accepted God into his life.

It was only a month and a half after my Dad passed on, in Nov. of 2002 that my Mom went to be with the Lord. I had been spending time with her in the hospital almost every day, and would wake up with an urgency to go see her. One morning, I didn't feel that urgency, and then the nurse called and said, "Your Mom has a taken a turn for the worse." I told her to tell my Mom, "I'm on my way" and quickly rushed to the hospital. However, she was already gone, when I arrived. The grief was unbearable. Losing both my parents so close together was heart wrenching. I loved them dearly, and miss them so much! Looking forward to seeing them again in the heavenlies.

As we go into our sunset years, I really hope and pray that our son will rededicate his life to God, meet an amazing woman to be his wife, and that they will have many children. It would be so wonderful if this happens soon, so I can get to know them before I leave this planet. It is my prayer that people will be impacted with God's love and truth. I just want to make a difference to expose this dragon called abortion, warn pregnant women, and save lives. I want to let this little light of mine shine in the world.

Chapter 4

GENESIS-What really happened?

S atan is the father of lies, and murderer from the beginning. Are you going to believe in his theory of evolution which declares that somehow all living things inadvertently, as well as mysteriously formed from deadness, nothingness, into the life of millions of plants, creatures and human beings, just by chance? In some way transforming from rock to bacteria slime into magnificent life with all its complexities, having seeds producing of its own kind, all by itself?

Or will you choose to believe that all things were created by God, by His intelligent design with a purpose? The Word of God states that; *"In the beginning God created the heaven and the earth. And the earth was without form, and void; and darkness was upon the face of the deep. And the Spirit of God moved upon the face of the waters. And God said, Let there be light: and there was light. And God saw the light, that it was good: and God divided the light from the darkness. And God called the light Day, and the darkness he called Night. And the evening and the morning were the first day.*

And God made the firmament (sky), and divided the waters which were under the firmament from the waters which were above the firmament: and it was so. And God called the firmament Heaven. And the evening and the morning were the second day.

And God said, Let the waters under the heaven be gathered together unto one place, and let the dry land appear: and it was so. And God called the dry land Earth; and the gathering together of the waters called He Seas: and God saw that it was good.

And God said, Let the earth bring forth grass, the herb yielding seed, and the fruit tree yielding fruit after his kind, whose seed is in itself, upon the earth: and it was so. And the earth brought forth grass, and herb yielding seed after his kind, and the tree yielding fruit, whose seed was in itself, after his kind: and God saw that it was good. And the evening and the morning were the third day.

And God said, Let there be lights in the firmament of the heaven to divide the day from the night; and let them be for signs, and for seasons, and for days, and years: And let them be for lights in the firmament of the heaven to give light upon the earth: and it was so.

And God made two great lights; the greater light to rule the day, and the lesser light to rule the night: he made the stars also. And God set them in the firmament of the heaven to give light upon the earth, And to rule over the day and over the night, and to divide the light from the darkness: and God saw that it was good. And the evening and the morning were the fourth day."

Have you been watching the amazing documentaries by Creation Ministries International, Reasons to Believe.org or Dr. Dino? It is so fascinating to hear about astronomy and how each of the planets in our solar system are so entirely uniquely diverse! The compositions are so different, the temperatures extreme, colours, sizes, and variances distinctive. Just like how each one of us are different and each snowflake is varied etc.

"And God said, Let the waters bring forth abundantly the moving creature that hath life, and fowl that may fly above the earth in the open firmament of heaven. And God created great whales, and every living creature that moves, which the waters brought forth abundantly, after their kind, and every winged fowl after his kind: and God saw that it was good.

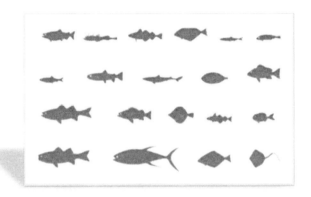

And God blessed them, saying, be fruitful, and multiply, and fill the waters in the seas, and let fowl multiply in the earth. And the evening and the morning were the fifth day.

And God said, Let the earth bring forth the living creature after his kind, cattle, and creeping thing, and beast of the earth after his kind: and it was so. And God made the beast of the earth after his kind, and cattle after their kind, and everything that creeps upon the earth after his kind: and God saw that it was good.

And God said; Let us make man in our image, after our likeness: and let them have dominion over the fish of the sea, and over the fowl of the air, and over the cattle, and over all the earth, and over every creeping thing that creeps upon the earth.

So God created man in His own image, in the image of God created he him; male and female created he them.

And God blessed them, and God said unto them, "Be fruitful, and multiply, and replenish the earth, and subdue it: and have dominion over the fish of the sea, and over the fowl of the air, and over every living thing that moveth upon the earth.

And God said, Behold, I have given you every herb bearing seed, which is upon the face of all the earth, and every tree, in the which is the fruit of a tree yielding seed; to you it shall be for meat. And to every beast of the earth, and to every fowl of the air, and to everything that creeps upon the earth, wherein there is life, I have given every green herb for meat: and it was so.

And God saw everything that he had made, and, behold, it was very good. And the evening and the morning were the sixth day." Genesis 1:1-31

And God blessed (spoke good of) the seventh day, set it apart as His own, and hallowed it, because on it God rested from all His work which He had created and done." Gen 2:3

Then we read how God commanded Adam and Eve not to eat from this one tree of knowledge of Good and Evil or they would die. But the Serpent put doubt into Eve's mind and he lied to Eve saying, *"You shall not surely die, [II Cor. 11:3.] For God knows that in the day you eat of it your eyes will be opened and you will be like God, knowing the difference between good and evil and blessing and calamity.*

And when the woman saw that the tree was good (suitable, pleasant) for food and that it was delightful to look at, and a tree to be desired in order to make one wise, she took of its fruit and ate; and she gave some also to her husband, and he ate.

Then the eyes of them both were opened, and they knew that they were naked; and they sewed fig leaves together and made themselves apron like girdles. And they heard the sound of the Lord God walking in the garden in the cool of the day, and Adam and his wife hid themselves from the presence of the Lord God among the trees of the garden." Gen 3:4-8

Notice that Adam was right there beside her, and he didn't try to stop her, or say, "No honey, don't defy God". Unfortunately, Adam stayed silent and he went along with Eve's decision to taste the fruit and disobey God. After this rebellion against God, they felt intense guilt and shame, and wanted to cover up. God asked Adam, "What did you do?" Adam basically said, "Don't blame me, blame this woman you gave me, it's all her fault." Then Eve replied with, "Don't blame me, blame the serpent..." The serpent didn't have a leg to stand on! Nothing much has changed throughout the centuries.

In March of 2013, I was in Israel for my second time, with an awesome group of pro-life friends from around the world. Caroline, a new friend from the USA, and I were on the beach, off the Kinneret (Sea of Galilee). While, thoroughly enjoying the shalom/peace of God, the beautiful scenery, and reading my Bible, I looked up as she approached. Caroline was holding a big glass jar with a live snake curled up inside it, saying, "Denise look what I found." Quickly, getting up I said, "Great, now we have to crush its head with our heel." (Gen. 3:15) She hesitated, and proclaimed, "I can't kill it." I replied, "No worries, he has a lot of brothers and sisters around here, and besides it will be good food for the wild cats and rats out here." Since I was wearing flip flops, Caroline had to do it, as a symbolic act confirming that we were going to defeat the spiritual enemy aborting children in the land of Israel, and globally.

That night the Holy Spirit revealed something very astonishing to me. He showed me how Satan was a serpent, (a snake) in the beginning, in the Book of Genesis; but by the Book of Revelation, the last book in the Bible Satan becomes an enormous red Dragon! His tail is so huge it can sweep a third of the stars away. Satan is growing! Why? How? I think he is getting fat and large from the shedding of innocent blood through the thousands of children's lives being aborted around our planet.

Throughout the Torah, the first five books of the Bible, God commanded His people to multiply and be fruitful and to subdue the earth for His Kingdom. After the flood, God gave that command again. There are 1,524 verses regarding children in the Bible, so they must be important to God. King David who had a heart after God stated this:

*"**Behold, children are a heritage from the Lord, the fruit of the womb a reward**." [Deut. 28:4.]* (Blessed shall be the fruit of your body/womb).

If children are the inheritance of the Lord, His reward to us, a prize, a gift, blessings, then how could we throw them back into His face and say, "No, I don't want this baby, this gift? I never want to have children. I only want one, or two, and no more. I don't want this one right now; take it back." So we take pills and insert IUD's and contraptions into our bodies or have well paid doctors abort those children, those precious gifts from God. Many of us will go to man to permanently sterilize us. Women getting their fallopian tubes clamped, and men getting vasectomies. We live in fear, and walk in fear…instead of living and walking by faith. Doing our will, and not HIS will. Not trusting God, but leaning on our own understanding.

Jeremiah 1:5 declares that God knew us before we were born, and has a purpose and a plan for every human being. There are no accidents with Him. You may not have been planned by your parents, but God chose you before the foundations of the world.

Psalm 139 also affirms that God knit us together in our mother's womb. We are all created in His image. He has a destiny for every person.

"As arrows are in the hand of a warrior, so are the children of one's youth. Happy, blessed, and fortunate is the man whose quiver is filled with them! They will not be put to shame when they speak with their adversaries [in gatherings] at the [city's] gate." Psalm 127:3-5

God says our children are as arrows, weapons in the hand of a warrior, to push back the enemy. Where have all our children gone, where have all our weapons gone? Who will fight for the Kingdom of God once we are all gone?

Over 30 times and in nine books of the Bible, God commands His children to multiply and be fruitful. So this must be essential to our Father God, Creator of Heaven and earth.

In a nutshell, Genesis describes the creation of earth and the creatures of the earth. The creation of mankind too. The fall and rebellion of mankind against God. The result manifested in plenty of sexual and immoral sins, worshiping other gods and sacrificing children. Then God sends a flood as judgment on mankind because of their evil and perverted ways; except for Godly Noah, Noah's family, and all of the creatures that were with Noah aboard the ark.

Through the generations God established a covenant with Abraham, Isaac and Jacob, testing them and mankind. Sending His Son, Yeshua, to fulfill the prophesies of old. He was conceived by the Holy Spirit, born of the Virgin Mary over 2,000 years ago. He did not come to start another religion, but rather He rebuked the Jewish religious leaders of the day, calling them hypocrites and vipers. He healed the sick, cast evil spirits out of people, and taught us to forgive and love. He loved us so much that HE gave His life, taking the 40 lashes, beaten and bruised beyond human recognition, paying the penalty for all of our sins on the cross. He also taught us how to fight evil and be in a personal relationship with God. He was God in the flesh, to make a bridge between man and God, redeeming mankind, to all who put their faith in Him. God is love! He loves you!

Have you ever thought about how the different races came to be? I personally believe that Adam, who was made from the dust of the earth, had a lot of melanin, which is the dark brown skin pigment. This is the main ingredient that separates the races. White people lack melanin. It is in the DNA of Africans. However, I recently watched a documentary on Albino (white) Black people. That was fascinating how there are Black African people who have white skin. It is in their DNA also, they lack melanin. Then God created Eve from the rib of Adam and she was woven more intricately, was shapelier and diverse than man, she may have even looked more oriental? But all of their DNA produced the varied humans of the earth.

Also, it is possible that after the flood, God may have created more peoples on different plots of land? The creation scientists have excellent materials explaining how the races came to be, and it is just intriguing. I recently watched a new DVD called, "Evolution vs. God" a great documentary asking atheists the right questions to get them thinking about the reality of a master architect.

God created one race of people on the earth, it is called, "the human race".

MALES

Men are God's handy-work, and for sure you quickly realize that he made their brains quite different than women's. Men usually love sports competitions, fights and have a knack for building and fixing things. Many like to be the boss, take charge, hunt, and explore. They are easily visually stimulated, and like to have most things fitting nicely into a compartmental box. They even have a "nothing" box. It's really true; when you ask a man; what are you thinking, and they say, "Nothing," believe him. LOL.

Sadly, there is a desensitizing of sin, clarity of the sexes, and condoning homosexuality even in some of the churches. With the legalization of same sex marriages, and the TV commercials and movies now making it common place…it has even crept into the church. There are many scriptures in the old and new Testaments which condemn homosexuality as a sin. It is an abomination to God. Romans chapter one declares it. Like any other sin, whether sex before or outside of marriage, lying, stealing or whatever, we need to love the sinner, but hate the sin. My Bible says that the wages of sin is death, but the gift of God is eternal life…IF, we turn from our wicked ways and repent.

I just wonder if all those birth control pills and estrogens women have been consuming and flushing down the toilets over the decades, are passing down those chemicals into children and feminizing some people?

God created Adam and Eve, not Adam and Steve. Adam was lonely, he needed someone to help him out…to encourage him…a beautiful woman to talk to and love. Adam had a hard time multi-tasking, and besides, he hated to do dishes and was cold at night too. He needed a warm, loving wife, a lover, a voluptuous woman to cuddle.

So God created woman.

FEMALES

God designed women to be multi-taskers, to nurture and carry the egg, which would be fertilized by the man by way of sexual intimacy, to reproduce the descendants of humanity in her womb. A woman is born with about one to two million immature eggs, or follicles, in her ovaries. When a woman 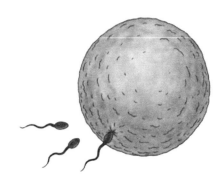 reaches puberty and starts to menstruate, only about 400,000 follicles remain. With each menstrual cycle, a thousand follicles are lost and only one blessed little follicle will actually mature into an ovum (egg), which is released into the fallopian tube, kicking off ovulation. That means that of the one to two million follicles, only about 400 will ever actually mature.

God fashioned Eve to carry the offspring of mankind in the secret place, the matrix, the spiritual incubator for the children of the Kingdom of God to grow and multiply to fill the earth.

God gave man the seed, (sperm) to sow, to reproduce. Have you watched the amazing video called, "The Great Sperm Race"? It is absolutely incredible how God arranged all this. A sperm is the smallest cell in a human body, and the woman's egg is the largest cell. But once they come together, (conception) there is a beautiful new person, who is fully human and fully alive.

The head of the sperm contains the DNA, which when combined with the woman's egg's DNA, will create a new individual. The tip of the sperm head is the portion called the acrosome, which enables the sperm to penetrate the egg. The mid-piece contains the mitochondria which supplies the energy the tail needs to move. The tail moves with whip-like movements back and forth to propel the sperm towards the egg. The sperm have to reach the uterus and the fallopian tube in order to fertilize a woman's egg. Wow.

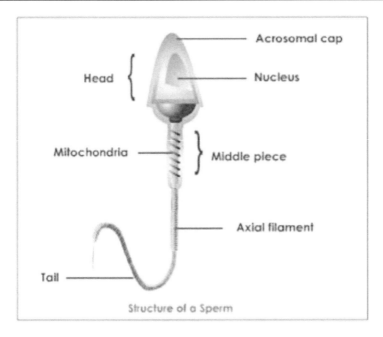

Structure of a Sperm

The Creator entrusted women to be the givers of life. Adam named his wife Eve which actually means 'Life Giver'. It is deplorable how Satan has influenced so many women to become life takers as abortion doctors have them sign the papers, and carry out the hideous deed. God also formed women uniquely to have fuller breasts that would become filled with milk to nourish her children, and please her husband. Women were fashioned to be the caregivers and primary teachers to their children. Thus, the most imperative unit on earth, the family, was created!

Mankind was designed by God to have dominion over the earth. He instructed man to work the land, to be creative and build cars, houses, cities, roads, and all manner of things, like infrastructure. Ideally, He built man to protect the women and children from enemies, and provide guidance and direction as the leader of the household, communities and nations. God's purpose in creating human beings was to be with us, love us and to be loved by us.

ROOTS & TRADITIONS OF MAN: Now I want you to get out of the box of westernized, religious, traditional, gentilized thinking when you read this book. I pray that you will open your mind and heart to hear what God hears, and see what He sees. He was GOD in spirit and God in the flesh, in physical form when He came and lived among mankind. He had a miraculous birth, a phenomenal life, and unparalleled death and resurrection from the dead.

God is a BIG God, and His ways are not our ways. The church, (the Bride of Christ) has picked up so many religious traditions and false teachings from man over the centuries that we need to get realigned and shifted back into position with His Word. We have drifted so far from our Hebraic roots that we need to be grafted back in according to the Word of the Lord.

"But now in Christ Jesus, you who once were [so] far away, through (by, in) the blood of Christ has been brought near. For He is [Himself] our peace (our bond of unity and harmony). He has made us both [Jew and Gentile] one [body], and has broken down (destroyed, abolished) the hostile dividing wall between us, By abolishing in His [own crucified] flesh the enmity [caused by] the Law with its decrees and ordinances [which He annulled]; that He from the two might create in Himself one new man [one new quality of humanity out of the two], so making peace.

And [He designed] to reconcile to God both [Jew and Gentile, united] in a single body by means of His cross, thereby killing the mutual enmity and bringing the feud to an end. Eph. 2:13 -16

Yeshua, our Saviour, integrating Jews and Gentiles (non-Jews) into "**one new man**" for His Kingdom is powerful. Since the Bible is the word of God, and it is our Owner's Manual for life, then we should abide by what it says, right?

"And whatever you do [no matter what it is] in word or deed, do everything in the name of the Lord Jesus and in [dependence upon] His Person, giving praise to God the Father through Him." Col. 3:17

However, translators did not keep His original name, but interpreted it to "Jesus". As the Lord has been sending me around the world with His message, I got a profound revelation of His Name several years ago. Whether I was in Israel, Moscow-Russia, Ghana-Africa, Germany or the Philippines... no matter what language they spoke, when the translators introduced me, or someone asked my name, I told them it was "Denise". My name is not Denisha, Roberta, or Julietto... it is Denise...and the Holy Spirit whispered in my ear... "And my name is Yeshua!" Wow! This is very interesting; Jehoshua is His formal name and Yeshua is short for Jehoshua, which is His real Hebrew name. (as from James to Jim, or Deborah to Debbie...)

Yeshua is related to the Hebrew word yeshuah which means "salvation". The angel, when announcing the Name of the virgin-born child, said *"You shall call Him Yeshua (salvation) for He shall save His people from their sins."* (Matt. 1:21) So the name of "Yeshua" is most powerful.

For centuries now we have been calling Him "Jesus" not His real name! Not to get all legalistic about it, I still sometimes pray or say "Jesus", but I am trying to use His real Hebraic name more and more in my prayers and speech. I am seeing and hearing more and more believers call Him by His real name too. For the last several years, when sharing the gospel with unbelievers, who are Muslims, Jews or First Nations peoples I have noticed that when I use the name "Yeshua", they seem much more receptive, than when I use the name of "Jesus". Sadly, there are many bad historical events that were done in the name of Jesus Christ, affecting these people groups.

And Yeshua said, *"So for the sake of your tradition (the rules handed down by your forefathers), you have set aside the Word of God [depriving it of force and authority and making it of no effect]."* Mat. 15:6

Yeshua was most likely born in the month of December, during the Festival of Lights, known as Hanukkah. His birth has nothing to do with Santa Claus and pagan rituals. Just don't start worshiping the Christmas tree. Another big anomaly is Easter. God commands His people to keep the Feasts of God, including the Passover and the Feast of unleavened bread. The New Testament also exhorts us to do this, and it is important to realize that Yeshua, actually became the Passover Lamb, for all of mankind.

So I plan on practicing the Passover with the inclusion of what Christ did for us.

Just as an overgrowth of yeast in the body may become a systemic infection and must be dealt with before it causes serious physical problems, the "leaven" or sin within the Body of Messiah (the Church) must be dealt with accordingly. Let's stop practicing the erroneous ways, as we learn more and more of the truth.

In the Bible, the Apostle Paul makes use of the imagery of Passover and the cleansing of the yeast to exhort the Believers in Corinth to get rid of the sin of malice and wickedness and live the holy life they are truly capable of living, free from the bondage to sin.

"Get rid of the old yeast, so that you may be a new unleavened batch—as you really are. For Messiah, our Passover lamb has been sacrificed. Therefore, let us keep the Festival [Passover], not with the old bread leavened with malice and wickedness, but with the unleavened bread of sincerity and truth." (1 Corinthians 5:7–8)

By the way, we should be observing the Passover, that is when Jesus Christ/Yeshua gave His life as the Passover Lamb for all mankind. To pay the penalty for our sins. He rose from the dead three days later. Not on the pagan holiday they call Easter.

We have many man-made customs that were started by Constantine, a Roman Emperor, who changed the dates and the times. He switched the Sabbath from the Seventh Day of the Lord, (Friday evening to Saturday evening) Shabbat to Sunday. GOD rested on the Sabbath, which was and always will be on Saturday. God commanded us to keep this time as a Holy Day unto the Lord, but we have switched it to Sunday. "Remember the Sabbath day, to keep it holy. Six days you shall labor and do all your work, but the seventh day is the Sabbath of the LORD your God." Exodus 20:8-10. The Sabbath Friday night to Saturday night is still practiced by Jewish people today, as we should also. Unless you can show me where God changed it in HIS word.

How did Jesus relate to the Sabbath when He was on earth? *"So He came to Nazareth, where He had been brought up. And as His custom was, He went into the synagogue on the **Sabbath** day, and stood up to read."* Luke 4:16.

On what day did Paul, long after the crucifixion and resurrection, worship and preach with both the Jews and Gentiles? *"So when the Jews went out of the synagogue, the Gentiles begged that these words might be preached to them the next **Sabbath**. Now when the congregation had broken up, many of the Jews and devout proselytes followed Paul and Barnabas, who persuaded them to continue in the grace of God. On the next **Sabbath** almost the whole city came together to hear the word of God."* Acts 13:42-44.

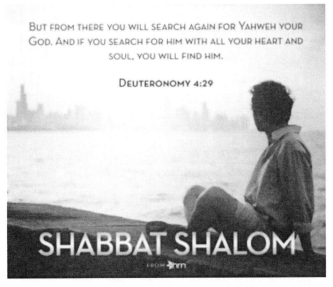

BUT FROM THERE YOU WILL SEARCH AGAIN FOR YAHWEH YOUR GOD. AND IF YOU SEARCH FOR HIM WITH ALL YOUR HEART AND SOUL, YOU WILL FIND HIM.

DEUTERONOMY 4:29

SHABBAT SHALOM

On what day will the redeemed worship God in the new earth? *"'For as the new heavens and the new earth which I will make shall remain before Me,' says the Lord, 'so shall your descendants and your name remain. And it shall come to pass that from one new moon to another, and from one **Sabbath** to* *another, all flesh shall come to worship before Me,' says the Lord."* Isaiah 66:22, 23.

Truth is, that 321 years after Yeshua was crucified, Constantine decided to pass the first Sunday law forcing all men, pagans and Christians, to worship on Sunday instead. "All judges and city people and the craftsmen shall rest upon The Venerable Day of the Sun." *History of the Christian Church* states, "Constantine reverenced all the gods as mysterious powers, especially Apollo, the god of the sun." Thus calling it Sun day. http://seventh-day.org/sabbath_bible_study.htm- Non-Jewish people are grafted into the vine to become one new man as the tremendous Apostle Paul explained. *"But now I am speaking to you who are Gentiles. Inasmuch then as I am an apostle to the Gentiles, I lay great stress on my ministry and magnify my office, In the hope of making my fellow Jews jealous, and thus managing to save some of them.*

But if some of the branches were broken off, while you, (Gentiles) a wild olive shoot, were grafted in among them to share the richness [of the root and sap] of the olive tree, Do not boast over the branches and pride yourself at their expense. If you do boast and feel superior, <u>remember it is not you that support the root, but the root [that supports] you.</u>

You will say then, Branches were broken (pruned) off so that I might be grafted in! That is true. But they were broken (pruned) off because of their unbelief (their lack of real faith), and you are established through faith [because you do believe]. So do not become proud and conceited, but rather stand in awe and be reverently afraid.

For if God did not spare the natural branches [because of unbelief], neither will He spare you [if you are guilty of the same offense]. Then note and appreciate the gracious kindness and the severity of God: severity toward those who have fallen, but God's gracious kindness to you—provided you continue in His grace and abide in His kindness; otherwise you too will be cut off (pruned away).

And even those others [the fallen branches, Jews], if they do not persist in [clinging to] their unbelief, will be grafted in, for God has the power to graft them in again. For if you have been cut from what is by nature a wild olive tree, and against nature grafted into a cultivated olive tree, how much easier will it be to graft these natural [branches] back on [the original parent stock of] their own olive tree.

Lest you be self-opinionated (wise in your own conceits), I do not want you to miss this hidden truth and mystery, brethren: a hardening (insensibility) has [temporarily] befallen a part of Israel [to last] until the full number of the ingathering of the Gentiles has come in, And so all Israel will be saved. As it is written, The Deliverer will come from Zion, He will banish ungodliness from Jacob. [Isa. 59:20, 21.] And this will be My covenant (My agreement) with them when I shall take away their sins. [Isa. 27:9; Jer. 31:33.]

From the point of view of the Gospel (good news), they [the Jews, at present] are enemies [of God], which is for your advantage and benefit. But from the point of view of God's choice (of election, of divine selection), they are still the beloved (dear to Him) for the sake of their forefathers. For God's gifts and His call are irrevocable. [He never withdraws them when once they are given, and He does not change His mind about those to whom He gives His grace or to whom He sends His call.]

Just as you were once disobedient and rebellious toward God but now have obtained [His] mercy, through their disobedience, So they also now are being disobedient [when you are receiving mercy], that they in turn may one day, through the mercy you are enjoying, also receive mercy [that they may share the mercy which has been shown to you—through you as messengers of the Gospel to them]." Rom. 11:13-31

Knowing that Gentiles are grafted into the Olive Tree (representing Jewish people); through Yeshua, Jews and Gentiles become one new mankind!

A friend and sister in the Lord lent me a copy of her book called, "*Healing Power of the Roots*" by Dominique Bierman, who is a Messianic Jew (that believes that Yeshua/Jesus is the Messiah). She lives with her Messianic Rabbi husband in Israel. It was about five summers ago, when I was reading this remarkable book in my back yard, and unintentionally forgot it out on a lawn chair, upside down. That night it poured rain.

The next morning, I walked outside and picked up the book, and it was soaking wet; the cover was all crinkly and water was dripping off of it. I thought, oh boy, I will have to buy her a new book now. Then I randomly opened it up…and to my great astonishment, right there in the center of the two open pages was a perfectly dry Star of David! Its outline was the wet, dark grey paper! Yes! It is known in Hebrew as the 'Shield of David'. This is the symbol for Israel today. I was like, WOW, this is incredible! This is a sign from God, a miracle! No way could this be a  coincidence! Paul, my husband was home. Jumping up and down with excitement, I quickly pointed, showing him the miraculous Star of David in this book, and he calmly replied, "Denise, but we are not Jewish" …I thought, oh boy…God help us understand the significance of our roots! Was the Lord trying to tell me I had Jewish roots? I think so!

By the way, Yeshua did not die on Good Friday either, Easter is a pagan holiday. No, He was crucified on Passover, He became the Passover Lamb! Yeshua Himself said, "You know that after two days is *the feast of* the Passover, and the Son of man is betrayed to be crucified." Mat. 26:2, "Purge out therefore the old leaven, that ye may be a new lump, as ye are unleavened. For even Christ our Passover, is sacrificed for us." 1 Cor. 5:7

GOD's Ordained Holy Days & the Link to the Development in the Womb

This is astonishing! Zola Levitt, a Messianic Jewish believer in Yeshua, was born again (John 3:3-8) in 1971. He had a spiritual awakening and believed that Yeshua was the prophesied Jewish Messiah. He wrote over 50 books. While he was preparing to write a book for new parents, he contacted a gynecologist for help in understanding how gestation works. He discovered an amazing correlation between The Feasts of Israel, God's Holy Days and the growth and development of every human baby, from conception to birth! The gynecologist showed him a series of pictures, the first one was where an egg and a sperm unite and he said, "On the fourteenth day of the first month, the egg appears." This statement struck a chord in his Jewish mind because that was the date of Passover, on the Jewish calendar. He remembered the boiled egg on his family table every Passover. Now, for the first time, he knew what it meant!

Passover commemorates the liberation of the Israelites from slavery in Egypt, as recorded in the Book of Exodus. On Passover, Jews also celebrate the birth of the Jewish nation after being freed by God from captivity. The Hebrew word *Pesach* means "to pass over." During Passover Jews take part in a meal known as the Seder, and are told to eat lamb, which incorporates the re-telling of the story of Exodus and God's deliverance from bondage in Egypt. Each participant of the Passover Seder experiences a national celebration of freedom through God's intervention and deliverance.

The Way to Deal with Sin–The sacrifices and offerings detailed in Leviticus were a means of atonement, or symbols of repentance from sin and submission to God. Sin required a sacrifice–a life for a life in the Old Testament. The sacrificial offerings had to be perfect, spotless, and without defect. These were a picture of Yeshua, the Messiah, the Lamb of God, who gave his life as the perfect sacrifice for our sins, so we would not have to pay this penalty.

In Luke 22, Jesus shared the Passover meal with his apostles saying, *"I have been very eager to eat this Passover meal with you before my suffering begins. For I tell you now that I won't eat this meal again until **its meaning is fulfilled** in the Kingdom of God." (Luke 22:15-16, NLT) Jesus is the fulfillment of the Passover. He is the Lamb of God, sacrificed to set us free from bondage to sin. (John 1:29; Psalm 22; Isaiah 53) His blood covers and protects us, and his body was broken to free us from eternal death. (1 Corinthians 5:7)*

As God commanded the Israelites to always commemorate his great deliverance through the Passover meal, we Christians were instructed by Christ as well, to continually remember his sacrifice through The Lord's Supper or Communion.

When the egg from a woman is released from the fallopian tube, it will either be: united and fertilized by a sperm to grow and live for eternity, or it will die, by itself. A woman in many ways dies to self, when she becomes a mother, putting her child/children first. She brings forth new life to carry on the future generations. Love is conceived when a child is conceived, as a baby is born with unconditional love!

Some authorities have interpreted the boiled egg as a symbol of mourning for the loss of the Holy Temples in Jerusalem. With the Temples destroyed, sacrifices could no longer be offered for sin. The egg symbolized this loss and traditionally became the food of mourners, as barren women grieve.

The gynecologist continued: "The egg must be fertilized within 24 hours or it will die." This reminded Zola of the **Feast of Unleavened Bread** and the seed or grain that "fell into the ground and died" in order to produce a harvest, the first fruits of which was presented to God. Next, the gynecologist said, "Within two to six days, **the fertilized egg attaches itself to the wall of the womb and begins to grow.**" And, sure enough, the Jewish evangelist thought, "The **Feast of First Fruits** is observed anywhere from two to six days after Passover!"

Next, he was shown a photo of an embryo **showing arms, hands, fingers, legs, feet, toes, a head, eyes**, etc. The caption said, "**Fifty days**." The gynecologist continued, "Around the fiftieth day, the embryo takes on the form of a human being." Zola thought, 'that's **Pentecost!** (Shavuot)

Celebrated on the fiftieth day after Passover, Shavuot is traditionally a joyous time of giving thanks for the new grain of the summer wheat harvest in Israel. The name "Feast of Weeks" was given because God commanded the Jews, in Leviticus 23:15-16, to count seven full weeks (or 49 days), beginning on the second day of Passover, and then present offerings of new grain to the Lord as a lasting ordinance.

Shavuot was originally a festival for expressing joy and thankfulness to the Lord for the blessing of the harvest; because it occurred at the conclusion of the Passover, it also acquired the name "Latter First-Fruits."

The next picture showed the baby at **seven months' gestation**. The gynecologist said, "On the first day of the seventh month, the baby's hearing is developed. For the first time, it can hear and distinguish sounds outside the womb." Zola knew that was the date for the Jewish **Festival of Trumpets.**

The Feast of Trumpets is the first of **God's High Holidays**, celebrating **Rosh Hashanah** (the Jewish New Year). According to one view in the Talmud, Rosh Hashanah commemorates the creation of man. In Jewish liturgy Rosh Hashanah is described as "the day of judgment" (*Yom ha-Din*) and "the day of remembrance" (*Yom ha-Zikkaron*) Rosh Hashanah is characterized by the blowing of the *shofar* (in ancient times it was also sounded on the Sabbath in the Temple). It is a trumpet made from a ram's horn or the horn of a goat or various types of antelope or gazelle (although not from a cow). It is intended to symbolically awaken the listeners from their "slumbers" and alert them to the coming judgment. Some connect the observance with the "sound of the trumpet" that they believe will occur at the return of Jesus Christ ("For the Lord Himself will descend from heaven with a shout, with the voice of an archangel, and with the trumpet of God," 1 Thessalonians 4:16).

The gynecologist continued, "On the tenth day of the seventh month, the hemoglobin of the blood changes from that of the fetus, to a self-sustaining baby to adult hemoglobin." Zola thought, 'that's the **Day of Atonement,** when the blood was taken into the Holy of Holies!'

Next, the gynecologist said, "On the fifteenth day of the seventh month, the lungs become fully developed. If born before then, the baby would have a hard time breathing." And Zola thought, 'That's the **Festival of Tabernacles**, a time of celebrating the Temple, home of the Shekinah glory or Spirit of God.' Throughout the holiday the sukkah (outside tent/shelter with a roof of branches and leaves) becomes the primary living area of one's home. All meals are eaten inside the sukkah and many sleep there as well. In the New Testament, our body is the temple of the Holy Spirit. The Greek term pneuma, normally translated as "breath," or wind is applied to the "Holy Spirit." The womb is the temple of every child until delivery.

Birth takes place on the tenth day of the ninth month. Eight days after birth, in Jewish families, a son is circumcised. Zola noted that the eight days of **Hanukkah** are celebrated right on schedule, nine months and ten days after Passover. This is no coincidence. The timing is precise. This is more likely to be the time when Yeshua our Christ was born; on Hanukkah…which is usually in the month of December.

No human being could have understood the intricacies of the gestational period thousands of years ago. The establishment of the Jewish Holy Days was given to Moses by Jehovah. Its correlation with the human gestation period is not only remarkable; it proves "Intelligent Design." It proves the existence of intelligence beyond this world. It proves that there is a Creator God that guides the affairs of mankind.

Zola Levitt in addition wrote, "When I read John's cosmic views of the Lord and the plan of salvation, I realized that I was reading Jewish writing about a Jewish Messiah, and a Jewish way to God…My prayer of 28 years ago was extremely simple. I said to God, "If you're there, show me. An open-minded look at the life I have led since that moment would have to conclude that He has indeed shown me wonders. The correlation between the Jewish festivals and the birthing of a baby was just one of those wonders." Awesome!

Chapter 5

Human Sacrifice Today

Years ago, I remember praying about God helping us to end the tragedy of abortion in our nation and the nations of the world. I realized that people were outraged about the horror of what has happened over the centuries by evil, atheist dictators, who committed massive genocides for communism, nihilism and racism etc.

The atrocities of slavery, the Holocaust and what happened to our own First Nations people in North America and so on.

Tragically, Native American children were forcibly removed from their families and taken to residential boarding schools across North America. Many of them suffered at the hands of wolves, in sheep's clothing. Many of those children were physically beaten and abused. Sadly, some children were also sexually abused by Catholic and Anglican Priests, peers and caregivers. Dreadfully, there are also testimonies of Priests getting some of the young women pregnant, then doing forced abortions on them. Yeshua warned us of wolves, dressed as sheep.

Many were poorly fed and not allowed to speak their native language or to each other. No wonder only 3% of First Nations believe in Jesus. My heart goes out to the First Nations peoples, they need healing from the Creator. A few years ago, our last Prime Minister, The Hon. Stephen Harper, made a public apology to them for the horrors and mistreatment they endured in Residential schools, many of them received some compensation, but it will never take away the scars and damage passed on to generations after.

Dreadfully, child molestation, incest and rapes are widespread all over, as well as in many reserves today. Now it is often the uncles and fathers and brothers doing most of the rapes and molestation to innocent unprotected children. Culturally, victims are told not to tell anyone, because it would bring disgrace to the families and community. Oh boy, the serpent always wants to keep his evil ways in the dark, in secret, so he can continue to defile and abuse his young victims. Then he plunges them into lifestyles of hopelessness, through alcohol, drugs and low self-esteem often leading to suicides. Sadly, the victims sometimes also become the predators offending others in the cycle of abuse. Yet, we have great news for victims of sexual abuse, neglect, substance abusers and the broken hearted…a new life in Christ.

We had the honour of hosting four First Nations and Inuit peoples in our home, during the "I Forgive Tour" with Kenny Blacksmith. The Holy Spirit told me that we are the salt and light of the earth, but they, (the First Nations peoples) are His Northern Lights, spiritually! God sees these *Believers* as more humble, more loving, more kind, gentler, more long suffering, more forgiving and more like Him in many ways. Inside, they are more brilliant and more spectacular, no wonder the devil wants to oppress and destroy them any way he can.

Aboriginal people believe that human life is sacred. Nonetheless, more and more of them are having induced abortions. We have had two First Nations women on the Board of Directors for Canada Silent No More. Many years ago, the Holy Spirit prompted me to reach out to First Nations peoples as the gatekeepers of the land.

Several years ago I attended a national meeting of Chiefs from across Canada, and spoke to many of them, asking about their outlook on abortion. 95% of them agreed that abortion is murder, and told me that human life is sacred. I pondered, if they would make a Resolution, or a Declaration that Human Life is Sacred, and renounce abortion, it would be a step in the right direction for our nation. Well, Praise God, to date we have 8 Bands, from northern Manitoba, who have made a Resolution that Human Life is Sacred and renouncing abortion, thanks to Maureen B. a First Nations woman who was on our Board, who got the ball rolling. However, there is much more work to do, and we need your help!

My prayer is that the cycle of sexual, alcohol, human/sex trafficking and drug abuse will end everywhere, and victims will become overcomers and move forward in forgiveness. We cannot go forward, if we are continually looking back. We must speak out as we have the victory with God on our side. We pray more will join us in this fight for life, healing and reconciliation.

Then the Holy Spirit reminded me that we weren't there when slavery was legal, and it was wrong. We weren't there when the Holocaust happened or when aboriginal children were forced out of their homes.

But we are here today, and the legal killing of children in the womb is happening right now, in our cities, on our watch. What will history record that we did about it? What are you going to do to stop the violence today?

Human Life

Science as well as God, the Creator informs us that human life begins at the moment of conception/fertilization! Whether a person is black, brown, yellow, red or white, we are all human beings. Everyone, should have the basic right to life, no matter what race, religion, sex, age or how small we are. Yet millions of children are being sacrificed and thousands of girls killed before they are born, just because they are girls!

The Bible records that thousands of years ago people chose to sacrifice their children to the gods of Molech and Baal, and it is recorded in the Bible as an abomination to God.

"They did not destroy the [heathen] nations as the Lord commanded them, But mingled themselves with the [idolatrous] nations and learned their ways and works And served their idols, which were a snare to them. Yes, they sacrificed their sons and their daughters to demons [II Kings 16:3.] And shed innocent blood, even the blood of their sons and of their daughters, whom they sacrificed to the idols of Canaan; and the land was polluted with their blood.

Thus were they defiled by their own works, and they played the harlot and practiced idolatry with their own deeds [of idolatrous rites].

Therefore, was the wrath of the Lord kindled against His people, insomuch that He abhorred and rejected His own heritage. [Deut. 32:17.]

And He gave them into the hands of the [heathen] nations, and they that hated them, ruled over them." Psalm 106:34-41 Think about it.

"Egypt shall be a desolation and Edom shall be a desolate wilderness for their violence against the children of Judah, because they have shed innocent blood in their land. Joel 3:19

"Thus says the Lord: Execute justice and righteousness, and deliver out of the hand of the oppressor him who has been robbed. And do no wrong; do no violence to the stranger or temporary resident, the fatherless, or the widow, nor shed innocent blood in this place." Jer.: 22:3

God is going to send His judgements on the nations that tolerate, condone and permit human sacrifices by way of legal abortions in the land. More wild fires, flooding, tsunamis, earthquakes, pestilences, droughts, poverty and evil will grow because we ignore and do nothing or little to stop this great crime against humanity, in our generation.

So what is a legal abortion anyway? Weapons of mass destruction such as deadly drugs/chemicals, forceps, suction machines and steel instruments are used with lethal force to dismember, poison, decapitate or crush a perfect little developing baby in the womb, until his or her death.

It is the brutal, systematic and deliberate taking of a fully human, fully alive, typically healthy child in his or her mother's womb. It is an unnatural, forced, pre-term delivery/birth of a child.

People who are called "doctors" commit this act of desecration, then attempt to remove all of the tiny body parts from the uterus. Some bones may inadvertently stick into the uterine wall; causing scarring and complications later. Often the cervix is also damaged as it is artificially stretched and forced open.

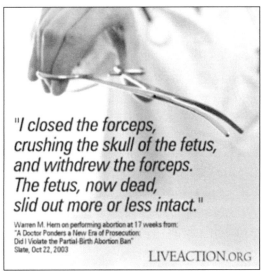

"I closed the forceps, crushing the skull of the fetus, and withdrew the forceps. The fetus, now dead, slid out more or less intact."

Warren M. Hern on performing abortion at 17 weeks from: "A Doctor Ponders a New Era of Prosecution: Did I Violate the Partial-Birth Abortion Ban" Slate, Oct 22, 2003

LIVEACTION.ORG

The remains are either sucked into a jar, or put into a pan, to make sure all of the extremities (arms, legs, head, hands and feet) are there, sometimes the bodily remains are just sent to a lab. The child's body is then discarded like garbage into Human Waste Disposal incinerators with all the other human waste.

In 2015, The Center for Medical Progress revealed and released 13 secret videos from undercover tapings of various employees and doctors who work for Planned Parenthood (a huge abortion mill business in the USA). These employees and abortion doctors are caught on tape talking about the sale of aborted baby body parts for profit. They get more money for older babies, and for heads, livers, hearts and extremities. There was lots of media coverage and outrage from the public about a dentist who killed a lion in Africa, around the same time, but rarely a peep about the sale of baby body parts by abortionists.

Not long ago, I met a young woman "M" who had an abortion in a hospital in Ontario about 6 years ago, when she was about 25 to 26 weeks pregnant. Healthy woman, healthy baby, but she felt pressured to abort as a single woman. Children are known to survive outside the womb at 24 weeks' gestation. After the procedure she went home and actually delivered the torso of this child with the arms and legs ripped off. Shocked, crying and panicking she called the hospital, and they told her to bring it in to them. So she took the remains back to the hospital and they told her they would bury this with the rest of the fetus. Now she wants justice for what was done to her baby.

Abortionists make it seem like it is a normal surgery, like getting a tooth pulled, and that it is not a child. However, when we actually see, what an abortion really is, and does it is revolting, it is abhorrent and it is unbelievable that we tolerate and pay for this cruel and brutal surgery. Sadly, it is frequently a violent form of birth control, and rarely a real medical necessity in this generation.

Occasionally, a baby aborted in the second and third trimester, by saline or other chemicals, actually survives, and is left to die, by neglect. There are now several You-Tube videos available showing doctors examining and poking tiny premature babies at 14-18 weeks. You can also watch an actual abortion take place, and be completely horrified as you see the humanity of these tiny children. But, pro-choicers tell you they are not alive until birth. That is an outright lie…surely you can vividly see these little boys and girls kick their legs and move their arms and bodies in reflex to being touched.

I personally know of three women whose mother's went for an abortion procedure, but somehow, miraculously their children survived...two of them were born with facial disfigurements as a result. One lady, Carrie Holland Fisher is bravely speaking out on how an abortion her mother had, almost killed her, and left her with a disfigured face and some other complications. She is seen here with her husband Richard on the Andrew Womack TV program. She told me that abortion should never be an option. She has the sweetest most forgiving heart.

Another well-known survivor is Gianna Jessen who was aborted at 30 weeks' gestation at 7 and a half months old! The doctor tried to poison her to death with a highly toxic saline injection into the amniotic sac, which forced her to swallow the poison, and it also causes burning to the sensitive skin. She was miraculously delivered alive, not dead as the doctor intended! She arrived alive on April 6, 1977 in Los Angeles, California. Though, rarely do children survive abortions. Go to www.theabortionsurvivors.com

Her medical records indicate she was born during a failed saline abortion attempt. Gianna's birth certificate is signed by the doctor who was performing the abortion. She only weighed 2 pounds at birth, which resulted in her ending up with cerebral palsy, a muscular/motor condition that affects various areas of body movement. She spent three months in the hospital before being placed in foster care. She was adopted at the age of four by a Christian couple. She is an incredibly anointed singer and shares her testimony worldwide. Oh, and by the way, she is totally against abortion too!

There is something terribly wrong when at one end of the hospital they do everything to save sick, pre-mature babies, while at the other end, they kill healthy ones! I call this schizophrenic health care!

The abortionists work really hard to make sure there are no accidental live births; this would be bad for their business. In second and third trimester abortions they often use a lethal dose of potassium chloride and inject this lethal poison into the baby's heart, using an ultra sound and long needle, these days. I wonder if they took lessons from the infamous Dr. Mengele, the German Nazi doctor. Or in the case of a partial birth abortion, the baby is pulled out of the womb, feet first, then the doctor pierces the back of his/her neck with a sharp instrument to cut the spinal cord and then they insert a tube to suck the brains out. Yes, this is really happening in our generation, in some hospitals and late term abortion clinics, and on our watch!

How can we be paying for these barbaric savage acts that not only kill a baby, that could survive outside the womb, but often times causes irreparable damage to the mother physically and psychologically? Abortion is not a "safe" procedure, nor is it a medical necessity, most of the time. If aborting children is a medical necessity, an obligation, then sound the alarm, there is a widespread epidemic on our hands, with thousands of children paying the price with their lives. Plus, we have millions of women suffering from mental and reproductive health issues in the aftermath, for the rest of their lives.

"These six things the Lord hates, indeed, seven are an abomination to Him: A proud look [the spirit that makes one overestimate himself and

underestimate others], a lying tongue, and **hands that shed innocent blood**," [Ps. 120:2, 3.] Prov. 6:16,17

I hold the abortion doctors most accountable, as they know it is a baby, a human being with potential. When we do not value human life in the womb, the disabled, or the weak, the elderly will be the next to go. This too, is a part of the "kill the unwanted" philosophy. Now we are not talking about heroic measures to keep terminally ill patients alive, but about active or passive ways to end the lives of others. It is already happening in countries like Albania, Belgium, Columbia, India, Luxemburg, Denmark, Switzerland, the Netherlands, four States in the USA, and now Quebec is trying to get it legalized too. You see once the doors open judicially for such things that go contrary to the ways of God, Satan begins to push them into other territories and regions…especially where there is little resistance from the people of God to oppose their works.

Years ago, the abortion clinics used to throw the human remains into garbage bags. And a guy I barely knew, went and opened up one of their garbage bags and took out this little one. He called me up, and we met because he wanted to show me what he found. He laid this little body, broken and ripped apart gently onto a paper towel that was folded in half. I remember just crying and grieving for the loss of this child. Today, they use Human Waste Disposal companies to collect the remains, and the blood is washed down the drains and into toilets. These bodies are either sold for body parts, or just heaped into garbage piles with cancer tissues and other human waste. Sadly, there are no funerals, no memorials, no eulogies, and no caskets or flowers. Nonetheless, most women will grieve in private, will suffer in silence and may never tell anyone about this deep sorrow, this deep dark secret.

In Canada, we sing, "God keep our land, glorious and free… we stand on guard for thee…" yet there are no laws or legal restrictions on the slaughter of innocent children while in the temporary residence of their mothers' womb.

WARNING: Graphic picture of an aborted child at about 14 weeks' gestation.

Abortion didn't just upset my life. It has also wounded an estimated 43% of women worldwide in one way, or another. By the time women reach 45 years of age many will have been coerced or deceived into having one or more of their children aborted in our generation. Think about the enormity of that per-centage-it's almost half of all the women of reproductive age!

Disastrously, even the Evangelical Christian community has not escaped the temptation to abort their children either. A George Barna survey states that "one in three women out-side the church have had an abortion and at least one in every six women sitting in Evangelical Christian churches have had abortions. Over 200,000 or 18% of American Christians each year choose abortion as the answer to an unplanned pregnancy.

These numbers are staggering to me! How could "Christians" be doing this horrible act? Unless, of course very few Priests and Pastors are teaching or preaching about the sin of abor-tion. Most leaders seem to just want to ignore the topic. They don't want to talk about it, or even think about it. In fact, it is so disheartening when Christian parents, including members of the clergy, pressure or take their own children for abortions. Even if it is to avoid the shame and disgrace that they or their children had sex before or outside of marriage, and an unplanned pregnancy might damage their "Christian" image or reputation.

I met a woman who attended one of our Healing & Equipping Conferences in Ontario several years ago. She and her husband went to church every Sunday, and they had three beautiful children. Her husband had lost his job, when she discovered she was pregnant with baby number four. They panicked. She asked three "Christian" friends what they should do, and all three, pretty much told them to "do whatever they thought was best." Of course with no scripture in God's word to back that up.

Her husband was complacent and did not stand up as the man of God and spiritual leader of the home and say, "No, honey, we cannot let someone kill our baby." Neither did he reassure his wife that they would manage somehow with God's help. They never considered how God had a plan for this child, and that He would never give them more than they could handle. No, instead her husband took her to the abortion clinic so their fourth child would be killed. She reluctantly went along in fear, thinking it must be

At least one in every six women sitting in Evangelical Christian churches have had abortions. Over 200,000 or 18% of American Christians each year choose abortion-why?

okay, because there was all this support and justification to have the abortion from her husband and "Christians".

Nevertheless, immediately after the abortion, she began to grieve the loss of this child. She felt the intense guilt and remorse of having their child murdered, and began to slide into a deep depression. She could not even look at her living children, knowing they had just had their sibling killed. She could not bear to look at or be with her husband either. Anger began to rage within her soul as she realized the horrible sin of child sacrifice they had committed on the altar of fear. Their marriage started to shatter big time. He did get a job, but their healthy baby was now dead, and they were responsible for that death. Their lives and family would never be the same. They needed to ask each other to forgive each other, and with God's help work at rebuilding their lives and family, never able to replace that child.

Another young woman contacted me because she had grown up in the Pentecostal church. When she was 14, she rebelled, had sex, and got pregnant. She did not tell anyone she was pregnant, but quickly booked an appointment herself, and with no opposition, had her first child aborted. There is no parental consent needed for underage children in Canada to have this invasive surgery that kills a healthy baby, and could leave a young woman sterile, depressed for years, suicidal, or with a much higher risk of getting breast cancer down the road. But if you want a Tylenol for a headache, you must have parental consent for that!

We have thousands of heart wrenching stories and testimonies from women broken and devastated after legal abortion.

Sorry to say, but for decades now, most Pastors and leaders in and out of the church do not want to think about abortion, talk about abortion or do anything to stop this diabolical systematic, ending of innocent human life.

Sadly, most Priests and Pastors are afraid to speak about it, just in case they might offend someone. Are they also afraid of being too political? Is there a fear of losing their charitable tax status, thus losing funds if they publicly renounce abortion and/or homosexuality from the pulpit today? The truth is, fornication is happening in our churches and communities, and therefore so are abortions and other immoral sins! Sex before marriage is rampant in the movies, on TV, /Hollywood, media and influencing young people, as a must do before marriage. Yet, in God's eyes it is a sin, and it is prohibited in His law and heart. Yeshua told His disciples that we are to be the light and salt of the earth. 2,000 years ago in context, salt was used as a preservative to keep fish and meat from rotting. Tragically, our society is rotting more and more, going from worse to worse, more debase, more sexually immoral and perverted, evil is more rotten and degrading than ever. Purity and Godliness is dying, if we continue in our selfish, self-centered ways. Are Christians staying in their comfy, cozy, happy salt shakers, instead of preserving God's ways, truth and word in our cities, and nations?

Have we lost our saltiness in the community, in our nation? "You are the salt of the earth; but if the salt has lost its taste (purpose), how can it be made salty? It is no longer good for anything, but to be thrown out and walked on by people." Mat. 5:13

Chapter 6

Abortion is NOT a "safe" procedure

According to the Merriam-Webster Dictionary, the word "safe" means: "Free from harm or risk, secure from threat of danger, harm or loss, affording safety or security from danger, risk or difficulty". Having an induced abortion is none of that…especially for the child about to be destroyed, or for the woman who may face immediate or future complications to her mental and/or reproductive health!

Many of my friends could never have any children after their so called, "safe" and legal abortion, making them infertile in the aftermath. Brokenhearted and lost motherhood and fatherhood.

My mission is to expose the lies of those who are out to kill, steal and destroy lives. It is about justice for children not yet born, and warning women about the dangers of this brutal act. As well, my heart is to bring hope, healing and recovery to women broken and devastated after abortion. It is only through the blood of Jesus Christ. He is the way, the truth and the life.

First of all, abortion is not safe for the children in utero, the first victim of abortion. A picture of a real 19 week old boy, who tragically was born too soon in a natural miscarriage. My friends, the parents, named him Daniel. We do not know why God allows some children to die naturally. Still, there is no denying his humanity. His perfect little arms and legs, fingers and toes, his cute face, beautiful nose and lips. They held a funeral for him, because he had worth and dignity as every child should.

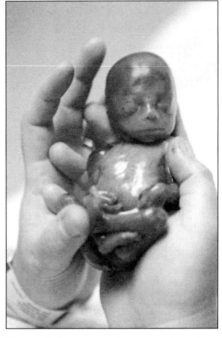

You began your life as the size of a . (dot). The abortion advocates advertise a lot on the internet, and tell people that it is a very "safe" and quick procedure. They publicize doing abortions up to 20+ weeks, which is five months along. In the USA they advertise abortions up to 28 weeks, or seven months' gestation. These are second and third trimester abortions! They do these late term abortions on many healthy babies that could survive outside the womb at 21+ weeks!

LINDA's Late Term Abortion: A few years ago, I got a frantic call from a woman in British Columbia who was so distressed about her abortion that she vividly recalled every detail of the procedure with me in an email she sent. She was also upset and crying in unbelief about what had just transpired a couple of weeks earlier.

Hundreds of women annually go through similar procedures. She was in her late thirties, and never wanted to have any kids she explained as she began to share her experience with me. About a month earlier, she went for a checkup and the doctor told her she was pregnant. She was shocked, she had no symptoms or signs that she was pregnant, and was told to go for an ultra sound. Like in that TV Reality Show, called 'Pregnant and Didn't Know it', that was her. She had often missed her periods, so it was not alarming to her to go for months without one.

Although she wasn't showing, and had no idea she was pregnant, the test disclosed that she was already seven months pregnant! The Radiologist knew that she was thinking of having an abortion, so when she asked to see the ultra sound, he would not let her see it. Perhaps if he would have let her see her baby, and hear the heartbeat, her daughter might probably be alive today. Bringing her much joy and love!

She was single and pregnant, and like many women, panicked. She began to search the internet for someone to help her get rid of this pregnancy, as this was not in her plans. After all, abortion is totally legal, millions of women are doing it, and the Government even pays for it. By the way, she was independent, a career woman on the go socially. She was healthy, and the baby was totally healthy too.

Soon she found an abortionist who would terminate the life of this baby, no questions asked. She informed them that she was already 28 weeks, or 7 months pregnant, and told them that there were no abnormalities with the fetus. She then asked if it was still okay to have the procedure done. "Not a problem" was the answer, and how soon could she come for the appointment, the sooner the better. It would be a 4-day procedure.

They made sure she would first get the documents faxed to them by the BC Provincial Government Health Care to cover the $12,500.00 fee. This exorbitant fee did not include her airfare to Boulder, Colorado or her hotel room either. She later wondered that if she had taken more time to really think about it, and if someone would have told her the fetal development and humanity of this child, she probably would have never have gone through with it.

By the time of the scheduled appointment she was now seven and a half months pregnant, the baby was now 30 weeks along.

She just felt an urgency to get this done as soon as possible, and did not think of or look into the facts of fetal growth. She was afraid, ashamed of being single and pregnant, afraid of what others would think of her, and stuck to her vow of never having any children.

On her way to the abortion clinic she felt the baby move, it was the first time she felt something, and ever so briefly. No one at the abortion clinic nor her own doctor suggested that she let the baby live, or call a pregnancy crisis center for help and get some education and awareness on what was happening with her child. She was not a teenager, or victim of rape or abuse. She was never informed about how developed her baby actually was. She was not told that babies born pre-maturely at this age can survive outside the womb as early as 24 weeks.

It was as if she got on this eerie treadmill and was not able to get off of it. She described the abortion clinic as "gloomy and cold".

The first day at the abortion clinic, they did an ultra sound, and she told them she wanted to see it, but they would not allow her to see the ultra sound or discuss it with her. Later she knew that she would have changed her mind after seeing a baby on ultra sound.

They had her sign lots of waiver forms etc. and told her to watch a 10 min. video on the procedure and birth control options, and to let them know when it was over.

They never even asked her why she wanted to have an abortion, or gave her any alternatives or options! That's not pro-choice, that is pro-death!

They used an ultra sound to find the baby's heart. When she turned to look at the screen, the abortionist yelled at her not to look. Then he inserted a long needle into her womb. She was so afraid, it hurt, and she began to squirm and shake a little. Her hands were shaking, he insisted she stop, but she could not control it. She was very anxious, tears were rolling down her cheeks, she was asking questions, but he just continued. The abortionist was extremely rude, and repeatedly told her to "Shut up, stay still or you will die."

This doctor who should be saving babies, injected a lethal dose of potassium chloride venom into this precious, healthy, baby's heart, with the intent to kill this child! Yes, this is happening in our generation! Yes, he killed this baby and hundreds, perhaps thousands more over the years!

What transgression did this child commit to deserve Capital Punishment like a prisoner on death row?

What kind of beast can kill the most vulnerable and innocent human beings on earth?

Who can do this routinely every day and justify it? As far as I am concerned, they are the biggest bullies on earth. Abortionists are blind, deceived and paid assassins, children of the devil, working hard for Satan, the father of lies, and murderer from the beginning.

Disguised as angels of light, they go to Medical school and dress in white coats. They have university degrees and are called "doctors". They claim they are doing women a favour. They claim it is a "safe" procedure. Well, it is certainly **not safe** for women, or the defenseless baby, powerless against these weapons of mass destruction. The choice to kill another human being, no matter how small should never be acceptable to any of us. These doctors are supposed to save lives, and help the hurting; not destroy lives and cause harm to the babies and to the mothers in one way or another, sooner or later!

They rake in millions of dollars...and you are paying for it with your money and silence.

Nazi doctors also felt they were doing Germans a favour by exterminating Jews, the sick and elderly etc. They used to systematically kill men, women and children with their lies and deception by telling the victims they were going for a shower, when in reality they were going into a gas chamber to be poisoned to death. Nazi Germany's T-4 Euthanasia Program used lethal injection also as one of several methods to destroy what the Nazi government dubbed as "lives unworthy of life". The victims were called "useless eaters and the unproductive" …

The abortionist then inserted laminaria seaweed into her cervix to begin to force it to dilate. Of course people who take the lives of the innocent want to downplay their acts of violence on the blameless, and never divulge the humanity of the baby in the matrix. These children are fully human and fully alive no matter how small.

On the website of this late term abortionist, it states, the injection "is an injection of medication into the fetus that will stop the fetal heart instantly." However, the definition of the word medication, means a 'drug used to treat an illness, or the treatment of an illness using drugs'. Since when is a lethal injection which will kill someone, a "medication"? How is this treating an illness? Since when is a baby in her mother's womb, an illness? Oh, how Satan uses euphemisms and lies to distort the truth.

He walked out of the room, and then it hit her like a ton of concrete…she had just made the biggest mistake of her life! She began to feel a tsunami of guilt and regret of what had just happened to her baby. It felt like she just woke up from a dream, a horrific nightmare, and realized what was happening. She just wanted to die. She couldn't stop crying for days… weeks…the crying continues. Another woman once told me she cried for 25 years after her abortion. You see we can never replace or bring back that aborted child. It is done. We never get to love, hug, cuddle, kiss, nurture or bless our child…it is the most unnatural thing for a pregnant woman to have her own child killed.

Linda did not want to return to the abortion clinic the next morning and face that monster doctor again. She was angry, she was upset, she was sick. When she didn't show up for the appointment, where they were going to insert more laminaria to force her cervix open more and more, they called her. She refused to go. A staff from the clinic knocked on her hotel door, and out popped the abortionist, who made his way into her room, and he pleaded with her to go back or she would die. He sure didn't want her going to a hospital in her condition and telling them that he had injected poison into her baby's heart to cause her demise. So she was coerced into going back and having the abortionist insert more laminaria to force her cervix wider and wider for the next 3 days, in order for the now dead baby to be delivered. She told staff that she wanted to see it; they said no, she can't.

When the deceased child was being delivered, after being poisoned to death by the doctor, Linda was trying to sit up to see it, the nurse pushed her down and they would not allow her to see the baby. When it was over, the doctor happily and proudly told her she was not pregnant anymore. She just cried.

The shedding of innocent blood is an abomination to God (Prov. 6:16,17), it also causes the womb to be empty/barren/desolate!

> *"So when you see the appalling sacrilege [the abomination that astonishes and makes desolate], spoken of by the prophet Daniel, standing in the Holy Place—let the reader take notice and ponder and consider and heed" [this]—[Dan. 9:27; 11:31; 12:11.] Mat 24:15*

Alone now, depressed, grieving and frantic, she began to search for help. She found our Canada Silent No More website and our Toll Free number and called me. Linda was very angry at herself, and the abortionist, she was severely hurt, broken, numb and was not able to go back to work…she was an emotional wreck. Linda isolated herself, and felt she could not face the world, knowing now what she did. Many of us go into shock after.

She had come to the realization that abortion actually killed her "baby" and from that moment a part of her died also. She was so distraught. She felt so much guilt, shame and deep remorse. The sorrow was extremely heavy. I too was angry asking, "How could this so called doctor even do such a brutal thing to a perfectly healthy baby who could easily survive outside the womb at that age?" How can anyone justify this contracted assassination/murder?

There is something terribly wrong when at one end of the hospital they are doing everything to save sick pre-mature babies, and down the hall they are killing healthy ones!

Linda is really having a difficult time trying to forgive herself, she has thoughts of suicide as the only way to ever see her baby. How could she have done this selfish, malicious thing she asks herself over and over? If only they had let her see an ultra sound, before the abortion procedure. If only the doctor had told her about how developed her baby was, and explain how the heart was beating, how she had perfect arms, legs, fingers and toes...and how she could survive outside the womb.

If only, she had someone to talk to about help for single Moms, and support services available for her. She totally took all the blame on herself, and could not even look at herself in the mirror, she felt less than worthy to live. I shared my pain of abortion with her, shared the vision I had of my aborted children with Jesus Christ, reassuring her that her child was in heaven. I led her in a sinner's prayer, and ministered God's love to her, although she still struggles with thoughts of suicide. She felt it was a girl, and has given her a name.

Yet, since we Christians, Jews, and Muslims and most religions know and agree that abortion is murder, how can we as citizens, be paying for these vicious, savage killings on little defenseless babies? Abortion is not a medical necessity 97% of the time. It cures no disease, but totally destroys a perfectly healthy human being, and wounds another.

How can they destroy a life, just because they are temporarily not "wanted" at the moment by someone? How can we tolerate this great EVIL happening in our cities, and nations?

In Canada, notorious abortionist and former holocaust survivor, Henry Morgentaler broke the laws to change the laws to bring in lawlessness. It worked. Tragically, a bunch of liberal judges struck down our abortion laws on Jan. 28, 1988. Sadly, most of the politicians here, have not had the courage to change the status quo, so there is still no law, or restrictions on abortion. We have total anarchy when it comes to abortion/human sacrifice in this country. The USA are miles ahead of us as they have many restrictions such as gestational age limits, parental consent laws, informed consent laws, and the right to know laws. Several abortion clinics have been shut down in the US. We need to follow suit.

Back in 1989, I think it was, notorious abortion doctor Henry Morgentaler sued 4 others and myself, for a million dollars because we were bad for their business. It was a strategy by Morgentaler and his lawyer to keep us away from his prospective clients and losing money. As we would warn pregnant women of the dangers of legal abortion and offer them help and alternatives to abortion.

I will show you how really unsafe abortion is for pregnant women and children in this book. Why are we paying for this diabolical procedure? Only one brave and courageous tiny Province in Canada, Prince Edward Island does not allow abortions on their land, so far. Abortion providers falsely claim that abortion is "safer than childbirth" itself. Certainly, it is not "safe" for the baby who is being poisoned or dismembered while alive! According to a Morgentaler-abortion clinic website, for decades they have given this false information to young pregnant women. As of March 12, 2016 they still publicize this fabricated statement; "Abortion is in the category of minor medical procedures and as such has one of the lowest rates of complication. To put things in perspective, abortion is considered to be twenty times safer than childbirth." http://www.morgentalermontreal.ca/index.php?page=faq&lang=_en

Can you imagine the young woman finds out she's pregnant, and in shock, wondering what to do, she begins a search about the possibility of having an abortion? She comes across this statement on the abortion clinic website, reading that abortion is 20 times "safer" than childbirth! Of course these abortion providers profit in the millions from susceptible, ill-informed young women who are usually pregnant for the first time. Wow, she thinks, I better have an abortion, it is so much safer for me. What a load of garbage!

Of course there are absolutely no references or links as to where they get this notion. Or is it just a good advertising and marketing ploy to entice young naïve pregnant women to go to them and get rid of the unexpected child? These are supposed to be ethical "doctors/experts" telling young pregnant women that induced abortion will be "safer" for their health and well-being, than to naturally give birth to their developing child?

Don't you think there is a huge conflict of interest here? Abortion clinics make their millions killing children before birth. It is big business! Who is most important to their success, babies who cannot speak for themselves, vulnerable, pregnant women, or doing as many abortions as they can squeeze into a day, to line their pockets with lots of money?

What a gross, misleading, disgusting LIE!! Yep, this really makes me angry, and it should stir you up too! How many pregnant women have they lured into these governments sanctioned death mills with that line? How many children have they brutally killed before they had a chance to fight for themselves? How many women have they maimed for life in the abortion procedure? How many will get, or got breast cancer or other complications in the after-effects? As you will see in the lines ahead, so many studies over the last few decades, along with thousands of former abortion patients testifying on how actually unsafe this intrusive surgery really is to our bodies and souls.

Remember, abortionists and their staff, are a little biased. They have a huge conflict of interest, since they make all of their income by doing abortions. It has become far too easy, and accessible to have ones' healthy child in utero dismembered and killed, without question. Vulnerable, young pregnant women just making appointments over the phone, with no prior consultation necessary, with no parental consent, no referral from a doctor, little wait times, and no medical necessity, just another form of birth control. Just a simple phone call to make an appointment that could ruin their life forever.

I pray that women will get the courage to sue these people who exploit young pregnant women. Abortionists will run for the hills, if they are sued. They are not helping pregnant women; they are ruining many lives and getting rich from the profits! It is abhorrent that we are forced to pay for these barbaric acts with our taxes!

I thank God for the abortionists who have repented, seen the error of their ways and stopped taking innocent lives. Doctors Beverly Mc Millan, Anthony Levatino, Bernard Nathanson, Joseph Randall, Yvonne Moore and more. I'm praying every abortion doctor will all be convicted by the Holy Spirit, and stop this violence against pregnant women and their children.

Carol Everett a former abortion clinic owner and operator of several abortion clinics in the USA. She publically discloses the secrets about the abortion industry, how it was always about sales, how many abortions they could do in a day. She also reveals how weekly women were injured and some had to go to hospital. There is a documentary called *Blood Money* that also exposes their deception and motives.

Greed overtook her and with her dream of being a millionaire, she opened a total of 5 clinics. She learned how to market abortions as the ONLY choice a woman had in her time of crisis. If it wasn't a crisis, they made her believe it was. Her employees that manned the telephones were called counselors, but were nothing more than telemarketers who had been trained to sell abortion as the only choice and it worked very well.

Virtually everything they told their clients were lies. When asked if it hurt, they just said it felt like any other cramping they had experienced. When asked if it was a baby, they said it was just a blood clot or a piece of tissue. The paperwork given to the girl asking for an abortion was specifically written to confuse her into not knowing what she was signing.

One woman even died from an abortion in one of her clinics. Then one day someone introduced her to Jesus Christ, and she left the abortion industry and began to expose the evil practices.

Read more at http://godfatherpolitics.com/8275/former-abortion-provider-confesses-horrors-of-abortion-industry/#5LUv5mOrTAqZctp0.99

Stefanie, a woman I know from British Columbia in her early 40's now, calls me regularly for prayer and emotional support. She had three abortions when she was younger. At the age of 32, I think it was, she had to have a total hysterectomy from complications of abortion, and will never be able to have children. This also makes her at a higher risk for getting breast cancer.

She fights depression, self-medicates and is now addicted to prescription pain killers. In my own darkest hours, I used to take pain killers, and drink, but it just numbs you out, it never really takes the pain away.

Abortionists specialize in killing pre-born children that is what these "doctors" do. It is a huge multi-billion-dollar industry. I would say they are very prejudiced, and not looking out for the best, healthiest interests of pregnant women, but rather on how many abortions they can do in a day, and how many baby body parts they can get paid for. I declare that they are NOT doing women a favour!

They should be sued for giving false and misleading information and made to remove their lies and misinformation from the websites and all their materials. It sickens me that many of them are in this for the love of money, really they are paid assassins, and the cost is innocent human life.

Do not believe their lies as they pronounce how so many hundreds of thousands of women are dying from "unsafe" illegal abortions. They fabricated and inflated those numbers greatly as Dr. Bernard Nathanson, a former abortion doctor and abortion activist confessed years ago. Their goal is to push abortion practices into every nation worldwide where it is still illegal or where there are restrictions to have abortion on demand as a form of birth control. They are now also pushing cancer causing chemical agents like The Pill, Patches, injectables and so forth into women as birth control and not letting women know about the hormonal cancer link!

Satan has, and still is out to kill women and children, since we are created in the image of God, and we bring forth children created in God's image, of whom He hates.

Where are the men to stand up and protect us women and children? They seem to be far and few between with courage and tenacity to face these goliaths getting away with murder.

Abortion is so prevalent these days. Nevertheless, there are some mighty men and women working tirelessly to be a voice for the voiceless today. I thank GOD for them!

There are now multitudes of credible studies proving abortion is harmful to women's mental and reproductive health and this research is mounting. All this scientific examination of proving the harm of induced abortion, is not good for the abortion industry, so of course they want to ignore it. They quickly deny and dismiss these studies, and keep this knowledge about all of the risk factors from their expectant customers.

It is also disheartening how the Media and Politicians also ignore and deny the science due to their own biased dogmas, agendas and ideologies.

Abortion is quite harmful to women! A huge study in Finland shows that **women who abort their child are approximately four times more likely to die in the following year, than women who carry their children to term.** This study "proves beyond a shadow of a doubt that abortion is not safer than childbirth," observed David Reardon, PhD of the Elliot Institute.

Researchers from the statistical analysis unit of Finland's National Research and Development Center for Welfare and Health (STAKES) examined death certificate records for all women of reproductive age (15-49) who died between 1987 and 1994 there was a total of **9,129** women. This is a HUGE significant study!

Then they examined the national health care database to identify any pregnancy-related events for the women in the 12 months prior to their deaths. The researchers found that compared to women who carried their baby to term; **Women who had an abortion in the year prior to their deaths were 60 percent more likely to die of natural causes, six times more likely to die of suicide, four times more likely to die of injuries related to accidents, and 14 times more likely to die from homicide.** Researchers believe the higher rate of deaths related to accidents and homicide may be linked to higher rates of suicidal or risk-taking behavior after induced abortions.

"Even though this important study was published in the top Scandinavian Obstetrics Journal, it has been completely ignored by the American press," Reardon continued. "Even worse, abortion counselors continue to lie to American women. They are telling women that abortion is safer than childbirth, when this and other irrefutable studies prove exactly the opposite. The entire body of medical literature clearly shows that abortion contributes to a decline in women's physical and mental health. Women are not hearing this! Nor are they being told that giving birth actually contributes to women's overall health, not only in comparison to those who abort, but also in comparison to women who have not been pregnant."

Reardon believes that abortion providers are collaborating with population control zealots to conceal the risks of abortion in order to advance their own financial and social engineering agendas. "If they were really pro-choice, they would want women to know about abortion's true risks," he said.

The Guttmacher Institute was founded by Allan Guttmacher, an abortionist and they do very biased research to promote their abortion agendas to legalize abortion in every nation. A multi-billion-dollar industry. They are population controllers. Nevertheless, the UN, media and other big organizations use their biased numbers and information to push their propaganda.

Please note that thousands of pregnant women have DIED from so called, "safe and legal" abortions! Abortion always has at least two victims, the dead child, and the wounded mother. Mark Crutcher from Life Dynamics has produced the 'Blackmun Wall' in Honour of some of the known women who have died from legally botched abortions in the USA. So far they have 348 women listed on this wall to date. With hundreds more they are following up on. Go to www.safeandlegal.com

In his telling book, *Lime 5*, Mark reveals that, "the USA Centre for Disease Control (CDC), an American Government agency, since the 70's has had dozens of abortionists and pro–abortionists in leadership staff positions in their Abortion Surveillance Department. Then we analyzed that list of names of people we knew to have links with the abortion industry. Not surprisingly, we discovered that a significant number of CDC employees, especially its leadership, are indeed involved in the abortion industry. Out of 68 upper-level employees of the CDC, we were able to identify 48 as medical doctors. Of these, 17 are actually practicing abortionists and nine others have an obvious connection with the abortion industry."

Crutcher further states, "This situation is clearly in violation of the government's code of employee ethics. While the public would never tolerate people with ties to the tobacco industry being in charge of an agency that monitors the impact of cigarette smoking on public health; but that is precisely what is happening at the CDC."

Crutcher knows of hundreds of women who have died from legal abortions, but no one is being informed about this! Why aren't these cases on talk shows or the daily news?

No wonder they always make excuses when abortion kills the mother. Tamia Russell, a 15-year-old in a Detroit suburb, died in January, 2004 as a result of a second trimester abortion. Dr. Leigh Hlavaty performed an autopsy on Tamia and ruled the death as "normal." The doctor explained, "I ruled it normal because these complications are expected with this type of abortion." However, It is not normal for 15-year-old healthy young pregnant women to die!

If abortion is a "medical necessity" then we better sound the alarm, and do a huge media prevention campaign, because there is an "epidemic" in the land!

The Canadian Morgentaler abortion websites propagate these following statements to susceptible pregnant teenagers online: "No, you do not need a doctor's referral to make an appointment. You can make the appointment at your convenience and at your request. There are no regulatory waiting times in place to prevent or restrict access to abortion services. No, you do not need parental and partner permission to book an appointment or to have an abortion." Yet, this surgery leaves some women sterile, some will get breast cancer and some young women will want to kill themselves in the aftermath.

They also deceptively state that abortion does not cause breast cancer, that the second trimester aged baby cannot feel pain, that abortion is safer than having your tonsils out, and that there is no Post Traumatic Stress Disorder etc. in the aftershock of abortion. How can this false and misleading advertising be tolerated?

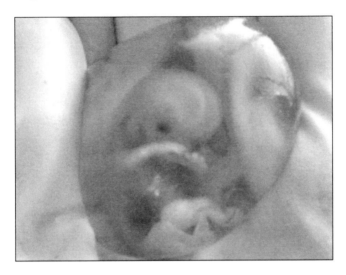

Science also proves that babies in utero do feel pain! Truth is, starting at four weeks after conception, pain receptors begin to develop, followed by nerve fibers that carry messages to the brain. Science demonstrates that as early as six weeks' gestation, the tiny baby responds to touch. The baby's cerebral cortex (pain center) starts developing at eight weeks. By ten weeks, if the baby is touched, his/her hands and eyes will close.

At twelve weeks the baby (Fetus-Latin word meaning the "little one") is able to smile, swallow and responds to simple stimulation of the skin. At 20 weeks, all the physiological connections are in place to feel pain.

Where are the laws protecting young pregnant teens and women from making the biggest mistake of their lives? This insidious procedure done in her most private parts could possibly result in irreparable physical and/or psychological damage? What does a teenager know about the risks and consequences of abortion? Most are also pressured to abort, like I was, at the age of 16.

Today, the euphemism of "choice" is chanted and touted as a great thing for women's wealth and health. Please think about this: The choice should be made on who to have sex with, why, when and where, but once conception takes place, now there is another human being there, with the potential to give you unconditional love and blessings. But the choice to have your baby dismembered, crushed and/or poisoned to death, should be unthinkable.

Just because something is "legal" doesn't make it right. Slavery was legal, when Africans were sold into slavery, beaten, worked to death and treated like animals. They were bought, sold and had no rights to property, no rights to freedom and no right to life.

The Holocaust was also legal, where Nazis killed the "unwanted" Jews. Millions of men, women and children were systematically starved, poisoned with gas, and exterminated by the millions. It was legal, but it was wrong.

The same "kill the unwanted" philosophy is manifested today through aborting children before birth, it is about population control and feeding off of the spirit of fear.

This horrendous industry is built on the blood of dead children and wounded women. Oh and for the record, for those rare number of women who think abortion is ok; and they claim to be happy they had their child(ren) killed by an abortionist... I think they are still in denial about fetal development and the humanity of children in the womb. I also believe that they are still trying to justify their abortion(s) so as not to contemplate the reality of what an abortion really is, and what it did to their child. However, one day, it will hit them. One day, they will get the revelation that abortion killed their child, and it is a wrong, and not a right.

Hippocrates, the celebrated Greek physician, was a contemporary of his time and left several valuable medical writings that are still used today to instruct young doctors. He was born between 460 and 470 B.C. He introduced the **Physician's Oath** and it was codified in the Declaration of Geneva (1948) by the World Medical Association This oath was in response to the atrocities committed by the Nazi physicians in Germany.

Notably, this oath requires the physician to "not use [his] medical knowledge contrary to the laws of humanity." This document was adopted by the World Medical Association only three months before the United Nations General Assembly adopted the Universal Declaration of Human Rights (1948) which provides for the security of the person. The legacy of the Hippocratic Oath for doctors' state:

> *"I will maintain the utmost respect for human life from the time of conception, even under threat, I will not use my medical knowledge contrary to the laws of humanity; I will neither prescribe nor administer a lethal dose of medicine to any patient even if asked, nor counsel any such thing, but will have the utmost respect for every human life from fertilization to natural death and reject abortion that deliberately takes a unique human life."*

Before Christ walked on the earth, some people were doing abortions, but real ethical doctors were told never to administer a lethal dose to any patient, and to reject abortion that deliberately takes a unique human life. Nevertheless, many medical schools have deleted the part about abortions and euthanasia, in the last few decades, how sad.

I hold the doctors most accountable for the shedding of innocent blood. They know it is a child. How could they be destroying human lives, when they should be saving human lives? I thank God for the brave doctors who say "No" to abortion, and who will not refer women to have their children's lives terminated. Far too many doctors protect and tolerate their abortion practicing colleagues.

Dr. Bernard Nathanson, a former abortionist from New York, and leader of National Abortion Rights League, (NARAL) who worked hard to legalize abortion in the USA, confessed that they lied about how many women were having complications and dying from illegal abortions in order to change the laws and get sympathy to legalize abortion on demand. He admitted doing over 60,000 abortions himself. Yet, when ultrasound technology began, he had a colleague do the ultrasound as he performed an abortion to observe what takes place during an abortion. He was shocked to see the 12-week old baby sucking her thumb; then, as the suction machine entered into the uterus, he could clearly see her opening her mouth wide as in a silent scream as she was ripped apart alive. This revelation turned him around, and he became a pro-lifer. I had the opportunity of hearing him share and meeting him personally. I also gave him a copy of my first book, *Forgiven of Murder, a True Story*. He did convert from being Jewish to being a believer in Yeshua.

I believe that whenever a man, a woman or a nation comes into an agreement with abortion, we are coming into an agreement with a spirit of death/murder and human sacrifice. Many times I have led post abortive men and women and Christians in a prayer to renounce the agreement with murder, and break this covenant with death.

Childbirth is the natural ending to every pregnancy. Giving birth results in the joy of a beautiful child that is full of unconditional love towards his or her mother and father. A child will never hurt anyone. Giving life to a child brings hope and a purpose, it even helps prevent breast cancer in women too! More on this later!

Recently, I was interviewed in a new documentary called, "HUSH" where it exposes how legal abortion causes Breast Cancer, Cervical Damage and Mental Health issues in the aftermath. I have prayed for years for this kind of a documentary to prove that abortion is not a "safe" procedure, and that it hurts women and killed my children. This documentary also reveals the cover-ups by Cancer Societies and the March of

Dimes (USA) who deny the abortion link, even though a mountain of evidence proves scientifically that abortion is significantly linked to breast cancer and pre-term births. This film also interviews an abortionist who blatantly denies the evidence and studies and the director is pro-choice woman, so it is really geared to secular audiences. It has several other testimonies from former abortion patients who declare that abortion hurt them, and took the lives of their children, some who could never have children after as a result. The Mental Health problems are real, and millions of women are suffering, often in silence.

It is well done, and has great conversations with scientists, doctors and researchers exposing these cover-ups by multi-million dollar organizations, who deny the connections. I attended the World Premiere at the La Femme Film Festival in Beverly Hills and the Malibu Film Festival at Universal Studios too. It just won a Gold Award in the World Documentary Awards. Please pray millions of people will see this and be astounded.

Most people have no clue, and have never heard about all these devastating consequences. For almost 30 years now, I have been telling people about the horrible aftermath of legal abortion, how it causes Breast Cancer, cervical damage and psychological damage. I am praying that at least one Celebrity sees it, gets it, and will help get this documentary and its valuable information into the marketplace and into theatres and television to warn pregnant women of the real medical risks involved in legal abortion.

A couple of years ago, I was praying, and asked the Lord about our last Prime Minister, apparently a conservative, supposedly a Christian, Stephen Harper. I was wondering why he was avoiding the "a" word and telling his Members of Parliament not to make motions or talk about the issue…and this is what the Holy Spirit showed me from the book of Revelation. Our elected Governmental leaders are supposed to make laws to protect every human being regardless of race, sex, age or how small or tiny they are. Yet sadly, most politicians are people pleasers, full of fear, and just want to keep their lucrative jobs.

They are too afraid to stand up against the loud, obnoxious pro-abortion lobbyists, or to that spirit of Jezebel. Instead of defending pregnant women and the lives of innocent children in the womb, most remain silent and ignore our cries for justice and restrictions. They tolerate the shedding of innocent blood in our land and make us pay for it.

Disappointingly, most Christians and politicians in Canada have done little to protect and rescue children in the womb. Yet, I am praying for them to become more brave and courageous to advance the Kingdom of God on this earth.

> ***"But as for the cowards, and the ignoble and the contemptible, and the cravenly lacking in courage and the cowardly submissive, and as for the unbelieving and faithless, and as for the depraved and defiled with abominations, and as for murderers and the lewd and adulterous and the practicers of magic arts and the idolaters (those who give supreme devotion to anyone or anything other than God) and all liars (those who knowingly convey untruth by word or deed)—[all of these shall have] their part in the lake that blazes with fire and brimstone. This is the second death."***
> *[Isa. 30:33.] Rev 21:8*

This is what God thinks of cowards, liars, perverts and murderers etc. They are going to hell, unless they ask God to forgive them, and change (repent).

However, I thank God for the few bold and courageous politicians and leaders who know their God and are attempting to do great exploits to save pregnant women and children. God bless Members of Parliament such as Rod Bruinooge, Maurice Vellacott, Brad Trost, Ken Epp, Mark W., Stephen Woodworth and others who stand up for Life and Godliness. We know that this massacre of legal abortion is happening every day in our cities, yet most will stick their heads in the sand and pretend it has nothing to do with us. This cruel and evil depraved act is carried on daily, without much resistance.

How does God put up with this? Good thing I am not God; I would have wiped us all out long ago.

With the exception of several thousand brave souls like the ones who participate in the Marches for Life, those who show the graphic pictures of aborted children and expose the link to genocides of the Jews and injustices of slavery and lynching's. I thank God for my pro-life friends and heroes like Linda Gibbons, Mary Wagner, Sissy, Peter, Don, Joanne, Sister Elisabeth, and all those who faithfully pray and do peaceful sidewalk counseling despite the man-made laws to stop them. Yes, like Paul and Silas, some of us have spent time in jail.

I was arrested once for peaceful protest during an Operation Rescue event in Toronto back in 1989, I think. I was more interested in doing sidewalk counseling; trying to talk to the pregnant women headed towards the abortion mill. I would tell them that I had abortions, and how it damaged my cervix and uterus. I told them abortion could hurt them too. I told them their baby had a beating heart, and we could help them, and urged them to let their baby live.

If I didn't have to do all this travelling to the United Nations, and around the world to bring this message exposing the damage of legal abortion to women's mental and reproductive health, I would probably be in jail for peaceful protests and trying to rescue children scheduled for death in front of those death camps, along with Linda and Mary right now. We are in good company with Mahatma Gandhi, Martin Luther King Jr. and Rosa Parks who all stepped out of their comfort zone to do the right thing against unjust laws.

One of my favourite parables from Luke 10:25-37. The Priest and the Levite, were purportedly Godly men in the Parable of the Good Samaritan. Here we have a lawyer, asking Yeshua, "How do we get **eternal life**?" Then Yeshua tells him to love God and to love his neighbor; "but who is my neighbor?" the lawyer asks. Then Yeshua proceeds to share this story about the Good Samaritan.

There was a man, a victim who was beaten and robbed, left bleeding to die in the ditch. Along came a Priest/Pastor, who saw him injured and dying, but for whatever reason, ignored him, and decided to cross the road and leave him there to die. He must have been too busy to help him. Then came a Levite, another Godly man, who also saw the victim, but perhaps he was on his way to Bible Study, or Worship practice or a prayer meeting, and also ignored him and left him there to die.

Today we ignore those being beaten and robbed of life, and just walk by the abortion mills and hospital killing centers, looking the other way, ignoring the bloodshed. However, it was the good Samaritan who went and rescued him, and brought him to a hotel and even paid to have him looked after, who was the Good Neighbour. He wasn't talking about the people next door either! It is the one who RESCUES them and even puts money towards their cause, is the one who loves his neighbor and gets eternal life, according to what Jesus Christ said here.

The Bible says that blood has a voice, and it cries out from the ground for justice. Justice is the foundation of HIS throne. Yet, mercy triumphs over justice. Christians walk and drive by the killing centers regularly, we know they are in our cities, yet hardly anyone prays or does anything that will stop it. Have you cried out to God on this issue yourself? While the blood of the innocents cries out to God for justice, the Blood of Yeshua cries out for repentance. Does anyone have ears to hear what the Spirit is saying? Does anyone see what God sees every time a baby is ripped apart alive and slaughtered in that secret place? Oh, that we would turn from our wicked materialistic, comfortable, self-centered ways, to be a voice for the voiceless? His Holy Spirit goes to and fro to see if anyone would stand in the gap. If we, the church, know the truth, and really believe that abortion is the systematic murder of innocent children, then, why aren't we acting like it is?

Wouldn't GOD want us to do everything possible to protect those children that He created? Doesn't He want us to be the salt and light of the earth, to preserve His way, truth and life, and expose this goliath getting away with cold blooded murder in our land?

Tragically, for many of us, who have succumbed to the lure of getting rid of an 'unplanned' pregnancy, we push down the feelings and memories. We go into denial, not believing it was really a baby, and we try to justify it. We come up with all the reasons why we thought it was okay to be rid of this unintended pregnancy. Most of us were convinced by others to do it.

Nonetheless, a pregnancy is really the condition of being pregnant, which is the physical condition of a woman carrying a baby temporarily inside of her body from the moment of fertilization until the birth or delivery of that child. Whether dead or alive, one day the child is delivered from the womb. From the moment of conception, all of the entire DNA is present with the potential for that person to live a full life span.

Abortion makes women and men, the parents of dead children. Abortionists who crush the life out of little children before their natural birth, are the biggest bullies to me. The abortionists must be atheists or humanists, children of the devil who have a seared conscience, and I pray that they will turn from their evil ways. They know it is a living baby, until they suck the life out of them.

Dr. Anthony Levatino, an Ob/Gyn and pro-choice advocate testifies that he aborted the lives of over 1,200 babies, many were from 14 to 25 weeks' gestation. Then one day his 6-year-old daughter was tragically hit by a car and killed. Then with the last abortion he did, he was repulsed with the reality of what he was actually doing as he ripped off an arm from the last child he killed. Now he describes the gruesome act of dismembering children in the womb. A powerful testimony which is exposing the truth.

If and when abortion becomes illegal again, there is no way that thousands or millions of women would start shoving coat hangers up their private parts, to abort their babies. We need to offer pregnant women love, education, support and practical help, not abortion.

Sooner or later, the reality arises. For some women, it is immediate, especially if they had doubts and did not really want an abortion. Studies show that over 64% of women do not even want an abortion, but are coerced or pressured into it by boyfriends, parents, husbands, doctors or others.

Sooner or later abortion devastates women and men. I know, we get the letters, emails and calls on our toll free number from broken women. Yet, most secular counselors tell women they did the right thing, and they should get over it… but deep down, they know it was wrong, and eventually the guilt, remorse and regret begin to surface…sometimes they suppress the pain and go into denial for many years; I did.

Chapter 7

Scientific Research Confirms the Damage

W e were designed to nurture and protect our babies, not have them brutally killed by someone. It can be unbearable as a woman, to realize one day that you had your baby legally murdered. It is not natural for women to come into agreement with this spirit of death, this contract with murder.

We, the church first need to encourage youth and young adults to hang on to their hormones! We are not animals. We also need to be there for single pregnant women, to offer help and hope and support for them in practical and loving ways. My heart is to one day open up a home for unwed mothers in every major city.

"Pure religion and undefiled before God and the Father is this; to visit/relieve the fatherless and widows in their affliction, and to keep himself unspotted from the world." James 1:27

For most women sooner or later, it does cause remorse, grief, deep sorrow and regret. Many studies confirm women suffer a lot of damage after an induced, legal abortion. There are over 100 possible physical complications. The deVeber Institute for Bioethics and Social Research in Canada, recently published a new extensive 433-page book entitled, **Complications-Abortion's Impact on Women** by Dr. Angela Lanfranchi, Prof. Ian Gentles and Psychologist Elizabeth Ring-Cassidy. It is a comprehensive collection of data and research on the aftermath of abortion. www.deveber.org

Abortion providers tell women it is a "safe" procedure, yet thousands of women are injured for life, and thousands are dying every year as a result. Many women end up aborting the only child they would or could ever have.

David Reardon from the Elliot Institute has also done a fabulous job collecting research on the after effects of legal abortion, see below:

According to a colossal Finnish study done from 1987 to 1994 by researcher, Mika Gissler, they found that there is a higher risk of **DEATH** for women who abort their babies, compared with pregnant women who let their children live:

Pregnant women who had their children aborted were...

- **3.5 TIMES more likely to die in the following year**
- **1.6 TIMES more likely to die of natural causes**
- **6 TIMES more likely to die of suicide**
- **14 TIMES more likely to die from homicide**
- **4 TIMES more likely to die of injuries related to accidents.**3

Another study found that, compared to women who gave birth, women who had abortions had a 62% higher risk of death from all causes for at least *eight* years after their pregnancies. Deaths from suicides and accidents were most prominent, with deaths from suicides being 2.5 times higher.

Causes of death within a week — the leading causes of abortion-related maternal deaths within a week of abortion are hemorrhage, infection, embolism, anesthesia complications, and undiagnosed ectopic pregnancies.

Physical Complications from induced abortion:

Cancer — significantly increased risk of breast cancer, cervical cancer, and lung cancer (probably due to heavier smoking patterns after abortion).

Immediate complications — about 10% suffer immediate complications; one-fifth of those are life-threatening:

- hemorrhage • infection • ripped or perforated uterus • cervical injury • embolism • anesthesia complications
- convulsions • chronic abdominal pain • endotoxic shock • second-degree burns • Rh sensitization

31% suffer health complications— A recent study published in a major medical journal found that 31% of American women surveyed who had undergone abortions had health complications.

80%-180% increase in doctor visits — Based on health care sought before and after abortion. On average, there is an 80% increase in doctor visits and a 180% increase in doctor visits for psychosocial reasons after abortion.

Self-destructive lifestyles after abortion, spiraling health problems — Increased risk of promiscuity, smoking, drug abuse, and eating disorders, which all put the woman at increased risk for other health problems.

Infertility and life-threatening reproductive risks. Abortion can damage reproductive organs and cause long-term and sometimes permanent problems that can put future pregnancies at risk. Women who have abortions are more likely to experience ectopic pregnancies, infertility, hysterectomies, stillbirths, miscarriages, and pre-mature births than women who have not had abortions.

Teens Face Higher Risks

Teenage girls are **6 TIMES more likely to attempt suicide** if they have had an abortion in the last 6 months than are teens who have not had an abortion.

Reproductive damage and other complications

Teens who abort are generally at higher risk of immediate complications and long-term reproductive damage after abortion than are older women.

Higher risk of Pelvic Inflammatory Disease (PID), 2.5 times higher risk of endometritis (a major cause of maternal death in future pregnancies)

Teens are at higher risk for dangerous infections such as PID (pelvic inflammatory disease) and endometritis after abortion. These infections increase their risk of infertility, hysterectomy, ectopic pregnancy, and other serious complications.

Pelvic Inflammatory Disease — Abortion puts all women at risk of Pelvic Inflammatory Disease (PID) is a serious, life threatening disease and a major direct cause of infertility. PID also increases risk of ectopic pregnancies.

Placenta Previa — after abortion, there is a seven- to 15-fold increase in Placenta Previa in subsequent pregnancies (a life-threatening condition for both the mother and her wanted pregnancy). Abnormal development of the placenta due to uterine damage increases the risk of birth defects, stillbirth, and excessive bleeding during labor.

Ectopic Pregnancy — Post-abortive women have a significantly increased risk of subsequent ectopic pregnancies, which are life threatening and may result in reduced fertility.

Endometritis, a Major Cause of Death — Abortion can result in endometritis, which can lead to hospitalization and infertility problems. It is a major cause of maternal death during pregnancy.

Death or disability of newborns in later pregnancies — Cervical and uterine damage may increase the risk of premature delivery, complications of labor, and abnormal development of the placenta in later pregnancies. These complications are the leading causes of disabilities among newborns. www. afterabortion.org/news

Pre-Term or Post Term Deliveries —Women who abort are twice as likely to have pre-term or post-term deliveries.

As abortion doctors force the cervix open, it causes cervical and uterine damage resulting in pre-mature births in subsequent "wanted" children. Many women also have miscarriages because they cannot carry the child to term. Or like in my case my cervix would not dilate due to abortion damage and I had to have an emergency C-section for our son to survive.

Women who had one, two, or more previous induced abortions are, respectively, 1.89, 2.66, or 2.03 TIMES more likely to have a subsequent pre-term delivery, compared to women who carry to term. **Pre-term delivery increases the risk of blindness, deafness, respiratory problems, autism, Cerebral Palsy and death for the 'wanted' babies.** The average hospital charge from delivery to discharge for a normal birth is $4,300.00 compared to the complications of a premature birth of $58,000.00 to a million dollars needed per child for longer critical care. Cases of pre-term births continue to escalate.

SETTLED SCIENCE remains SETTLED SCIENCE

Summary of the May 2016 Dr. Gabrielle Saccone et al. abortion-preemie 'study of studies':

There is no more prestigious U.S. medical journal in the REPRODUCTIVE HEALTH field than the American Journal of Obstetrics & Gynecology.

They have just published in the May edition, the 2016 SACCONE 'study of studies' (medical jargon: 'meta-analysis') for the premature birth risk of prior induced abortions:

A. Surgical Induced Abortions (SIA): 28 prior studies supplied data for 913,297 women subjects. They found that Prior surgical induced abortions multiply pre-mature delivery Risk in subsequent "wanted" pregnancies by 1.52 (i.e. 52% higher relative odds); this result was statistically significant (since 'SACCONE' was at least 95% confident of increased preterm birth risk).

B. CHEMICAL Induced Abortions (referred to as some as 'medical' abortions): examined 10,253 subjects from prior studies and discovered that a Prior CHEMCIAL (aka 'medical') abortion multiply 'preemie' risk by 1.50 (i.e. 50% higher odds). A very serious finding!

C. The 2016 SACCONE 'abortion-preemie' study is the fourth such 'study of studies' with 100% of the 4 studies by Shah, Swingle, Lemmers and Saccone now, all finding that prior induced abortions significantly raise future risk of a preterm birth. ZERO 'study of studies' find that prior induced abortions reduce pre-mature/term birth risk. 4

ABORTION-PREEMIE risk = SETTLED SCIENCE, so why aren't pregnant women being told this vital information when considering an abortion?

Provided by Brent Rooney (MSc) Research Director, Reduce Preterm Risk Coalition
3456 Dunbar St. (Suite 146), Vancouver, Canada, V6S 2C2
Other Damage to women after induced abortion includes:

Suicide

- 6 times higher suicide rate. Two national records-based studies from Finland revealed that aborting women were 6 times more likely to commit suicide in the following year than were delivering women.
- Up to 60% have suicidal thoughts. According to a recent study in a major scientific journal, 31% had thoughts of suicide after abortion. In another survey, approximately 60% of women with post-abortion problems reported Suicidal thoughts, with 28% attempting suicide and half of those attempting suicide two or more times.
- Another study of more than 173,000 American women who had abortions or carried to term found that, during the eight years after the pregnancy ended, women who aborted had a 154% higher risk of suicide than women who carried to term.

Depression

- 65% higher risk of clinical depression. A longitudinal study of American women revealed that those who aborted were 65% more likely to be at risk of long-term clinical depression after controlling for age, race, education, marital status, history of divorce, income, and prior psychiatric state.
- Depression risk remained high, even when pregnancies were unplanned. Among a national sample of women with unintended first pregnancies, aborting women were at significantly higher risk of long-term clinical Depression compared to delivering women.

Trauma

- 65% report symptoms of post-traumatic stress disorder. In a study of U.S. and Russian women who had abortions, 65% of U.S. women experienced multiple symptoms of PTSD, which they attributed to their abortions. Slightly over 14% reported all the symptoms necessary for a clinical diagnosis of abortion-induced PTSD, and 25% said they did not receive adequate counseling.
- 64% said they felt pressured by others to abort.
- 60% of American women reported that they felt "part of me died" after their abortions.
- **Twice as likely to be hospitalized**. Compared to women who deliver, women who abort are more than twice as likely to be subsequently hospitalized for psychiatric illness within six months.
- More outpatient psychiatric care. Analysis of California Medicaid records show that women who have abortions subsequently require significantly more treatments for psychiatric illness through outpatient care.
- **Multiple disorders and regrets**. A study of post-abortion patients only 8 weeks after their abortions found that:

127

44% reported nervous disorders, 36% experienced sleep disturbances, 31% had regrets about their decision, and 11% had been prescribed psychotropic medicine by their family doctor.

Im Fine.

- Generalized anxiety disorder. Among women with no previous history of anxiety, women who aborted a first, unplanned pregnancy were 30% more likely to subsequently report all the symptoms associated with a diagnosis for generalized anxiety disorder, compared to women who carried to term.

Elliot Institute: AfterAbortion.org Fact Sheets, Outreach: TheUnChoice.com

Psychological Risks

Traumatic After-effects of Abortion

- **Sleep disorders**. In a study of women with no known history of sleep disorders, women were more likely to be treated for sleep disorders after having an abortion compared to giving birth (nearly twice as likely in the first 180 days afterwards). Numerous studies have shown that trauma victims often experience sleep difficulties
- **Disorders not pre-existing.** In a New Zealand study, women had higher rates of suicidal behavior, depression, anxiety, substance abuse, and other disorders after abortion. The study found that these were not pre-existing problems.

Eating disorders & substance abuse

- 39% had eating disorders. In a survey of women with post-abortion problems, 39% reported subsequent eating disorders.
- Five-fold higher risk of drug and alcohol abuse. Excluding women with a prior history of substance abuse, those who abort their first pregnancy are 5 times more likely to report subsequent drug and alcohol abuse vs. those who give birth.

Substance abuse *during subsequent pregnancies.*

Among women giving birth for the first time, women with a history of abortion are five times more likely to use drugs, twice as likely to use alcohol, and ten times more likely to use marijuana *during* their pregnancy, compared to women who have not had an abortion.

- Alcohol abuse linked to other problems. Alcohol abuse after abortion has been linked to violent behavior, divorce or separation, auto accidents, and job loss.

Coercion, guilt, repressed grief

- Coerced to violate their beliefs, values and conscience. The "decision" to abort is often based on the demands or threats of others — even when it violates the woman's own moral beliefs and desire to keep the baby. This is a known risk factor for psychological complications after abortion.
- 64% of abortions involve coercion. A recent study of women who had abortions found that 64% of American women reported that they felt pressured by others to abort.
- Common negative reactions. In a survey of women reporting post-abortion problems, 80% experienced

guilt, 83% regret, 79% loss, 62% anger and 70% depression.
- Forbidden grief. After abortion, societal expectation, personal shame and public and professional denial result in repressed grief, causing serious problems including clinical depression, eating disorders, self-destructive lifestyles and suicide.

Divorce and chronic relationship problems

- Women with a history of abortion are significantly more likely to subsequently have shorter relationships and more divorces. This may be due to lowered self-esteem, greater distrust of males, sexual dysfunction, substance abuse, and increased levels of depression, anxiety, and volatile anger.
- More poverty and single parenthood after repeat abortions. Women who have more than one abortion (nearly half of those seeking abortions each year) are more likely to become single parents and to require public assistance.
- 30-50% of post-abortive women report experiencing sexual dysfunctions such as promiscuity, loss of pleasure from intercourse, increased pain, and aversion to sex and/or men.

Not counseled before or after the abortion, many wanted alternatives

In a study of American and Russian women who experienced abortion:
- 67% of American women reported that they received no counseling beforehand
- 84% reported they received inadequate counseling beforehand
- 79% were not counseled about alternatives
- 54% were not sure about their decision at the time.

Unresolved trauma and child abuse

- 144 % more likely to abuse their children. One study found that women with a history of induced abortion were 144% more likely to physically abuse their children than women who had not had an abortion.
- Child abuse linked to unresolved trauma. Abortion is linked with increased violent behavior, alcohol and drug abuse, replacement pregnancies, depression, and poor maternal bonding with later children. These factors are closely associated with child abuse and would appear to confirm a link between unresolved post-abortion trauma and subsequent child abuse.

Repeat abortions, self-punishment and risk factors

- 48% of aborting women have had a previous abortion. Women who have had an abortion are 4 times more likely to abort a current pregnancy than those with no prior abortion history. This may reflect aspects of self-punishment.
- Studies have identified factors that put women at risk for negative reactions to abortion, including feeling pressured into unwanted abortions, lack of support, being more religious, prior emotional or psychological problems, adolescence, being unsure of her decision, and receiving little or no counseling prior to abortion. An analysis of 63 medical studies that identify risk factors concluded that the number of women suffering from negative emotional reactions could be dramatically reduced if abortion clinics screened women for these risk factors.5[1] The Elliot Institute

---

[1] www.afterabortion.org, www.bcpinstitute.org and www.abortionbreast-cancer.com

The prestigious British Journal of Psychiatry published the results of a gigantic Meta-analysis done by Professor Priscilla Coleman, Ph.D. and colleagues. They examined 22 worldwide studies on abortion and mental health. These experts brought together data on 877,181 participants, of whom 163,831 experienced an abortion.

They found that women who aborted their child, compared to women who gave birth to their unplanned child, had an **81% increased risk in mental health problems afterward**.

Truth is, a MOUNTAIN of STUDIES REVEAL the TRUE CONSEQUENCES of Legal Abortion to women's mental and reproductive health. The cost to women, families, society and healthcare is enormous!

Chapter 8

Breast Cancer Cover-up

THE PILL, a known carcinogen!

As you know sexual immorality, along with Birth Control Pill consumption, injections and patches etc. as well as the number of induced abortions have sky-rocketed since 1973?

The sixties pushed for free sex, drugs and rock and roll. Today, Hollywood and the liberal media produce more films with adultery, fornication and homosexuality promoting and endorsing sex before marriage. Pornography is rampant, sex trafficking is rampant and Sexually Transmitted Diseases (STD's) are over the top. And sadly divorce rates are high too. Fatherless children abound.

We have had sex education up to our necks, for decades on how to put on condoms, and where and how to get the pill, or other forms of birth control. Seems they are encouraged to just have sex before marriage, and told to take your birth control pills, and you'll be fine. NO! Our developed liberal world has never seen so many promiscuous teenagers, so many cases of STD's, computer abuse, teen suicides and unplanned pregnancies resulting in massive abortion cases, as birth control. Totally, thousands of broken hearts.

UN agencies at the WHO and IPPF are pushing for Comprehensive Sexuality Education which promotes the sexualization of children, instead of teaching them to Hang on to their Hormones. As of December 2015 the World Health Organization (WHO) stated that: *Sexually transmitted infections (STIs) have a profound impact on sexual and reproductive health worldwide, and continue to cause a major burden of disease. Global estimates, published in the journal PLOS ONE today, show that an estimated* **357 million new infections** *occur every year with one of 4 Sexually Transmitted Infections: chlamydia, gonorrhea, syphilis and trichomoniasis.* Please read that again! **357 million NEW Sexually Transmitted INFECTIONS every year!**

There are more than 30 different sexually transmissible bacteria, viruses and parasites.

Every year, one in 20 adolescent girls gets a bacterial infection through sexual contact.

ORAL CONTRACEPTIVES (OC's) **ARE ALSO AN ESTABLISHED RISK FACTOR FOR BREAST CANCER**: First of all, The World Health Organization (WHO) put out a statement in 2005, that long term use of The Pill, is a known carcinogen.

Evidence for an estrogen–breast cancer link was published in a New England Journal of Medicine review, "Estrogen Carcinogenesis in Breast Cancer" (Yager and Davidson 2006). Estrogen levels are 10–50 times higher in breast tissue than in blood, and are higher yet in cancerous tissue than normal tissue. OC's are known to accelerate cell division in girls and young women who take them before their First Full Term Pregnancy (FFTP).

A Mayo Clinic Proceedings meta-analysis by Dr. Chris Kahlenborn et al. demonstrated a 52 percent increase in the risk of premenopausal breast cancer among women who had given birth, and used OCs for four or more years before their first full-term pregnancy (FFTP) Kahlenborn et al. 2006. In the Linacre Quarterly 81 (3) 2014 the accompanying editorial noted, "that a higher risk of breast cancer for OC use was first described more than 25 years ago" (Cerhan 2006). In other words, this overview finding by Kahlenborn et al. reflected a long-standing, even if seldom discussed, scientific understanding.

Despite a huge cover-up by Cancer Societies and Foundations who rake in billions of dollars in donations annually and who deny or belittle the Abortion-Breast Cancer Link, the evidence is astounding. The TRUTH is there are not one or two, but dozens of credible, published, worldwide studies connecting Breast Cancer to induced

abortion! As of Nov. 2013 there were a whopping total of **57** scientific studies showing a positive correlation between induced abortion and Breast Cancer! 34 of these being "Statistically Significant".

The first one was published in 1957 from Japan. It showed a 2.6 relative risk or 160% increased risk of breast cancer among women who'd had an induced abortion. [Segi et al. (1957) GANN 48 (Suppl.):1-63] See: The Breast Cancer Prevention Institute: www.bcpinstitute.org-http://www.bcpinstitute.org/PDF/BCPI-FactSheet-Epidemiol-studies_2014.pdf

This is huge. This news should be shouted from the rooftops and on every newscast globally. However, since most cancer societies deny the link, for political reasons, women are not being warned of the connection! Of course, it doesn't mean that every woman who has had an abortion will get breast cancer, or visa-versa, however there is a notable risk factor.

Here is my lay term explanation: A girl has immature breasts, until her first full term pregnancy. Women who never have any born children, will also have a higher risk of getting breast cancer. However, once a woman gets pregnant, two thousand times the estrogens are naturally pumped into the breasts in the first trimester, to become milk for the baby in a few months, thus reducing the risk, making more cancer resistant cells.

BREAST CANCER IS MUCH MORE COMMON TODAY: There were an estimated 68,000 new cases of breast cancer among U.S. women in 1970 (Silverberg and Grant 1970). By **2014**, there was a **242 percent increase** with **232,670 in new cases** of female breast cancer (Siegel, Zou, and Jemal 2014). During this period, from 1970 to 2014, the U.S. population increased 56.8 percent (203,392,031 to 318,892,100). Thus, the rate of increase in female breast cancer has been more than 4-fold (i.e., 4.26-fold) the increase in the U.S. population during the same period. One in eight women will get it now.

Also, The Journal of the American Medical Association reported that the incidence of advanced breast cancers (cancers that had spread to distant locations by the time of diagnosis-life threatening) or what they term 'aggressive or invasive cancer' has surged nearly 90% in young women aged 20-39 within 33 years between 1976 and 2009! (Johnson R, et al. JAMA 2013;309(8):800-805)

The author, Rebecca Johnson, had been diagnosed herself at age 27 with breast cancer.

Furthermore, in-situ cancers, had risen by 300% since 1975 according to the SEER data collected by the National Cancer Institute. In-situ (localized) cancers are treated with mastectomy or partial mastectomy with radiation and at least 5 years of hormonal therapy. In-situ (in one location) cancers progress into invasive cancers, spreading to other organs and areas, if not treated.

First Way Abortion Causes Breast Cancer
Biological Evidence

Researchers were able to demonstrate that 77.7% of a group of rats given abortions began to develop breast cancers with the carcinogen DMBA. Among a group of 9 rats allowed to have a full term pregnancy and nurse their pups, only one developed a tumor. Among two groups of virgin rats, 66.7% and 71.4% developed tumors after being exposed to the carcinogen. Rats with abortion histories were at the greatest risk of all 5 groups. The experiment demonstrated that an induced abortion resulted in close to an 80% risk elevation among rats. [Russo J, Russo IH (1980) Am J Pathol. 100:497-512

These studies suggest that an induced abortion causes biological changes to occur in a woman's breasts which make her more susceptible to breast cancer. This is one of two ways in which abortion causes breast cancer. The biological rationale for this phenomenon can be found on the Abortion Breast Cancer (ABC) Summary page; www.abortionbreastcancer.com

Delayed first full term pregnancy is a second way in which abortion causes this disease. "Abortion is an "elective surgical procedure and a woman's exposure to the hormones of early pregnancy — if it is interrupted — is so great, that just one interrupted pregnancy is enough to make a significant difference in her risk" [Professor Joel Brind, President, Breast Cancer Prevention Institute, Endeavour Forum Public Meeting, August 24, 1999, Malvern, Victoria, Australia].

Approximately 1 in 100 women procuring an abortion are expected to die as a result of abortion-induced breast cancer. Wow!

In 1986, government scientists wrote a letter to the British Journal Lancet and acknowledged that abortion is a cause of breast cancer. They wrote, **"Induced abortion before first term pregnancy increases the risk of breast cancer."** (Lancet, 2/22/86, p. 436)

In my research, I discovered that Professor and Researcher, Joel Brind, headed up a research team in 1996 to examine the data and literature on abortion and breast cancer. They published a comprehensive review and meta-analysis of 23 worldwide studies on the subject. They found a statistically significant, **30 percent increase in breast cancer** among women who had had an abortion! However, it prompted a major, decade-long backlash from many mainstream medical organizations, medical journals, and government public-health ministries who did not want to hear this information as it went against their pro-abortion ideology.

The main study all the cancer societies and abortion clinics refer to, is the 1997 Mads Melbye study from Denmark. However,

I found out from another researcher that they only interviewed women who had an induced abortion just 1 to 10 years previously. It usually takes over ten years for cancer lumps to manifest. Furthermore, the Brind team argued in a letter to the New England Journal of Medicine that serious errors of misclassification and data adjustment in the Melbye study likely masked a significant risk increase. This study was debunked by published correspondence that demonstrated that 60,000 women in the study who had legal abortions on record were misclassified as not having had an abortion, many of whom developed breast cancer subsequently. They also reported that **"with each one-week increase in the gestational age of the fetus...there was a 3 percent increase in the risk of breast cancer."** The researchers, nevertheless, reported no overall positive association between abortion and breast cancer. [Melbye, et al. "Induced Abortion and the Risk of Breast Cancer," New England Journal of Medicine (1997);336:81-5] Read more at: http://www.nationalreview.com/article/415140/abortion-and-breast-cancer-stubborn-link-returns

Mads Melbye team also neglected more than two dozen published studies at that time which did find risk elevations. Yet, of course the abortion industry uses this Melbye study to deny a link; as this evidence would be bad for their business, and add another conflict of interest.

Isn't one ounce of prevention, worth a ton of cure? Women have the right to know that if they choose an abortion, they could be choosing breast cancer too! Common sense reveals this is a risk, and it has to do with the hormones! Tragically, Estrogen Positive Breast Cancer is widespread.

The only study of American women which relied entirely of medical records of abortion (not interviews after the fact) reported a 90% increased risk of breast cancer among women who had chosen abortion.

The Royal College of Obstetricians and Gynecologists has acknowledged the finding of the 1996 "Comprehensive review and meta-analysis" by Dr. Joel Brind et al. 36: a significant, 30% average increased risk with abortion. The Guideline reads: "the Brind paper had no major methodological short-comings and could not be disregarded." 37

The Association of American Physicians and Surgeons, issued a statement in 2003 calling on doctors to inform patients about a "highly plausible" relationship between abortion and breast cancer. General Counsel for that medical group wrote an article for its journal warning doctors that three women (two Americans, one Australian) successfully sued their abortion providers for neglecting to disclose the risks of breast cancer and emotional harm, although none of the women had developed the disease yet.

As of 2006, eight medical organizations recognize that induced abortion raises a woman's risk for breast cancer, independently of the risk of delaying the birth of a first child (a secondary effect that all experts already acknowledge).

China does the most amount of abortions in the whole world, by a long shot. In November of 2013, China published a large systematic review and meta-analysis of 36 Chinese studies by Dr. Yubei Huang and his colleagues in the prestigious journal, *Cancer-Causes-Control.* On top of all these other studies on the ABC link, this new systematic review and meta-analysis by Dr. Huang and associates examined 36 studies from 14 provinces across CHINA, and this is what they found this in their CONCLUSIONS:

"Induced Abortion (IA) is significantly associated with an increased risk of breast cancer among Chinese females, and the risk of breast cancer increases as the number of induced abortions increases. High rates of induced abortions in China may contribute to the increasing breast cancer rates there."

They discovered a colossal **44% increased risk for Breast Cancer for one legally induced abortion, a 76% increased risk for two induced abortions, and an 89% increased risk of Breast Cancer** if the woman has had THREE or more Induced Abortion's.

As well more recently, Bangladesh, India and Mexico also had scientific studies published in Medical Journals reporting a high risk elevation of breast cancer risk for women with a history of abortion. Why the cover-up?

This NEWS should be on CNN, CBC, Global, Oprah and every TV news station if they really cared about women's health-despite their "pro-choice" biases!

http://www.nationalreview.com/article/368490/shades-pink-interview

Why wasn't this NEWS proclaimed from CNN, Oprah Talk Shows, CBC, CTV and so forth?

Please help me get this valuable information out there!

China does a massive amount of induced abortions on pregnant women. They do the most abortions per capita in the world. In 2013, I submitted an official complaint to the High Commissioner on Human Rights in Geneva against China's One Child Policy. We had testimonies and evidence from Chinese women who were forced to abort their babies, because they did not have a "pregnancy permit". One woman was about 30 weeks along, and devastated. Today they have a two child policy, but still this is also horrible as women will still be forced and coerced to abort if they are pregnant with a third child. Millions are suffering depression and they also have the highest suicide rate per capita in the world, for women. No wonder.

Take heed! Not one or two, but over **57 studies revealing a positive correlation between breast cancer and abortion, and 34 of those being "statistically significant!**

So why the deadly silence from media and cancer foundations? Really? Is it still politically incorrect to say anything negative about the "a" word-even if thousands of women are suffering and dying? I will never keep silent about these cover-ups. "Have nothing to do with the fruitless deeds of darkness, but rather expose them." Eph. 5:11

Why all the hoopla to find a cure, and raise billions of dollars for research-when a mountain of studies already shows a huge connection between induced abortion and breast cancer?

It makes total sense when you examine the hormonal factor, especially when most breast cancers are "estrogen positive". Shouldn't they err on the side of caution, whether it agrees with their ideology or not?

Why aren't our governments, medical associations, all doctors and the Cancer Society's and the church blowing the trumpet and warning women not to have induced abortions to be on the "safe" side to prevent breast cancer? By the way, I have written many letters over the years to politicians, cancer organizations, the media and to Pastors and leaders about this critical information; they ignore me...but I will not stop.

At least five women have now successfully sued their abortionists for keeping them clueless about the risks of breast cancer and emotional harm. If you have had an abortion(s) and subsequently got any lumps removed, breast cancer or had a pre-term birth, or any other complications, please contact me.

It is unconscionable that Cancer groups continue to deny the abortion breast cancer link, while dozens of studies and common sense can see the connection. Are they afraid of losing individual, corporate or government donors? Nothing new. The late Karen Malec, former President of the Abortion Breast Cancer Coalition declared, "Cancer groups lied to women about the risks of using combined (estrogen + pro-gestin) hormone replacement therapy and 'the pill' when con-clusive evidence of a breast cancer risk became available in the 1980s, and they are still lying about abortion today." said Karen Malec, the late president of the Abortion Breast Cancer Coalition.

"I realize that the breast cancer epidemic has been tre-mendously profitable for the cancer establishment," continued Malec "but those who've participated in this cover-up should be deeply ashamed of themselves for the incredible suffering they've inflicted. These people are not pro-choice. They are cold, calculating abortion zealots driven by greed and fear of widespread medical malpractice lawsuits. Some cancer groups' officials formerly worked for the abortion industry."

141

The Coalition on Abortion/Breast Cancer is an international women's organization founded to protect the health and save the lives of women by educating and providing information on abortion as a risk factor for breast cancer.

It's undeniable that most women who have abortions, abort their first child, which means they forego the protective effects of early FFTP. She may never be able to have any born children as a result of that abortion. It delays childbearing, and she will certainly not be able to breast-feed that aborted child.

Yet, despite these truths, there is not one anti-cancer organization which uses this phrase, "Abortion causes breast cancer." Why not?

Why do they use flawed studies to denounce the ABC link? Are they afraid of the backlash of anger from mouthy feminists, who want to protect abortion as a woman's right to have her babies killed? Or are they afraid of breast cancer survivors and their families suing them, for keeping people in the dark about this mountain of research? Are they worried about losing big corporate donors and the millions of dollars they rake in annually to 'Find a Cure'? Check out the Documentary called, "Pink Ribbon Inc." an expose' on the breast cancer business enterprises, and the new documentary I am in called, "Hush" and hear the evidence from researchers, doctors, scientists and women like me.

The ESTROGEN Connection:

Dr. Angela Lanfranchi is one of my heroines. She is a Breast Surgeon and co-founder of the Breast Cancer Prevention Institute. She has been teaching this information for many years at the UN:

"The reason why induced abortions raise breast cancer risk, while natural miscarriages don't: The female sex hormone called estrogen is the most potent stimulator of breast cell growth. In fact, the actions of most known risk factors for breast cancer are attributable to some form of estrogen positive over-exposure. Hormone replacement therapy, the Birth

Control Pill, Birth Control patches, injections and other hormonal drugs are known carcinogens, (cancer causing agents).

In a normal pregnancy, the mother's ovaries begin producing extra estrogen within a few days after conception. The level of estrogen in her blood rises naturally by 2,000% by the end of the first trimester-to a level more than six times higher than it ever gets in the non-pregnant state.

It is the un-differentiated cells in the breasts which estrogen stimulates to proliferate, so that there will be enough milk-producing tissue to feed the baby after birth. Only the undifferentiated cells are vulnerable to carcinogens, and can ultimately grow into cancer cells. An induced abortion, artificially terminates the pregnancy, and those cells never get to differentiate, and become the milk they were intended to be, and over time can make for more cancer vulnerable cells.

However, what is very important, is the fact that during the last 8 weeks of pregnancy, other hormones differentiate these cells into milk-producing cells. In the process the growth potential-and cancer-forming potential-of these cells is turned off. That is why a full-term pregnancy lowers the risk of breast cancer.

Therefore, if a woman who has gone through some weeks or months of a normal, healthy, pregnancy, then chooses abortion; she is left with more of these cancer-vulnerable cells in her breasts than were there before she got pregnant, which increases her risk of breast cancer later in life. Never giving birth also increases the risk of breast cancer.

In contrast, most pregnancies which abort spontaneously do not generate normal quantities of estrogen. Thus most miscarriages (at least 1st trimester miscarriages) do not raise breast cancer risk."

Breast Cancer Prevention

The majority of Breast Cancers are "estrogen positive". It has to do with the hormones, estrogens and reproductive health. Today's medical experts and cancer societies agree that the best way women can reduce their lifetime risk for breast cancer is by:

1. **Having your first child under the age of 24, reduces breast cancer.** The longer you delay that first full term pregnancy, the more you increase your risk of breast cancer. One study illustrates that breast cancer risk increases 3% for every year you delay that first full term birth.
2. **The more children you give birth to, the better.**
3. **Breast-feeding** also reduces the breast cancer risk.

Let your children Live-One ounce of prevention is worth a TON of Cure!

However, an induced abortion, artificially terminates the pregnancy, and usually it is the first pregnancy, thus leaving more cancer vulnerable cells, then if she would carry that baby to term.

There is a huge cover up that I want to expose, we need to find partners and raise funds to produce feature films and documentaries made for Television in order to reach the masses and save lives. Can you help support this cause for true women's health and well-being? Will you?

Sandra Barrett sent me an email on November 17, 2006 9:16 AM.

*"**I was 14 when I had an abortion. It changed my life forever.** I was raped and got pregnant. I was told it was alright, the best thing to do, by my parents, doctors and friends to have an abortion. I was told I should not bring a child of rape into the world. No choices for me...After, I immediately knew it was wrong. I may not then have been able to look upon the face of my child without seeing the trauma, but adoptive parents would not know the circumstances of the conception. **This child was innocent!!***

Instead, I looked upon myself every day for more than 2 decades with pain, guilt and remorse. I may not have been given a choice in conception, but I did have the ultimate choice in the outcome of life. I could have stood my ground; I could have adopted out. I could have stopped the pain.

Years of depression, self-loathing, destructive behaviour and counseling followed. The grief is with me still almost 30 years later. The son I had after the abortion was born pre-maturely and frail. Scar tissue and infections in my uterus caused me to have to have a total hysterectomy at the age of 22!

My mother had cancer. Then I was diagnosed with stage 3 estrogen positive breast cancer at the age of 34 and have now relapsed at the age of 41 to an advanced stage.

Women are not told about the link between abortion and breast cancer.

There is not a year that goes by I do not think of the child lost due to my own uneducated decision... on abortion. Think before you act, search before you decide, it's a baby, and you are the mother. The decisions made today will affect you every day after. Sandra

Sadly, Sandra died of Breast Cancer on April 20, 2008 at the Age of 43

If you have a family history of breast cancer, you should never take The Pill or any hormonal drugs, as well as never have an abortion as this will only increase your risk factor for breast cancer substantially, according to the data.

www.abortionbreastcancer.com, www.bcpinstitute.org, www.polycarp.org

Cancer society's should be promoting Motherhood, and denouncing abortions, if they really want to prevent breast cancer!

Cancer society's rake in billions of dollars to "find a cure," yet are deadly silent and deny the mountain of studies exposing the abortion breast cancer link. If they truly cared about women's lives and health, they would sound the alarm, and warn young women about the Abortion Breast Cancer Link. Whether it is "politically incorrect" or not, women have a right to know! There have been a few lawsuits settled out of court in the USA and Australia where former abortion patients sued the abortionists for not informing them about the abortion breast cancer link, mental health problems and other complications in the after effects. Although, they had not got breast cancer yet, (and may never get it) the fact that they were never informed about this significant risk, was enough for the courts to grant compensation to these women. As well the abortionists made sure everything was settled out of court, so as not to set a precedent.

If you had an abortion and were never informed by the abortion clinic or hospital about the Breast Cancer link, even if you have not got breast cancer, you can sue them for no informed consent. Most clinics deny the risk, despite the evidence. Furthermore, if you have had any lumps in your breast, cervical or uterine damage, resulting in a hysterectomy, infertility, pre-term birth as well as suffered any emotional/mental health issues such as depression, suicidal ideation, eating or anxiety disorders, substance abuse etc., after abortion, please contact me at dmountenay@telus.net, or get a lawyer. You had a right to know about all of these risk factors.

It is time to hold them accountable. Women have a RIGHT TO KNOW!

Chapter 9

Expert Witnesses Testify

"We defeat Satan by the Blood of the Lamb and the word of our testimony..." Rev. 12:11

A huge Thank you to Mr. Allan Parker, Cindy Collins, Myra Meyers and all the Operation Outcry Women, The Texas Justice Foundation and Canada Silent No More Women who have collected over 5,000 testimony/declarations from former abortion patients who have been injured physically and/or psychologically after their abortion(s).

We still need more testimonies-so please contact us to include your pain and injuries of legal abortion at: ***www.canadasilentnomore.com***

Debbie

One day I got a call from a woman whose daughter was in college. She told me that her daughter had been a very upbeat, happy young woman until right after her abortion. The mother was ambivalent about the abortion, and told her to do whatever she thought was best…and to think about her future, her courses, and her career. A baby right now would ruin all that, she thought.

So, with the boyfriend in agreement, Debbie went for it… made an appointment, had the induced abortion and within 36 hours she was a patient on the Psychiatric floor in the hospital. Her mother was frantic and very troubled and after a short conservation, urged me to come and see her daughter. Her daughter suffered a mental breakdown after her abortion. She was curled into a fetal position and would not talk to anyone. They began to administer anti-depressant drugs. Her mother was very worried and concerned; this was so not like her daughter at all, she had snapped.

Drawings by Shannon Moody, BC.

When we walked into her private room, she was still in a fetal position. Her mom introduced us, but she kept her head down, and ignored us at first. Then I began to tell her how sorry I was about the loss of her baby. I told her I knew that pain, as I had an abortion too when I was younger... tears began to well up, and she began to cry. I asked if I could sit on her bed, she said, "Sure". Although she and her mom were not Christians, I told them I was, and suggested she first ask God to forgive her for having the abortion. They agreed, and I led them in a sinner's prayer. Debbie said, she felt a huge weight lift off of her. I encouraged her to begin a new life with God and to know that one day she would see her child in heaven.

Linda

Another day I got a frantic call from a woman so distressed about her abortion that she vividly recalled every detail of the procedure with me. She was also upset and crying in unbelief about what had transpired.

Hundreds of women annually go through similar procedures. She was in her late thirties, and had never wanted to have any kids, she explained as she began to share her ordeal with me. A few weeks earlier, she went for a checkup and the doctor told her she was pregnant. She was shocked, as she had no symptoms or signs that she was pregnant, and was told to go for an ultra sound. Like in that TV Reality Show, called 'Pregnant and Didn't Know it', that was her. She had often missed her periods, so it was not alarming to her to go for months without one.

Although she wasn't really showing, and had no idea she was pregnant, the test disclosed that she was already seven months pregnant! The Radiologist knew that she was thinking of having an abortion, so when she asked to see the ultra sound, he would not let her see it.

She was single and pregnant, and like many women, panicked. She began to search the internet for someone to help her get rid of this pregnancy, this was not in her plans. After all, abortion is totally legal, millions of women are doing it, and the Government even pays for it. By the way, she was independent, a career woman on the go socially. She was healthy, and the baby was totally healthy too.

Soon she found an abortionist who would terminate the life of this baby, no questions asked. She informed them that she was already 7 months pregnant, and told them that there were no abnormalities with the fetus. She then asked if it was still okay to have the procedure done. "Not a problem" was the answer, and how soon could she come for the appointment, the sooner the better. It would be a 4-day procedure.

They made sure she would first get the documents faxed to them by the Provincial Government Health Care to cover the $12,500.00 fee. She later wondered that if she had taken more time to really think about it, and if someone would have taken the time to give her support and options, to tell her the fetal development and humanity of this child, she probably would have never have gone through with it.

By the time of the scheduled appointment she was now seven and a half months pregnant, the baby was now 30 weeks along.

She just felt an urgency to get this done as soon as possible, and did not think of or look into the facts of fetal growth. She was afraid, ashamed of being single and pregnant, afraid of what others would think of her, and stuck to her vow of never having any children.

On her way to the abortion clinic she felt the baby move, first time and ever so briefly. No one at the abortion clinic nor her own doctor suggested that she let the baby live, or call a pregnancy crisis center for help and get some education and awareness on what was happening with her child. She was not a teenager, or victim of rape or abuse. She was never informed about how developed her baby actually was. She was not told that babies born pre-maturely at this age can survive outside the womb as early as 21 weeks.

It was as if she got on this eerie treadmill and was not able to get off of it. She described the abortion clinic as "gloomy and cold".

The first day, they did an ultra sound, and she told them she wanted to see it, but they would not allow her to see the ultra sound or discuss it with her. Later she knew that she would have changed her mind after seeing a baby on ultra sound.

They had her sign lots of waiver forms etc. and told her to watch a 10 min. video on the procedure and birth control options, and to let them know when it was over.

They never even asked her why she wanted to have an abortion.

They used an ultra sound to find the baby's heart. When she turned to look at the screen, the abortionist yelled at her not to look. Then he inserted a long needle into her womb. She was afraid, it hurt, and she began to squirm a little. Her hands were shaking, he insisted she stop, but she could not control it. She was very nervous, tears were rolling down her cheeks, she was asking questions, but he continued…the abortionist was extremely rude, and repeatedly told her to shut up, be still or she would die.

This doctor who should be saving babies, injected a lethal dose of potassium chloride venom into this precious, healthy, baby's heart, to kill this child! Yes, this is happening in our generation!

What transgression did this child commit to deserve Capital Punishment like a prisoner on death row?

The doctor then inserted laminaria seaweed into her cervix to force it to dilate. Of course people who take the lives of the blameless want to downplay their acts of violence on the innocent, and never divulge the humanity of the baby in the matrix. These babies are fully human and fully alive no matter how small, until an abortionist kills him or her.

On the website of this late term abortionist, it states, the injection "is an injection of medication into the fetus that will stop the fetal heart instantly." However, the definition of the word medication, means a 'drug used to treat an illness, or the treatment of an illness using drugs'. Since when is a lethal injection which will kill someone, a medication? How is this treating an illness? Since when is a baby in her mother's womb, an illness?

He walked out of the room, and then it hit her like a ton of concrete…she had just made the biggest mistake of her life! She began to feel a tsunami of guilt and regret of what had just happened to her baby. It felt like she just woke up from a dream, a horrific nightmare, and realized what was happening. She just wanted to die. She couldn't stop crying for days…weeks…the crying continues. Another woman once told me she cried for 25 years after her abortion. You see we can never replace or bring back that aborted child. It is done. We never get to love, hug, cuddle, kiss, nurture or bless our child…it is the most unnatural thing for a woman to have her own child killed.

She was coerced into going back and having the abortionist insert more laminaria to force her cervix wider and wider for the next 3 days, in order for the now dead baby to be delivered. She told staff that she wanted to see it; they said no, she can't.

When the baby was being delivered, after being poisoned to death by the doctor, Susan was trying to sit up to see it, the nurse pushed her down and they would not allow her to see the baby. When it was over, the doctor happily and proudly told her she was not pregnant anymore.

What kind of beast can kill the most vulnerable and innocent human beings on earth? Who can do this routinely every day and justify it? As far as I am concerned, they are the biggest bullies on earth. Disguised as angels of light, they go to Medical school and dress in white coats. They have university degrees and are called "doctors". They claim they are doing women a favour. They claim it is a "safe" procedure. Lies.

Well, it is certainly **not safe** for the defenseless baby, powerless against these weapons of mass destruction. The choice to kill another human being, no matter how small should never be acceptable to any of us. These doctors are supposed to save lives, and help the hurting; not destroy lives and cause harm to the babies and to the mothers in one way or another, sooner or later! They rake in millions of dollars...and you are paying for it with your money and silence.

Nazi doctors also felt they were doing Germans a favour by exterminating Jews, the sick and elderly etc. They used to systematically kill men, women and children with their lies and deception by telling the victims they were going for a shower, when in reality they were going into a gas chamber to be executed. Nazi Germany's T-4 Euthanasia Program used lethal injection also as one of several methods to destroy what the Nazi government dubbed "lives unworthy of life". The victims were called "useless eaters and the unproductive" … Today, they are on a new campaign to legalize Euthanasia in Canada and globally. So who will be the next to go?

The shedding of innocent blood is an abomination to God (Prov. 6:16,17), it also causes the womb to be empty/barren/desolate!

> *"So when you see the appalling sacrilege [the abomination that astonishes and makes desolate], spoken of by the prophet Daniel, standing in the Holy Place—let the reader take notice and ponder and consider and heed" [this]—[Dan. 9:27; 11:31; 12:11.] Mat 24:15*

Alone now, depressed, grieving and frantic, she began to search for help. She found our Canada Silent No More website and our Toll Free number and called me. She was very angry at herself, and the abortionist, she was severely hurt, broken, numb and was not able to go back to work...she was an emotional wreck...she isolated, and felt she could not face the world, knowing now what she did. Many of us go into shock after.

She had come to the realization that abortion actually killed her "baby" and from that moment a part of her died also. She was so upset. She felt so much guilt, shame and deep remorse. The sorrow was extremely heavy. I too was angry asking, "How could this so called doctor even do such a brutal thing to a perfectly healthy baby who could easily survive out-side the womb at that age?" How can anyone justify this con-tracted murder?

Joanne

Joanne and Bill were happily married with 3 children. They went to church every Sunday. Unexpectedly, Joanne was preg-nant with baby number four. However, her husband had recently lost his job and they went into a dread about having another child now. They sought advice from three other "Christians" who basically told them to do what they felt was the right thing to do. No scriptures, no word from God, just what was right in their own eyes.

> ***"There is a way which seems right to a man and appears straight before him, but at the end of it is the way of death."*** Pro 14:12

Stressed and afraid of the future, Joanne reluctantly went for the abortion. Her husband was passive and in total agreement to do this. But deep down she knew it was wrong. Immediately after the abortion, she felt the heavy weight of death/murder on her conscience. She began to grieve the fact that this baby, their fourth child, was killed and how could she have let this happen? What kind of a mother was she, how could they as Christians have done this horrible thing to their baby? Their marriage was severed big time from that horrible day. She totally lost respect for and was very angry that her husband permitted this to happen. Why didn't he stop her, why didn't he say, 'Honey, don't worry, I will get a job, let's pray, God allowed this baby to be here, and He has a purpose and a plan for her/him.' Why didn't they walk by faith, instead of running in fear? She was so depressed and distraught after that she could not even hold or cuddle her other children bearing the guilt of murder, she was crushed.

For most women it can take years for the reality of what abortion did, to hit us. We suppress the memories and feelings and thoughts for many years. The pain is so great and con-suming that we do not want to go there, but one day we must.

Ruth Ann

Ruth Ann reluctantly, driven by fear, had an abortion in a Toronto abortion clinic. The following day as she was having a shower, blood along with little human body parts from the baby came out, including a leg with a foot. She went into shock, never told anyone for years, but immediately turned to drugs and alcohol and has never been the same since.

Lori, Dee, Marie, Melody, Melony, Diane, Heidi, Cindy, Janelle, Barb, Chris, Kim, Julie, Darlene, Heidi, Kaili, Sue, Anita, Ann, Kathy, Linda, Maureen, Marielle, Norma, Maria, Brenda, Molly, Vicky, Stephanie, Liz, Faye, Whitney, Gwen, Chantal, Susan, Carolyn, singers, movie stars, executives and thousands of other women including myself have suffered from abortion by self-medicating and trying to numb the guilt, regret, grief and pain with booze and other drugs etc. Studies show that women who abort are six times more likely to become addicted to drugs and have substance abuse problems after their abortion.

Several women I know aborted the only child they would or could ever have. Abortion affected their fertility and made them unable to conceive or bear children…many have miscarriages. This is not a "safe" procedure!

Karly

Karly grew up in a family that attended a Pentecostal Church. They went to church every Sunday. She had sex with a guy when she was 14, and got pregnant. (Sadly, a lot of people would say it's okay to abort at that age, because they are too young to have a baby. But, for whatever reason, God allows the conception to take place, He knew us before we were born. He has a plan for that child and parents.) Without telling a soul, she got out the phonebook and booked an appointment to have an abortion. Although underage, and even though you cannot have an aspirin without parental consent at a school. She went on to have this abortion with no questions asked, and with no parental consent! Legally. Where are the laws to protect youth and children?

Soon after the abortion she rebelled against the church, God and her parents, turning to alcohol, drugs and an independent lifestyle. She still struggles with the guilt, remorse, shame and anger, years later.

Chantel

Chantel has been calling me regularly for about 6 years now. She began to call us not long after she had her abortion. She lives in another Province and had some depression when she was a teenager. In her twenties, she fell in love, lived common-law and got pregnant when she was 26 years old. He pressured her to have this abortion, she was crushed, felt rejected by him, and did as he said. Soon after they broke up. She could not bear to drive by the hospital where her baby was killed, and had to move. Very few relationships survive an abortion, because now you become the parents of a dead baby that you had killed. It can affect your sex life, because abortion is also connected to sex.

Chantel has been devastated by her abortion. She had an emotional breakdown and is preoccupied with thoughts of doom and gloom; she misses her baby, her little girl. A friend of hers was also pregnant about the same time, and let her baby live. Chantel walks in grief and is tormented with clinical depression and suicidal thoughts. She has tried a ton of different anti-depressants and medications to no avail over the years. A couple of times I have called 911 to have her rescued. I am always try to bring hope and encouragement to her. Multitudes of women are fighting depression and suicidal thoughts. Please pray for these women.

There was a documentary on TV where a happy, enthusiastic, energetic young woman in College had her whole life ahead of her. She got pregnant, and took the morning after pill. Her baby was successfully aborted, and she began to spiral downhill. She actually recorded her descent on her webcam as depression, grief, and regret grew in her heart. She jumped into the Ottawa River and her body was found weeks later.

Several women have confided in me that they tried to commit suicide after their abortions because of the anguish and deep sorrow they felt for having their child killed. How many more women have taken their lives after abortion that we don't even know of? Many women go into self-destructive behavior after induced abortion. Only God knows how many.

How can politicians be protecting and condoning this systematic massacre? How can the church be silent while the murders go on and on, at a rate of over 300 every day in this nation? Where are the activists to protect the innocent? Where are all of the nice people who should be outraged that such a calamity is taking place daily in the land?

There is something so sinister about hospitals killing healthy children in the womb, on request.

What are you doing to stop this slaughter of the innocents? What will you do to make a difference?

Every day around the world, especially in developed countries abortion doctors and nurses and staff are getting away with the destruction of human life, and doing harm to women also. How can we support and accept this great evil in our generation with our money and silence?

"They did not destroy the [heathen] nations as the
Lord commanded them,

But mingled themselves with the [idolatrous] nations and learned their ways and works, And served their idols, which were a snare to them. Yes, they sacrificed their sons and their daughters to demons [II Kings 16:3.] **And shed innocent blood, even the blood of their sons and of their daughters, whom they sacrificed to the idols of Canaan; and the land was polluted, with their blood.**

Thus were they defiled by their own works, and they played the harlot and practiced idolatry with their own deeds [of idolatrous rites]. Therefore, was the wrath of the Lord kindled against His people, insomuch that He abhorred and rejected His own heritage. [Deut. 32:17.] And He gave them into the hands of the [heathen] nations, and they that hated them ruled over them." Psalm 106:35 -41

Tragically, during the writing of this book, a friend of mine and a Canada Silent No More representative in Ontario, Carolyn George committed suicide at the age of 59. How many others have taken their lives because of the deep pain of abortion?

What if the woman was raped, and got pregnant? For whatever reason God has allowed that conception to take place, and He has a plan and purpose for that child and mother. Two wrongs do not make a right. Rebecca Kiessling, Juda and other women I know who were conceived in rape, and who got to be born, and adopted into wonderful families, or with mothers who let them live, are so happy to be alive. Rebecca is beautiful, and became a lady lawyer who tells people that she wants to be the face of children conceived in rape. Besides, why should the baby get a death sentence, for the crime of the sperm donor?

- The right to have your baby killed by a doctor, or anyone should be unthinkable.
- Why someone should be killed based on their temporary place of residence? Or killed because of how young or tiny they are? A person is a person, no matter how small.
- Should a person be killed just because they couldn't survive on their own? What about people on insulin, or people using a pace-maker to survive, or people who are paralyzed and need assistance, are they less human? No!
- Sadly, 90% of children diagnosed with Down's Syndrome are killed before birth.
- Should a doctor abort a child, just because the mother thinks it may be too expensive or take time from her school or career to raise a child? People are not allowed to kill a puppy, kitten, colt or eagle eggs just because it's their choice to...but it is ok to kill the baby humans?

What if the child has Down's Syndrome or is disabled? Sadly, 90% of Down's children are killed before birth. Why should a child be killed because he is disabled? Is it okay to take all the disabled people and kill them? Although we may not understand it, they are happy to be alive and are used to their conditions.

Do children in the womb feel pain as they are poisoned or dismembered? An industry that regularly rips children apart for profit, does not like the idea of people knowing that babies in the womb actually feel pain.

According to published research by Blackburn, Vanhatalo, Van Nieuwenhuizen et al. on *Fetal Pain and Neonatal Physiology*; as early as six weeks after conception, the baby responds to touch. By a mere ten weeks if the baby is touched, he/she will close his/her hand and eyes. By 20 weeks Dr. Paul Ranalli, a neurologist at the University of Toronto reports that "the fetal brain has the full complement of brain cells present in adulthood, ready and waiting to receive pain signals from the body, and their electrical activity can be recorded by standard electroencephalography."

Thank God that recently Texas legislated a limit of 20 weeks for abortions, a step in the right direction. The USA are leaps and bounds ahead of Canada for laws protecting at least some children in the womb. So when someone tries to tell you that a "fetus" is not a person, and is not entitled to the right to life, tell them these amazing facts:

- The baby has his own blood type and his/her own unique DNA from conception!
- The baby's heart starts beating at around three weeks after conception and beats about 54 million times before birth!
- By sixteen weeks, the baby is grasping with his/her hands, kicking, and doing somersaults!
- By eighteen weeks, his/her vocal chords are functional. He/she can cry!

It's not just good to know these facts about human life. It's our job to know and to teach others. If we're going to be pro-life, we need the tools to defend the weakest and most vulnerable among us.

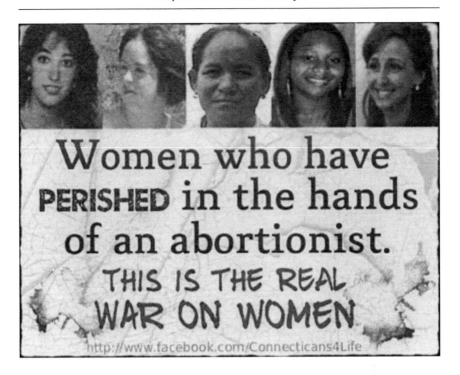

The Abortionists

In 2011, former abortionist Dr. Kermit Gosnell, alongside various co-defendant employees, was actually charged with eight counts of murder resulting in part from gross medical malpractice in the treatment of patients at his clinic. He was also charged with 24 felony counts of illegal abortions **beyond the 24-week limit,** and charged with 227 misdemeanor counts of violating the 24-hour informed consent law. The murder charges were related to **a patient who died** while under his care and **seven newborns, said to** have been killed, **after being** born alive, **during attempted abortions on them.** In May 2013, he was convicted on only three of the murder charges, 21 felony counts of illegal late-term abortion, and 211 counts of violating the 24-hour informed consent law. After his conviction, Gosnell waived his right of appeal in exchange for an agreement not to seek the death penalty. Gosnell himself, sentenced thousands of innocent children to the death penalty, but selfishly pleaded for life in prison; and got it.

Below are revealing statements made by former abortion industry personnel. These are direct quotes from men and women who worked in abortion facilities. These former abortion providers are now pro-life. They regret their involvement with abortion so much that now they are speaking publicly to warn people about what goes on before, during and after abortions. Their statements were made at a videotaped conference called, "Meet the Abortion Providers."

1) Former abortionist, Anthony Levatino, M.D., says, *"I want the general public to know that the doctors know that this is a person, this is a baby. That this is not some kind of blob of tissue . . ."*

2) Former abortion counselor, Nita Whitten, says, *"It's a lie when they tell you they're doing it to help women, because they're not. They're doing it for the money."*

3) Former abortion counselor, Debra Henry, says, *"We were told to find the woman's weakness and work on it. The women were never given any alternatives. They were told how much trouble it was to have a baby."*

4) Former abortionist, Joseph Randall, M.D., says, *"The picture of the baby on the ultrasound bothered me more than anything else. The staff couldn't take it. Women who were having abortions were never allowed to see the ultrasound."*

5) Former abortionist, David Brewer, M.D., says, *"My heart got callous against the fact that I was a murderer, but that baby lying in a cold bowl educated me to what abortion really was."*

6) Former abortion counselor, Kathy Sparks, says, *"The counselor at our clinic could cry with the girls at the drop of a pin. She would find out what was driving them to want to abort that child and she would magnify it."*

7) Former abortionist, McArthur Hill, M.D., says, *"I am a murderer. I have taken the lives of innocent babies and*

I have ripped them from their mother's wombs with a powerful vacuum machine."

The most important thing for former abortion patients and abortionists is to know that Yeshua/Jesus paid the penalty for our sins, including abortion. He also took our shame and guilt on the cross with Him. **The most difficult thing is to forgive ourselves.**

The Lord showed me, that we do not forgive ourselves, then what we are really saying is that what Yeshua did on the cross, how HE gave HIS Life for all of our sins...wasn't good enough! So we must by faith, forgive those who pressured us, and those that did it, those that lied, and then forgive ourselves... even though we don't deserve it. God's love for us is amazing!

Chapter 10

Ambassador To The United Nations

I n 1987, I gave my life to God. One Sunday at Queensway Cathedral Pentecostal Church in Toronto, the Pastor called people to come up to the altar for prayer. I was singing my heart out, *"Here am I, send me to the nations, as an Ambassador for you, Ambassador for you..."* and I remember going forward, laying down my life for God, with my whole heart poured out to do His will. Crying and sobbing in commitment to serve Him, no matter what the cost.

For years I have been praying for GOD to open doors no man can open, and to make a way for me to bring the truth and tragedy of this genocide to the forefront. Many times I have cried out on my living room floor to GOD for help and to provide the funds for me to go where ever HE wanted me to go. Often I prayed Lord, we just need one millionaire who gets it. Now I pray we need several millionaires who get it, and want to help us change hearts, minds, laws and history for such a time as this.

The Lord began to connect me with strong Pro-Life, Pro-Family Generals like Allan Parker, Babette Francis, Molly White, Cindy Collins, Rebecca Porter, Peter Smith, Patrick Buckley, Bill Fowler, Sissy, Brett, Pastor Paul, Pastor Tony, Ted and Dr. Bert Dorenbos along with many others globally in this fight for life, truth and justice for children yet to be born.

For the past ten years or so, God has opened many doors for me to host workshops and lead teams of women into the **United Nations Headquarters** in New York City during the Commission on the Status of Women (CSW) meetings. He has called me out of darkness, and into His light to meet with UN Ambassadors and delegates. It has been so humbling, so amazing, and I just love meeting them. I share the scientific research we have on how legal abortion is injuring women in so many ways. My purpose is to also bring humanity to children in the womb, along with giving my personal testimony on the pain of legal abortion.

That spirit of Jezebel, and those staunch pro-abortion radicals do not like us at the United Nations. The opposition is fierce; we can sometimes feel the spiritual hatred towards us. Nevertheless, we continue to press in, and press on, regardless, in love and joy. One time I had one of them following me around, so I told Glenisaah, let's turn around and see if she still follows us, and sure enough she did...then I turned about quickly going toward her and started asking her what she wanted...and she fled, almost running away.

One time I was sent on assignment to Berlin, Germany, to attend a Women Deliver (death) conference as they push to legalize abortion in every nation worldwide. They even propagate do it yourself abortions with chemical poisons. There was such a dark presence in the place we could really feel it.

It so happened that only three of us on the side for life, could get registered, and interestingly, we were all former abortion patients. The very first day we arrived in Berlin, we decided to go for a walk to check out the scenery, when suddenly Katie began to get chest pains. We quickly prayed over her for healing and commanded those pains to dissipate. We would walk another 10-15 feet and she would start to get the pains again. She told us she has had this before, but not so bad, and 3 or 4 of her siblings have had heart attacks and by-passes. "Oh boy, Katie, I sure hope you bought Medical Travel Insurance," I asked. "No," she calmly responded. Well, that night we had to rush her to Emergency in the Berlin

Hospital, and we prayed hard that God would supply all of the funds needed to cover her medical costs. She needed a miracle, or two now.

Immediately, they hooked her up to the heart monitors and IV's. Soon they reported that she would be staying for a while and that she had heart blockages and needed three stints inserted. Katie, did not speak a word of German, and I told her we were so sorry, and prayed God's ministering angels would minister to her and guide the doctors in Yeshua's/Jesus name. Leaving her in good hands. We could not even stay there and hold her hands, as we had to get back to the hotel to prepare for the conference the next morning and register, etc...

Again, we prayed over her, for the doctors and those attending to her and for God's shalom peace. The next day when I told the conference administrators at the registration desk, that our "colleague" had to be rushed to the hospital for heart surgery, the night before, the one young lady said, "Please wait here a minute, I must check something." Soon she returned with that thick German accent, to tell us the good news.

The conference organizers had not only paid the airfare, accommodations and food for all of the people coming from Africa and developing nations, they had also bought travel, medical and baggage insurance for every registrant, including ours. "Halleluiah" I shouted. They were also covering our food, but we had to pay our hotel accommodation and airfares as we were from Canada and the USA. Have you ever heard of this before? We were thrilled that they were going to cover our sister's medical costs, which would have been many, many, thousands of dollars a day! Yahoo, God provided another miracle for us.

While Katie was recuperating, Mary and I were planning to go to the workshop on "Abortion". We sat at different locations in the room and hoped to be able to make a comment or ask questions at the end. It was very upsetting for us to hear all of the same old rhetoric and lies to promote abortion as a woman's right to have her baby killed, and push their agenda into the nations. Anyway, there was such a heaviness in the atmosphere. My heart was pounding, and I just wanted to get out of there, but I knew God wanted me to stand up and share my testimony and expose their lies.

I glanced over to see where Mary was for moral support, I was shocked to see that she was GONE! What? She had taken off out of that room, and somehow, I didn't notice her leave. I felt so isolated and abandoned, and yet I knew I just had to speak up. So, with trepidation, when the opportunity came for questions/comments, praying quietly in the spirit, and with my heart almost beating out of my chest, I quickly put up my hand first, and was allowed to speak.

Of course, I thanked them for the presentations, and then began to share how I had been pressured into abortions and believed the lies, but then learned that my children had a beating heart by three weeks, arms, legs, fingers and toes by eight weeks and how I ended up with an infection, damaged cervix as well as suffering years of depression because of legal abortion in Canada...

The Jezebels began to squirm and gasp, as I went on speaking. I asked if they were aware of the dozens of studies linking breast cancer, pre-term births and depression to induced abortions. One woman burst out calling me a "Liar". My heart was about to explode with fear, but I got everything out God wanted me to, and then as soon as I could, I got out of there, and went up to our room. A couple of women who were sitting close to me, thanked me for sharing, but I could feel the daggers flying from across the room.

After a couple of hours, I went back down to the lobby, and several women were waiting and looking for me, they quickly surrounded me asking why I was there, who I was, where I came from and who I was with etc.

Anyway, God gave me the grace and courage to answer all their questions in love, and share my testimony and infor-mation on how abortion was hurting women.

The Holy Spirit also led me to start attending the Commission on Population and Development (CPD) meetings at the UN in New York City; as well as making a way for me to give Oral Statements to that assembly the last four years. What an amazing opportunity to share this truth at this level. I call this the "population control freaks conference". With a lot of prayer and the help of the Holy Spirit, we have had so many divine appointments with Ambassadors, delegates, doctors and Ministers of Health.

While in New York City, a city I love, I usually attend the Times Square Church the one David Wilkerson started. The praise and worship is anointed and fantastic. The sermons are strong and relevant. One time, the Holy Spirit instructed me to go to the Visitors Reception after the Service, so I did. I was in the line getting a cup of tea, and as usual began to speak to the person in front of me. Asking where she was from; "Uganda" she promptly replied, then invited me to join her and her friends at their table. So I did. It wasn't long when one of the ladies asked what brought me to New York. So I began to share how God had opened doors for me to come to the United Nations and to meet with Ambassadors and Delegates on the pain of legal abortion, and how it is damaging women's mental and reproductive health, and is NOT a "safe" procedure for pregnant women or their children.

It turns out that the lady I introduced myself to, was in fact the Ambassador to Uganda's wife! Halleluiah, I exclaimed, then told her I would sure love to meet her husband. She said, "That can be arranged, and would you be able to join us for dinner, tonight?" She had her friend pick me up and drive me to their home that evening for a lovely dinner with their family and I shared my testimony and information with His Excellency, who was also a doctor, and like most people, not aware of all of the damage legal abortion can bring to women's health. It was a divine appointment for sure.

For several years now the abortion lobbyists are trying to push to legalize abortion throughout Africa, South and Central America and into every nation where it is still illegal or there are plenty of restrictions. They have already conquered all the developed nations. I thank God for my colleagues Sharon,

Scott, Jeanne, Ruben, Patricia, Ildi, Colleen and a few others who have worked at the UN. I just love meeting all the people, and God has given me a supernatural favour as well as a boldness to approach and love them, so I can expose the lies, and share the truth and knowledge I have on this issue as an expert witness.

Allan Parker, a mighty man of God, and attorney with the Texas Justice Foundation and lawyer Sam C. from the USA and a coalition of us, submitted an official complaint against China. We submitted 37 cases of women forced and coerced into abortions and sterilizations because of the One Child Policy. Thank God now there is a two-child policy, so they are moving in the right direction, albeit slowly.

The Lord also sent me on an assignment to intervene for Life at the UN Headquarters in Bangkok, Thailand a few years ago. I was to meet and train a young lady lawyer fresh out of law school on UN protocol and matters. We were to attend a high level UN Women's meeting. However, we missed the deadline to register, but I had a peace about it, and felt that GOD would make a way for us to get in there regardless. After praying in our room for some time, I felt the ok to head to the UN, my first time at this location. Just as we were approaching the main gate, a Thai Catholic Nun was also coming at the same time. I began a conversation with her, explaining that this was our first time, that we were pro-lifers and here to attend this High Level Women's meeting. She responded with, "Me too, come follow me." We went right past the guards, and into the main lobby where a woman at the registration desk, asked what our names were. She looked up and down the long list, and said, "Funny, they are not on here." I said, "Really?" She said, no worries, I will just make you up new badges!" And we were in.

In March of 2013, while at the CSW, I was randomly speaking to a woman about our work and mission, and she quickly interrupted me and said, "Wait, you have to talk to my producer." I asked, "What producer? What kind of a pro-ducer?" and she informed me that they were at the UN making a documentary on population trends around the world and how seven billion people would impact our planet... They were featuring three people, a man from China who was having a difficult time trying to find a wife. A female journalist from Uganda, where they have the highest number of children per capita, and now they were wanting to feature me. Denise Mountenay this passionate Christian pro-life activist from Morinville, Alberta, Canada...oh boy.

On meeting the producer, and sharing my heart, she was interested and wanted to hear more...so I invited her and her crew to come to our scheduled Parallel Event. They filmed the whole session, then interviewed me for half an hour afterward.

We had another packed out workshop with delegates and representatives from around the world. Tricia shared her testimony, followed by Maureen talking about the sacredness of Human Life from an aboriginal point of view, along with sharing her own testimony on the pain of abortion. Dr. Sandy Christiansen, an OB/GYN gave an excellent power-point presentation on how abortion is damaging women's mental and reproductive health.

As MC, I also shared my testimony divulging the lies and violence of abortion to women and the child in the womb.

Part of my presentation included the fact that we are very troubled by some of the language in the UN documents that pertain to "Comprehensive Sexuality Education" (CSE) as I discovered this term originates from the International Planned Parenthood Federation (IPPF) curriculum where they want to teach young children about sex, and show them pornographic illustrations, and sexualize their innocent minds. I am not even going to tell you the garbage they are putting into 10 year olds, and the mindset to believe that same sex relationships and marriages are a good and wonderful thing. When clearly studies show that homosexuals have a much shorter life span due to anal diseases, HIV/AIDS and other problems. As well as studies show children are best adjusted with a Mother and a Father. You would be shocked at the indoctrination they put on children. We also asked them to delete references to "reproductive rights"; which is code for 'abortion on demand'.

We had appointments with the Ambassadors to Argentina, Nicaragua, Sri Lanka, El Salvador and Canada.

We were invited to a Reception for the UN Ambassador to Nigeria, where I also had the opportunity to speak to her Excellency as well as with the Minister for Women's Affairs on the pain of legal abortion and bringing humanity to children in the womb. All of these countries are being pushed to make abortion legally on request, as birth control.

We also met with delegates from China, Germany, Thailand, Romania, Guatemala and Israel... Leaving them with information packages and resources to examine. We exposed the lies and rhetoric propagated, and proclaimed God's truth at the UN level.

Elsie, the film producer emailed and called me to see if I would be going back to the UN to attend the Commission on Population and Development (CPD) meetings the next month. I let her know that if God wanted me back there, He would have to supply the funds, and I would keep her posted.

The donations came in, so I let Elsie know I was going back...she asked if she and her film crew could come to my house and film me getting ready to go to the UN. They could not believe that I was so passionate, yet I had no salary, no corporate sponsors, no funding, no doctorate, and no commercial offices, but was meeting with UN Ambassadors and trying to educate people on the pain of legal abortion, expose the myth of over population and try to change hard hearts on the issue going against the mainstream.

Elsie, two camera people, and two sound people came to our little hamlet to film me teaching our son how to make homemade soup. They filmed our prayer meeting in my living room, filmed me getting my hair and nails done then flew back to Los Angeles.

A week later they met Glenisaah, a beautiful, striking tall black woman from Alberta and Cecilia, an attractive Latino woman from Florida both former abortion patients and myself in lower Manhattan, New York City as we booked into our three-star hotel and began to put our information packages together for the delegates and ambassadors we would meet there that week.

It was another marathon as we had late nights and early mornings speaking to dozens of delegates. Monday began with the film crew following me around the UN with their cameras and microphones, just like the paparazzi. It was an adventure! We attended the International Planned Barrenhood meeting where they were pushing their Vision 2020 propaganda program featuring abortion on demand, without restrictions in every nation, same sex marriages, and "Comprehensive Sexuality Education (CSE)". We are outraged, and so should you be if you saw the materials they are unleashing on young children. They rake in billions of dollars annually from UN agencies, corporations and governments. We spoke to a few key people there, and dozens during the week.

We met with delegates one on one from Hungary, Croatia, India, Romania, Korea and Israel. Several were in on the CPD negotiations for the final agreed conclusions, so we hoped and prayed that they took out the propaganda on reproductive rights (code for abortion on demand) and comprehensive sexuality education. Apparently, our efforts worked, thanks to Sharon, Peter, Jeanne, Ramon and our other colleagues who, all together, influenced enough delegates not to include the CSE in the documents...a huge victory for our side.

We also had the privilege of meeting with the UN Ambassador to Bangladesh, who agreed to have the camera crew. It was very interesting how he knew all about the CSE, and added it looked like they were using porno-graphic videos too. The Ambassador also shared with me how they have reduced "poverty" by not 5 or 15 %, but by 50%! By implementing good infrastructure which was creating jobs and fixing sewer, water and other problems, as well they were providing micro-financing and assisting farmers to grow sustainable food sources to end poverty.

Praise the Lord, I got to make another Oral Statement at the CPD! In my report I spoke about how legal abortion is damaging women and killing innocent children, and I ended with this; "If poverty is the enemy, let's eliminate poverty, not the children!" Thanks for listening. The film crew shot me giving my statement too.

Then after the crew left for Los Angeles, we celebrated with dinner at a Chinese Restaurant close to our hotel. OMG, that night I was so sick! I got food poisoning, and felt like I was getting purged. Enough of that part...

Well, they completed the documentary April of 2014, and have called it, *"Misconception"*. I just love the title. My son and I were invited to join the film crew for dinner, and attend the World Premiere of "Misconception" at the Tribeca Film Festival in New York City! I am so excited, and a little apprehensive... but deep down I know that God planned this. Hoping and praying that I did a good job getting this message out. Please go see it if it comes to a Movie Theatre or you see it on Netflix ok. I think it was very well done. It features a man in China having trouble finding a wife because of the 30 million missing women from sex-selected abortions, a woman from Uganda

who is helping abandoned children get reunited with their families. She is the heroine in the film, and myself, a former abortion patient, activist. They discuss family planning, but have a
statistician who tells us to calm down, don't worry, we are not
over-populating the earth...

In May of 2013, I had the opportunity to go once again
to the World Health Organization (WHO) annual Assembly in
Geneva, Switzerland and lobby at the UN Headquarters also
while there. I met with delegates, doctors, Ministers of Health
and health care leaders and scientists to talk about the pain
and damage of legal abortion.

There was an interesting big display and new campaign
which caught my eye. "***Born Too Soon-The Global Action
Report on Preterm Birth-Executive Summary***". Quickly, I
raced over to talk to the representatives, ask questions and
get their report...I grabbed the last one! The full color displays
and booklet revealing a tiny baby's hand holding an adult's
finger was intriguing. It included a big list of partner organizations such as March of Dimes, Save the Children, WHO,
Bill & Melinda Gates Foundation, Johns Hopkins Bloomberg
School of Public Health, UNICEF, UKAID, UNFPA, USAID, the
Government of Canada and Women Deliver to name a few...

My heart was racing as I opened the report and read the
Headline Messages: "**15 million babies are born too soon
every year**" Wow, this is an epidemic! That means one in ten
babies are born prematurely, affecting families all around the
world. Over 1 million of these children die, due to complications of pre-term births. Premature newborn babies (under 37
weeks' gestation) have elevated risk of MACE (Mental retarda-
tion, Autism, Cerebral Palsy, Epilepsy) disorders, plus higher
odds of deafness, blindness, respiratory distress, gastrointes-
tinal injury, and serious infections.

It continued, "**Rates of preterm births are rising**" globally.
This despite all of our big advances in medicine and health
care. **This is the leading cause of newborn deaths.**

I began to get upset as I read on...knowing what I have
known for about 10 years now. Thanks to medical researcher

Brent Rooney, who has kept me abreast of the abundant number of studies on how induced abortion causes children to be born too soon. Brent calls it "settled science." Abortion damages a woman's cervix as they force it open to insert sharp, deadly instruments to dismember and tear the babies' limbs apart, causing weakness of the cervix, making it incapable to carry or hold a subsequent "wanted" child to full term.

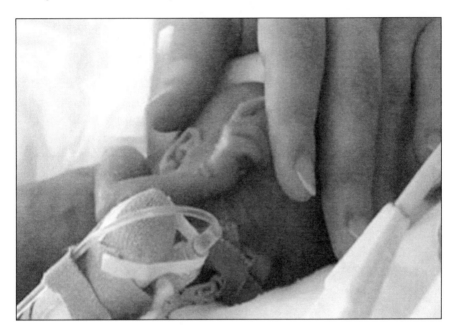

The uterus is often scarred with bone fragments from the aborted child's remains that get lodged in there, as well as sometimes causing Placenta Previa, and the list of complications goes on and on!

One legally induced abortion increases the risk of a pre-term birth by over 36%! Two or more abortions increase the risk by 93%!!

A February 2013 study by three Canadian researchers at The Department of Obstetrics and Gynecology at McGill University in Montreal reviewed the records of 17,916 women who delivered babies between April 2001 and March 2006 using data from the McGill Obstetric and Neonatal Database.

The researchers found that, on average, **women who had one prior induced abortion were 45% more likely to have pre-mature births by 32 weeks, 71% more likely to have pre-mature births by 28 weeks, and 117% more likely to have pre-mature births by 26 weeks**. [6, Hardy; http://www.jogc.com/abstracts/full/201302_Obstetrics_5.pdf]

The prestigious Institute of Medicine lists **"Prior first trimester induced abortion"** as one of 14 **"Immutable Medical Risk Factors Associated with Preterm Birth".** [7, Behrman] HELLO!

There are now a total of 4 Systematic Review Meta-Analysis (SMRA) confirming a significant connection between cervical damage from induced abortions and subsequent Pre-Term Births. The first one published in Feb. of 2009 by Dr. Hanes Swingle et al. Then another one published in the British Journal of Obstetrics & Gynecology in October of 2009 by Dr. Prakesh Shah's of the University of Toronto, Ontario, Canada. Their teams each examined the pre-term birth risk, after prior surgical abortions, including 'suction' abortions, revealing statistically significant links.

The 3rd SRMA was in 2015, authored by Dr. Marike Lemmers et al. and gave preemie risk numbers for Dilation & Curettage induced abortions.

The 4th SRMA was just conducted by Dr. Gabrielle SACCONE et al. and gives astounding evidence, it was just published May, 2016 in The American Journal of Obstetricians and Gynecologists.

Saccone inspected 28 prior studies of 913,297 women. They found that women who never had an abortion only have a 3.15% risk of having a natural miscarriage. This increases to 24% for women who abort. Women who had one induced abortion had a 52% higher risk in having a premature delivery in a subsequent pregnancy! This is huge.

They also discovered that women who have Chemical/Medically Induced abortions using the Emergency contraceptive or Morning after Pills etc., also have a 50% increased risk of having a pre-mature birth in a subsequent pregnancy. Who has heard of these facts as more and more teenagers and young women are popping so called Morning after Pills as another form of birth control and endangers the lives of their future children?

The next paragraph in this "Born Too Soon-Executive Summary" from the World Health Organization campaign talked about the urgency to prevent preterm births...but do they really want to do that? Tragically, there is not one word about the mountain of studies linking pre-term births to induced abortions!

In the Born Too Soon Executive Summary, they don't mention one of the SMRA studies proving induced abortion causes Pre-Term Births, instead they start pushing their birth control, women's rights to abortion and population control agenda, and I quote: *"Family planning, and increased empowerment of women, especially adolescents...can help to reduce preterm birth rates."* WHAT?? When they say family planning, they are referring to women ingesting cancer causing agents i.e. The Birth Control Pill, inserting painful IUD's and when those fail, abort your babies. This is what they call empowerment that will reduce preterm birth rates? What a lie!

You have no idea how upsetting and frustrating it is for me to see these falsehoods made over and over, and to hear this propaganda from high levels of government and feminists. Every day they put a gag order not to tell women and the public about these studies means more children will become disabled, more children will die and more women and families will be heartbroken!

I am driven by love, justice and facts to keep testifying, to keep speaking out and to try to bring these to the forefront in the Media! Please pray for me...please help me...God knows I need help in this war against pregnant women and children.

Do you realize that as of March of 2016 there are not 2 or 3 studies, or 20 or 30, or 80 or 100 studies...? No, there are currently

Over 140 **studies reporting women with prior Induced Abortions have an elevated risk of a future preterm delivery or a low birth weight (under 2,500 grams) newborn baby;**

URL: http://justiceforkids.webs.com/chap450studies.htm

So why isn't this breaking news on CNN? The CBC, CTV, Oprah, Dr. Phil, or Dr. Oz...? Why isn't this mentioned as a risk factor by doctors or abortionists when women think they want an abortion? Over 40 current studies just since the year 2000, and seven so far this year. Yet, NOT one word publically warning pregnant women of this significant connection between abortion and pre-mature births to save future children from disabilities or death. Shame on doctors, researchers, media and governments for the cover-ups! Millions of disabled and dead children's blood are on their hands for the silence!

Newborns delivered between 28 & 31 weeks' gestation (very preterm) have 55 times the risk of having Cerebral Palsy then a full-term newborn. [5, Himpens]. Women have a right to be fully informed about all of the risk factors of this dangerous procedure called abortion, but they are not even informed the majority of the time. Do you realize that there is not ONE study that says abortion is beneficial for women's reproductive health? Yet there's a colossal number of studies showing its detriment to women's mental and physical health.

It would be great to find a mathematician to calculate all the medical costs of every one of these problems associated with legal abortion; especially as women suffer the physical and psychological trauma to our bodies and minds in the aftermath of having our children aborted.

Chapter 11

The Seed of the Serpent

From the Book of Genesis to the Book of Revelation, it is the continuing saga of the Seed of the Woman and the seed of the Serpent go to WAR!

People who reject God, who believe that we evolved from slime and put their faith into the theory of evolution, instead of into the Word of God, or Christ, are rooted in the spirit of anti-Christ. The emergence and teaching in schools and amongst people that mankind evolved from slime, sow seeds of doubt and unbelief in a divine creator. They choose to believe the lies, and think they are gods, rather than believe that everything is made from intelligent design. They deny a Holy Creator, a loving eternal Father with a purpose and a plan for everything, and everyone. Besides, it's easier to sin if you have no accountability to God in the end.

If you believe there is no God, no judgment, no eternity, then it is much easier to lie, steal a little, cheat now and then, and become hedonistic and self-centered.

All creatures and plants are so incredible with distinction, with purpose, and having their own particular inherent DNA to reproduce after their own kind. This is not taking billions of years, but rather days, weeks and months to happen. It is amazing to examine!

Most people, who believe in the Theory of Evolution, or Macroevolution, do not believe in God, the creator who has a purpose and a plan for every living creature. We have no problems with the proven small changes in adaptation; called microevolution which are minor variations in species due to environmental challenges.

Most evolutionists are atheists and visa, versa. I hope that the Holy Spirit will open the eyes of our understanding and give us revelation knowledge of the wonder and brilliance of a Master Creator and His amazing artwork and majesty on earth. Everything is divinely inspired for His Kingdom on this planet.

Atheists do not believe in God at all. Agnostics aren't sure, they are very skeptical about everything… and many function as atheists.

That is how I used to be, until I examined the big picture of how our world is so perfectly put together in the universe, and how we rotate around the sun and are just the perfect distance away from it...all the way to the micro, minute cells that know how to build each cell, repair skin, fight infection etc... and learning about the evidence of creation through science.

Atheists and many agnostics further believe there are no moral absolutes…such as what is wrong to you, may not be wrong to me. Some people believe that there is absolutely nothing wrong with a woman choosing to have her baby killed by an abortionist. Many people support this right to have a baby slaughtered in his or her mother's womb, and also demand the government pay for these killings.

The problem is this; what you might call right and good, is not what I would call right and good…it is relativism; everyone is right in their own eyes.

> *"There is a way which seems right to a man and appears straight before him, but at the end of it, is the way of death."* Proverbs14:12

Unfortunately, most teachers in the public school system, professors, doctors, lawyers and politicians are atheists these days. They have flooded the classrooms for decades now to push their speculations and beliefs of Darwinism as the absolute truth to generations of students. And we usually trust and accept what those professionals in authority say. *"But, the wisdom of this world is "foolishness (absurdity and stupidity) with God, for it is written, He lays hold of the wise in their [own] craftiness;"* 1Cor. 3:19

This could be why so many more Christians are resorting to Home Schooling their children. Wish I would have done that.

Yeshua/Jesus Christ is a historical figure. He existed, no doubt about that. Over 2,000 years ago, He talked about the spirit of "anti-Christ" which was already in the world. The Greek definition is "an opponent of the Messiah". In my research for this book, I found a host of people who were networking to promote the theory of evolution and atheism to deposit doubts into the minds of people back in the 1700 and 1800's, and this same spirit is operating today.

These wealthy individuals were also proponents of 'utilitarianism'. Which means that in all acts there must be what is known as the "hedonic calculus" in order to achieve "the greatest pleasure for the greatest number". It is totally self-indulgent; it is all about self-pleasure as a way of life.

They rebelled against Christian teachings. They formed societies and organizations to propagate their anti-Christ agenda.

Yet, over the years, I have heard so many atheists tell me that it was the religious people who had started so many wars, and killed so many people...that is not true! Read on friend.

In the last century, some of the top intellectuals of the Western world supported brutal dictators like Hitler, Stalin and Mao. They supported eugenics, deconstructionism, speech codes, using rhetoric, values clarification education, and the voluntary human extinction movement, to name just a few of their pet projects.

Atheists mock those who believe in God, and want us to "Get rid of God," they argue. They have insisted God be taken out of the classrooms, out of the government, out of the community. Now, in this generation we have many teenagers who come from broken homes, are fatherless, and who are fixated on brutal graphic video games, dark demonic music, addicted to pornography which is easily available, and of course bullies, gangs and plenty of alcohol and drugs. Most families today only have one child, or prefer dogs and cats to having children. Many children spend many hours without their mommies and daddies daily. Have we become too materialistic? The infiltration and influence of promiscuity, adultery, fornication and homosexual perversion propagated on television, in the music, media and in the arts and movies are resulting in an immoral and godless society, getting more desensitized. Tragically, we have more and more bizarre episodes of young adults shooting and killing children in schools...

Nations and societies which adopt the evolutionary philosophy see a breakdown of families, broken homes, sexual immorality, lack of respect for the sanctity of human life, increasing crime, anarchy and chaos.

The Seed of the Serpent: Connecting the dots

David Hume was an atheist philosopher who held terrible views of Christianity, and argued against the existence of God in 1779. Hume was a friend of Thomas Robert Malthus, the father of fear mongering about Population Control.

In 1805 Malthus became Professor of History and Political Economy at the East India Company College. Influencing his students to fear 'over population' in the world. Malthus became hugely influential, and controversial, in economic, political, social and scientific thought. He spurred on the speculation of population explosions.

Malthus argued that two types of checks hold population within resource limits: *positive* checks; which raise the death rate; (sickness, disease, wars, famines...) and *preventative* checks; which included abortion, birth control, prostitution, postponement of marriage and celibacy which all lower the birth rates. Today we could add homosexuality to this list. He totally disregarded the sovereignty of God, and sarcastically criticized the notion that agricultural advancements could expand without limit to provide for larger populations to sustain people.

He was a population control freak, in my books. His anti-God social theory influenced the idea of the survival of the fittest, and others. Many evolutionists read his books and articles; notably Charles Darwin.

Darwin's father was a wealthy doctor and financier who married his cousin. His grandfather and father were probably atheists too. They were non-conformist. His mother had him baptized in an Anglican church as a baby, but she took him to the Unitarian church (a cult) which denies the divinity of Jesus Christ. When he was eight years old his mother suddenly died. That must have been horrible. So he and his brother were sent to an Anglican boarding school for boys.

By June of 1838, the strain of debates took a toll, and Darwin was sick for days on end with stomach problems, headaches and heart symptoms. For the rest of his life, he was repeatedly incapacitated with episodes of stomach pains, vomiting, severe boils, palpitations, trembling and other symptoms, particularly during times of stress, such as attending meetings or making social visits. The cause of Darwin's illness remained unknown, and attempts at treatment had little success.

Darwin wrote of Malthus, "In October 1838, that is, fifteen months after I had begun my systematic enquiry, I happened to read for amusement Malthus on Population... I had at last got a theory by which to work..."

He published his theory in 1859 in the infamous book, "On the Origin of Species by Means of Natural Selection, (including the subtitle) Or the **Preservation of Favoured Races in the Struggle for Life**".

Please read that subtitle again. The preservation of "Favoured Races" that sounds quite racist to me! The scientific community and much of the general public came to accept this hypothesis as fact in his lifetime. Ever since, there has been a broad consensus developed by secular humanists which unfortunately still teach this evolutionary propaganda in schools today!

Darwinism=Atheism=Racism

*"**The fool hath said in his heart,** there is no **God.**"* Psalm 14:1

Another total atheist and a staunch believer in the theory of evolution was Fredrich Nietzsche born in Germany in 1844. However, Nietzsche's father died from a brain ailment when Fredrich was only five years old. His younger brother died the following year. This must have been dreadful for a little boy.

In 1862, after reading articles by other atheists, it put more doubt and unbelief into his mind. Nietzsche became a lifelong rebel against Christianity. He became a nihilist. Nihilism is the total rejection of established laws and institutions. It rejects established moral beliefs and religion, therefore anyone can do what they want, when they want, how they want, with few repercussions. It believes that life is pointless and human values are worthless. It can involve anarchy, terrorism, total and absolute destructiveness toward the world at large and including oneself (this manifested in Hitler's last years). It is an extreme form of philosophical skepticism, including the denial of all real existence or the possibility of an objective basis for truth, and no God.

Nihilism also incorporated the principles of a Russian revolutionary group, active in the latter half of the 19th century, holding that existing social and political institutions must be destroyed in order to clear the way for a new state of society (**communism**) and employing extreme measures, including terrorism and assassination. This was one of the roots to communism!

Tragically, nihilism is evident in this generation through many secular heavy metal band lyrics, websites, TV and movies talking and singing about it. When I read about Nietzsche, I hear one irritated man. His notorious view about the "death of God" resulted from his personal life tragedies, in a move from traditional beliefs in God, to a deeper trust in science and commerce. Nietzsche put down Christians all the time and belittled them as weak and irrelevant.

Yet, not surprising to me, in January of 1880, Nietzsche went crazy, had a mental breakdown, and was sent to an asylum. He also had syphilis. Nietzsche spent his last ten years in mental darkness then died.

The Nazis, welcomed Nietzsche's view of "Herrenmensch," a new type of man, who with his robber instincts, was able to manipulate the masses and who was a law unto himself. Adolf Hitler kept a bust of Nietzsche. When Elisabeth Nietzsche died in 1935, Hitler participated in the funeral ceremony. Hitler was a frequent visitor to the Nietzsche Museum and used some of his quotes in his notorious book, *Mein Kampf*.

The First World War began in 1914 to 1918 and killed over 15 million people due to fascist leaders and European Empires for power and dominance; not Christian rulers. The first Marxist-run nation state was the Soviet Union, which began in 1917, was enforced in 1922 following the Russian revolution. Atheist leaders Vladimir Lenin, Leon Trotsky and Joseph Stalin formulated the theoretical trends of Marxism-Leninism.

From 1932-39, Josef Stalin (USSR,) not a Christian, had 23 million people killed through purges including Ukraine's famine.

Stalin followed the position adopted by Lenin that religion was an opiate that needed to be removed in order to construct the ideal communist controlled society. To this end, his government promoted atheism and still do.

The LINK between Evolution, Atheism, Marxism, Communism, Fascism, Humanism, Racism, Nazism and Nihilism is unquestionable.

In the Marxist-Leninist interpretation, communism was completely atheistic and explicitly anti-religious. Did you know that Russia became the very first country in history to make atheism the official ideology of a nation? This trend was also reflected in policies in the Eastern Bloc and China.

Karl Marx was born into a middle-class home in Germany on May 5, 1818. Marx met with Friedrich Engels another German; together co-founding Communism. They produced The Communist Manifesto in 1848. Marx outlined a humanist conception of communism. Another close friend of Marx was Bruno Bauer who openly taught atheism as a Professor of Theology, until he was fired.

In 1887 Vladimir Lenin studied law, and read Karl Marx's books. He became a Russian/Marxist revolutionary and communist politician who led the October Revolution of 1917. As leader of the Bolsheviks, he headed the Soviet state (1917–1924), as it fought to establish control of Russia. Lenin was responsible for the murders of millions of people! He was highly critical of religion, saying in his book Religion; "Atheism is a natural and inseparable part of Marxism, of the theory and practice of scientific socialism."

After Lenin died in 1924, Stalin become the dictator of the Soviet Union. From the Soviet archives, it is estimated that nearly 700,000 ordinary people including priests and farmers were executed between 1937 and1938. Stalin was the first General Secretary of the Communist Party from 1922 until his death in 1953.

Stalin personally condemned to execution some 40,000 people. Once, while reviewing a list, Stalin reportedly muttered to someone, "Who's going to remember all this riff-raff in ten or twenty years' time? No one. In addition, Stalin dispatched a contingent of operatives to Mongolia, and unleashed a bloody purge in which tens of thousands were executed as 'Japanese Spies.' It is estimated that over **20 million people** were killed, and/or starved to death during the anti-God, Stalin reign of terror!

The religious persecution in the Soviet Union began in 1929 with the drafting of new legislation that severely prohibited religious activities, and called for a heightened attack on religion, in order to further spread atheism.

Joseph Stalin was an ardent atheist, and believer in evolution, he criticized the party for failure to produce more active and persuasive anti-religious propaganda. The main target of the anti-religious campaign in the 1920s and 1930s was the Russian Orthodox Church, which had the largest number of members. Almost every priest and minister, along with many of its believers, were shot dead, or sent to labour camps, just because they were followers of Christ! Theological schools were closed, and church publications were prohibited.

In the period between 1927 and 1940, the number of Orthodox Churches in the Russian Republic fell from 29,584 to less than 500!

It is also quite interesting to discover that in 1920, Russia became the first country in the world to allow abortion in all circumstances, but, over the course of the 20th century, the legality of abortion changed more than once, with a ban being enacted again from 1936 to 1954. Russia had the highest number of abortions per woman of child-bearing age in the world for decades according to the UN.

It is so interesting to see how all these atheists and their hatred towards Christians and the word of God, took the lives of millions of people. They used the media and journalism to promote their atheistic ideas then, and now.

Chapter 12

Wars And Rumours Of Wars

"Have nothing to do with the fruitless deeds of darkness, but rather expose them."
Ephesians 5:11

The next time you hear someone tell you that "Christians" or "Religions" have started more wars and killed more people than anyone on earth, please correct them with these particulars below! Communists/atheists and have burned hundreds of churches down and killed millions of innocent men, women and children.

More PAGAN DICTATORS

Leopold II, of Belgium, an atheist, had over **10 million** people killed in a hostile takeover of the Congo, Africa where he enslaved its people and forced them into labour camps. In the 23 years (1885-1908) Leopold II ruled the Congo he stole their rubber and natural resources, had millions massacred by cutting off their hands and genitals, flogging them to death, starving them into forced labour, holding children ransom and burning villages.

About **63 million** people were killed in the Second World War. This horrific war, initiated by secular humanist evolutionist,

Adolf Hitler also caused unknown thousands to starve to death. Adolf Hitler, himself had 17 million civilians killed in concentration camps in WWII (Germany, 1939-1945)

So many evil dictators such as secular humanist and Communist **Mao Zedong** who was responsible for **49-78 million deaths in Communist China** from 1958 to 1969!

Other terrible atheist dictators include: Hideki Tojo, from Japan who approved of eugenics and had millions of people killed there. Ismail Enver Pasha, a Muslim Turkish Military Leader, lead the Armenian Genocide where 2.5 million deaths occurred. Pol Pot, another Communist this time from Cambodia, had 1.7 million people killed from 1976 to 1979.

Also, Kim Il Sung, of Communist North Korea, has killed over 1.6 million people, and we are getting more horrible reports as the people are still in bondage today. And the list goes on and on!

They were all godless rulers who detested God, rather they wanted to get rid of God, so to speak. They tortured, murdered, intimidated and tormented Christians through fear-mongering, by burning and destroying churches, persecuting Priests, Pastors and coercing Christians to be silent.

These vile atheists (children of the devil) embarked on orgies of mass murder that wiped out over <u>100 million people</u> over the centuries!

Between 1917 and 2001, wicked, malicious leaders and their governments murdered and starved more people than all of the world's empires put together managed to kill in several thousand years.

However, oh yes, the Catholics...There were two major Roman Catholic Inquisitions, the Medieval Inquisition and the Spanish Inquisition. Although there are no exact numbers, scholars believe they have estimated Inquisition deaths reasonably accurately. The secular press has exaggerated and come up with numbers up to the millions with absolutely no data to back it up.

The Catholic crusades were, in part, a response to the territorial cravings of the Muslims. Like most wars, they were wars

191

about land disputes, dominant takeovers, power and politics. Sometimes religion was more of an annoying factor, rather than a cause or justification.

Jesus never told us to kill anyone. He told us to love our enemies, and to pray for those who despitefully use us...

Investigating the Medieval Inquisitions, I discovered that they have been grossly exaggerated to demonize the church. However, truth is, Bernard Gui, one of the most notorious medieval inquisitors, had tried 930 people. Out of which 42 were executed that is (4.5%) of those accused. Another famous Inquisitor was Jacques Fournier who tried 114 cases of which 5 were executed (4.3%). Using numbers that were recorded, scholars have been able to surmise that approximately 2,000 people died in the Medieval Inquisition. (1231-1400 AD)

According to public news reports regarding the Spanish Inquisition, they state that about 125,000 persons were investigated, of which 1.8% were executed, that is about 2,250 people. Most of these deaths occurred in the first decade and a half of the Inquisition's 350-year history.

During the high point of the Spanish Inquisition from 1478-1530 AD, scholars found that approximately 1,500-2,000 people were found guilty. From that point forward, there are exact records available of all "guilty" sentences which amounted to 775 executions.

In Portugal of the 13,000 tried in the 16th and early 17th century 5.7% were said to have been condemned to death. Between the years 1540-1700, 775 people (1.7%) were actually executed while another 700 (1.4%) were sentenced to death in effigy.

If we add the figures, we find that the entire Inquisition of 500 years, caused about a grand total of about 6,000 deaths. These atrocities are horrible, as real Christians should never kill innocent people, no matter their ethnicity or religion etc. Nevertheless, these numbers pale in comparison to the **100 MILLION+ people killed by cruel, atheistic dictators!**

Sadly, today radical jihadist Muslims are committing genocides against Christians in Africa and the Middle East.

They are inflicted with brutal beatings, persecutions, killings and beheadings. They carry the spirits of anti-Semitism and anti-Christianity.

Catastrophically, there is another war occurring in the nations today. A conflict where pregnant women and innocent tiny human beings are the targets. In most developed "Christian" countries we have tolerated and paid for the sin of induced abortion/child sacrifice on demand.

Today there is a concerted effort by abortion providers and population controllers to target the mainly Christian nations who still have abortion as illegal, or with many restrictions. We stand to keep abortion out of Northern Ireland, Malta, Poland, several countries in South America and most African nations who have not bowed down to the intense pressure to legalize the killing of the innocent children, as a "choice".

As Believers in GOD and His word, through the Holy Bible we know that abortion is murder. A fetus is a *living* and growing being with a heartbeat and developing features. For God knew us before we were born, He has a purpose and a plan for each child knit together in his or her mother's womb. God has commanded us not to kill.

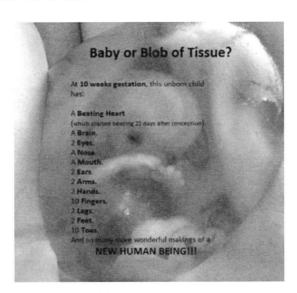

"For You did form my inward parts; You did knit me together in my mother's womb. I will confess and praise You for You are fearful and wonderful and for the awful wonder of my birth! Wonderful are Your works, and that my inner self knows right well. My frame was not hidden from You when I was being formed in secret [and] intricately and curiously wrought [as if embroidered with various colors] in the depths of the earth [a region of darkness and mystery]. Your eyes saw my unformed substance, and in Your book all the days [of my life] were written before ever they took shape, when as yet there was none of them." Psalm 139: 13-16

Usually it is young women who are having sex outside of marriage, who are mainly on some kind of birth control, that fails, and as a result get pregnant, and for whatever reason, God allows this baby to be created in His image with a destiny. Sometimes it is married women having an affair. Sometimes it is women who only wanted one or two children, and have their third or fourth child aborted. Rarely, pregnancy is a result of rape or incest.

However, studies show, and we have found that the majority of pregnant women do not really want an abortion, but are pressured by boyfriends, husbands, parents, doctors or friends to abort their babies. Many of us were lied to and deceived about fetal development, told abortion was a fast and easy fix to an unplanned pregnancy. We were told the baby was "just a clump of tissue" a product of conception, no big deal. We were told it was a "safe" procedure and we could always have children later.

Women have been deceived like Eve in the Garden of Eden, who believed the lies of the Serpent who put doubt in her mind, who seduced her and said, *"Can it really be that God has said, You shall not eat from every tree of the garden?"*

Then he said, *"You shall not surely die, For God knows that in the day you eat of it your eyes will be opened, and you will be like God, knowing the difference between good and evil and blessing and calamity."* Gen. 3:1-5. Then she disobeyed God, ate and gave it to Adam, while he was standing right there next to her, and he partook also. Adam did not try to stop her, nor did this first man of God stand up against the serpent either.

Sound familiar? Is it really a baby? Is it really a person? Besides, it's your choice, your body; you can do whatever you want, whatever is right in your own eyes. Besides it is okay with your boyfriend, parents, the doctors and the government, so it must be okay. Wrong!

Nevertheless, abortion is the deliberate killing of an innocent child. It is really a paid assassin (the doctor) who performs this homicide and gets paid for it, either by the mother of the child, or the Government and its taxpayers.

Once we recognize the humanity of the child in the womb, from the moment of conception, we must not permit or tolerate this destruction of human life. All pregnancies do terminate eventually, either with a live baby, or a dead one. Abortion isn't about the termination of a pregnancy, but it is the termination of a human life! It is the sin of murder.

"You shall not commit murder." Exodus 20:13

> *"So you shall not pollute the land in which you live; for blood pollutes the land, and no atonement can be made for the land for the bloodshed in it, but by the blood of him who shed it."* Num. 35:33

AND THE Lord said to Moses,

"Moreover, you shall say to the Israelites, Any one of the Israelites or of the strangers that sojourn in Israel who gives any of his children to Molech [*the fire god worshiped with human sacrifices*] shall surely be put to death; the people of the land shall stone him with stones.

I also will set My face against that man [*opposing him, withdrawing My protection from him, and excluding him from My covenant*] and will cut him off from among his people, because he has given of his children to Molech, defiling My sanctuary and profaning My holy name."

> ***"And if the people of the land do at all hide their eyes from the man when he gives one of his children [as a burnt offering] to Molech [the fire god] and they overlook it or neglect to take legal action to punish him, winking at his sin, and do not kill him [as My law requires], Then I will set My face against that man and against his family and will cut him off from among their people, him and all who***

follow him to [unfaithfulness to Me, and thus]
play the harlot after Molech." **Lev. 20:1-5**

Governments have laws, police, military and responsibilities to avert armed robberies, to protect property, to prevent terrorists from plotting and destroying people and places, etc. It also has the responsibility to prevent the killing of innocent human beings, no matter how small, including those waiting to be born.

Moreover, God's word commands us to *"Deliver (rescue) those who are drawn away to death, and those who totter to the slaughter, hold them back [from their doom]. If You [profess ignorance and] say, Behold, we did not know this, does not He Who weighs and ponders the heart perceive and consider it? And He Who guards your life, does not He know it? And shall not He render to [you and] every man according to his works?"* Proverbs 24:11, 12

How long will GOD put up with the enormous amounts of innocent bloodshed on the earth? How long will He hold back His judgments? Let us not be lukewarm in these days, but brave and courageous to save precious lives. IF we do not protect the most vulnerable and innocent amongst us, who will? Who will be the next to go? The clock is ticking…

"Clouds and darkness are round about Him, righteousness and justice are the foundation of His throne." Psalm 97:2

Do you realize that there is another massive genocide taking place in most developed nations today? In 1946 just after the Nazi Holocaust, The UN General Assembly Resolution 96, defined "genocide" as a "denial of the right of existence of entire human groups, as homicide is the denial of the right to live of individual human beings." It further states that genocide is a "crime", whether committed on religious, racial, political or any other grounds. So whether it is done just because a pregnant woman wants her baby dead and gone, or by "doctors" willing to do the killing, for a fee of course, is another case for "genocide".

Today, the biggest crime against humanity on earth is the war against innocent children alive and growing in utero. Like the genocides of the Nazi holocaust, doctors systematically kill children before birth, in abortion clinic camps, where women are told lies, like it is a "safe" procedure and a quick fix to their problems. The Nazis told the Jews that they were going in to have a shower, while poisonous gasses filled their lungs, and killed them and their children.

Margaret Sanger – Founder of Planned **Barrenhood,** oops, I mean Parenthood, started the largest birth control, and abortion business in the USA. She wrote; *"Birth Control: to create a race of thoroughbreds".* Like Adolf Hitler, Sanger considered herself to be part of a genetically superior elite, and was totally racist.

The founders of Planned Parenthood had more ties to Hitler than just a shared vision as population controllers. Their board of directors included avowed Nazi supporters like Dr. L. Stoddard, who authored, *"The Rising Tide of Color Against White Supremacy,"* and another article praising the Nazi sterilization law. They used their official publications to spread Nazi propaganda. In April of 1933, the Birth Control Review published an article by Dr. Ernest Rubin, who was Hitler's director of genetic sterilization and a founder of the Nazi Society for Racial Hygiene. In this article Dr. Rubin wrote:

> *"The danger to the community of the un-segregated feeble-minded woman is more evident. Most dangerous are the middle and high grades living at large who, despite the fact that their defect is not easily recognizable, should nevertheless be prevented from procreation. . . In my view we should act without delay."*

The founders of Planned Parenthood printed Dr. Rubin's article in the same year that he worked with SS chief Heinrich

Himmler to draw up German's 1933 sterilization law which called for the sterilization of all Jews and "colored" German children.

In 1952 Sanger became the founder/president of International Planned Parenthood Federation (IPPF). Planned Parenthood has exterminated millions of lives globally. They also get over a billion dollars annually to promote their unrestrained sex education, birth control and abortion business. They do about 340,000 induced abortions every year, just in the USA.

Is it any coincidence that the founders of Planned Parenthood were racists and Nazi propagandists?

The United Nations talks a great deal about population control, and many population control agencies will give humanitarian aid only to those poor women who accept birth control and sterilizations.

Planned Parenthood has branches all over the world through IPPF. They continue to work to make abortion free, a woman's right on request, without question, without real informed or parental consent.

With abortion, the "entire human group" that is being murdered are the unwanted, pre-born children! When we honestly compare mass injustices and genocides from history we quickly see that whether it was in the killing fields of Cambodia, China, Russia, the Holocaust, Africans forced into slavery, then raped, lynched or Native Americans killed or forced into residential schools, it all comes from the same spirit of racism. It is always linked to demonic spirits and ideologies of atheism, racism, and the "kill the unwanted" philosophies.

The rhetoric is similar…the victims are dehumanized, belittled and the bullies perform the atrocities, which are often government sanctioned.

But, we weren't there in 1857 when the Supreme Court of the USA declared that Blacks were an inferior and subordinate class of beings in the Dred Scott v. Sandford case. We weren't there when Slavery and Segregation was legal, and it was wrong. One of my beautiful African-American sisters told me that it is deplorable that none of her ancestors have any of their real African names, but were forced to all take on the Slave Masters last name. They have no idea from what area or tribe in Africa they came from.

We weren't there when the Supreme Court of Germany declared that Jewish people had no rights to their own land, to their private possessions, to life or freedom, and essentially the court legalized the Holocaust.

But, we are here now, in this generation while every day babies in their mother's womb are being unjustly sentenced to death and exterminated on our watch. These are the same evil spirits operating today to kill the "unwanted" children before they are born.

Think about this: Why should someone be killed just because they are smaller than others and cannot protect themselves? Is a fat man or woman more of a "person" because he or she is bigger, than a smaller person?

Is a teenager more of a "person" than a two-year-old, because he/she is more mature?

Is a newborn, or pre-maturely born child in a hospital incubator more of a "person," than a pre-born child in his or her mother's womb (a natural incubator)? Just because he or she is in a different temporary location, doesn't make them any less human, or less alive?

Is a healthy man or woman more of a "person" than another man or woman with a heart pacemaker or dependent on insulin? Of course not.

The word, "person" is defined in the Merriam-Webster Dictionary as a "human, individual".

I just love this saying, "A person, is a person, no matter how small!"

My heart is not to condemn anyone; God will do that. I just pray that the Holy Spirit will convict people of the sin of abortion, and for you to rise up to be a voice for the voiceless, for such a time as this. I pray that there will become a huge evangelistic outreach to the millions of former abortion patients who are suffering, often in silence because they are so hurt about the fact they had an abortion, or several in their lifetime. My heart goes out to them to be forgiven and healed through the mercy and grace of our loving heavenly Father.

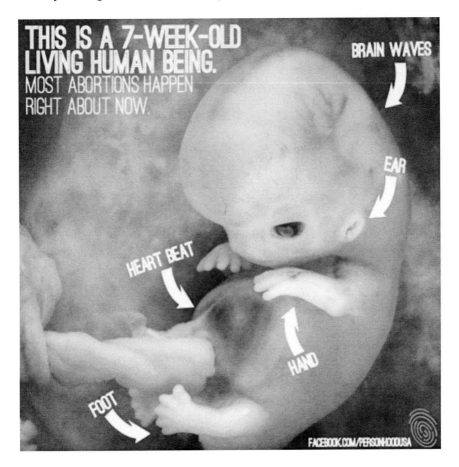

Then for those people who pressured them or who were complacent in the act, to come forward and join us in this effort to bring education, awareness and hope to encourage and help single Moms and their babies. Also, we need to reach the teenagers and young adults with a message to Hang on to their Hormones!

Will you help be a voice? Will you support this great cause for Life?

Chapter 13

THE Dragon Wars against the Church

"They lay crafty schemes against Your people and consult together against Your hidden and precious ones. They have said, Come, and let us wipe them out as a nation; let the name of Israel be in remembrance no more. For they have consulted together with one accord and one heart; against You they make a covenant." Psalm 3,4

The Serpent keeps growing

The National Secular Society (NSS) was founded by Charles Bradlaugh in 1866 in England. It is a secular Humanist campaigning organization that promotes atheism and pressures governments in the separation of church, and state. Of course, Satan does not want the morals of the Bible included in State laws. They want lawlessness. The society is a member organization of the International Humanist Association of which Dr. Henry Morgentaler infamous abortionist in Canada, was the President of it for some time.

In the 1800's, Anne Besant, from London, England also studied Darwin's Theory of Evolution. In the midst of her readings, she met this Charles Bradlaugh, who was also a Member of Parliament, who started Besant in journalism and in political action for the National Secular Society. She went to jail for publishing a pamphlet/book on birth control as it contained instructions on how to insert certain chemicals into the vagina after intercourse, to cause an abortion. She also went on lecture tours advocating Marxism and atheism. By the late 1930s it had become dangerous to be publicly associated with any religion, in the Communist/Marxist/Fascist nations.

Early, in 1941, the Society of the Godless, (S.0.G) developed in communist Russia, also known as the League of Militant atheists, had about 3.5 million members around the world consisting of 100 nationalities. No God means, no consequences, you can do whatever you want and there is no eternal punishment…and no hell in their religion of belief, and so it was very popular to the masses.

In the books of Mathew, Mark and Luke, Jesus warned us about wars and rumors of wars. *"And when you hear of wars and rumors of wars, do not get alarmed (troubled and frightened); it is necessary [that these things] take place, but the end is not yet."* Mark 13:7

He also told us that many would come in His name and not be of Him. Yeshua also warned us that there would be wolves in sheep's clothing too.

In July of 2013, I read this quote from the current Executive Director of the NSS website, "…the only way to prevent the kind of religious power-seeking that leads to conflict is to make both religious discrimination and religious privilege constitutionally impossible.

We need a secular constitution that will:
- End the privileged input of religious bodies to policy making and law-making
- Keep all public services free from religious control so that that they remain equally available to all on the same terms
- Abolish the established Church and all its privileges…

The enemy of God is still working hard today, to keep the church quiet and ineffective in politics, and from being an influence in our governments and nations which is so important. The Ecclesia, is the government of God…we are of another government, we are of the Kingdom of God on earth.

As you can see they clearly intend to dismantle and tear down the authority and influence the Church has on governments, and instill their godless beliefs instead! They are full of the spirit of Anti-Christ. They cannot tolerate the role of salt and light in the earth today and want to stop religious broadcasting on television and remove God from the courts, from oaths, and so on. They are totally pro same-sex marriage, pro-abortion rights and pro-euthanasia.

Our spiritual enemy certainly does not want Christians involved in Education or Politics at all, so they can continue to sexualize children, push birth control and abortions, then ultimately do away with the sick and elderly, as population controllers always pushing for godlessness. Do you have eyes to see? Ears to hear?

Jesus/Yeshua taught us to love our enemies, to love our neighbor, to rescue those who are beaten, robbed and bleeding in the ditches of our streets. (Luke 10) He taught us to feed the poor and visit the sick and those in prison. He commanded us to love God and love others and this meant to be patient, kind, gentle, long suffering and self-controlled… His way is more about dying to self, and laying down our lives for others. Giving and doing things His way, not our way.

He also taught us to walk by faith, and not by sight. God loves everyone, but not everyone is adopted into His Family. This is a gift from GOD, as it is our sins that separate us from God. This is why Yeshua gave His life and died on the cross for our sins to redeem mankind and make a way, a bridge back to our heavenly Father.

God wants us to *"Rescue those being unjustly sentenced to death, don't stand back and let them die, don't disclaim responsibility by saying you never knew about it. For God knows you knew, and He will reward everyone, according to their deeds."* Prov. 24:11,12

He also commands us to speak up for those who cannot speak for themselves. Prov. 31:8

The United Nations originated to bring unity and order after Hitler's diabolical extermination camps were exposed; and to ensure those atrocities would never happen again. It sadly has been hijacked by the pro-abortionists. It has become a platform for the population controllers to push their radical godless ideologies. For years they have been pressuring all the undeveloped nations to legalize abortion on request. It is interesting that The First Director-General of United Nations Educational, Scientific and Cultural Organization (UNESCO), was an atheist, humanist, evolutionist; Julian Huxley. He pushed for population control in his book, on *Evolutionary Humanism* (1964).

Humanism rejects anything that is supernatural, like God or Christ, therefore appealing to agnostics, atheists and secularists. Pray God sends workers across their paths and they come to know His way, truth and life.

Tragically, in Israel, also known as the Holy Land, over 30,000 abortions a year are taking place within her borders. As in many developed nations, they pay for it too...they are killing off future Israeli defense soldiers. Yes, of all peoples to tolerate this great crime against humanity, they too have become hardened and deceived by allowing abortion on demand. It is the shedding of innocent blood, and God declares in the Bible that He hates it. Israel too has succumbed to a philosophy of "kill the unwanted" before they are born. This is the same spirit that Hitler used to kill the "unwanted" Jews. Can they afford to kill off generations of offspring, and incite the wrath of God?

Nonetheless, there is a people group, who do not believe in birth control or abortions and they are multiplying, and want to subdue the earth for Allah.

Today, most western nations are now concerned about the radical Muslim terrorists who have attacked, threatened and killed thousands of people many of them Christians in Europe, the USA, Africa and Middle Eastern countries. They want to annihilate Israel, and take it over; they cry out "Death to America" publicly.

In Muslim culture there is the belief that Mohammed was born and began the religion about 570 years after the death and resurrection of Jesus (Yeshua) Christ. Muslims say they believe that Yeshua (Jesus) was a mighty prophet of God. However, they do not believe what Jesus, the Prophet said. There are many wonderful, nice Muslims around the world; however, many are given false teachings that do not line up with the Holy Scriptures written hundreds and thousands of years before Mohammed came along.

If this movement of Islam continues, they will not have to resort to violence anymore to take over non-Muslim nations. They will just move in, many under the guise of refugees, and democratically vote in their leaders, by the sheer numbers of their population.

Then the radicals will enforce the cruel Sharia Laws, as they are doing in several European nations now, until the Lord Jesus Christ returns. This is not good news for Jews and Christians, as there are places in the Qur'an that exhort Muslims to chop off the heads of people who do not believe that Mohammed is the Messiah.

Qur'an:8:12

> "Your Lord inspired the angels with the message: 'I am with you. Give firmness to the Believers. I will terrorize the unbelievers. Therefore, smite them on their necks and every joint and incapac- itate them. Strike off their heads and cut off each of their fingers and toes."

Here are a few more reasons why I would never become a Muslim: Muhammad had 9 wives that we know of. Other Muslims are only allowed to have 4 wives. He actually married a little six-year-old girl! "The Prophet married Aisha in Mecca ... At the time she was six." Ishaq:281 Tabari IX:128 She reports that he consummated the marriage with her at the age of nine. Tabari IX:131

Sorry, but who has a 6-year-old WIFE? To me, only a pedophile would do such a vile thing to a little girl.

I was raped one time at the age of 13, and it was a horrible, event, leaving me feeling dirty and defiled. Marrying a girl at the age of 6 years old and consummating a marriage with her at the age of 9 years old would be imposing on that child repeated sexual assaults and rapes.

Oh, and it's okay to lie if you want to according to Mohammad, so how can we trust them?

Ishaq:365
Tabari VII:94

> "Muhammad bin Maslamah said, 'O Messenger, we shall have to tell lies.' 'Say what you like,' Muhammad replied. 'You are absolved, free to say whatever you must."

At his direction some Muslims groups will continue to terrorize the world until there are no more non-Muslims according to the Qur'an they follow.

Qur'an:9:5

> "Fight and kill the disbelievers wherever you find them, take them captive, harass them, lie in wait and ambush them using every stratagem of war."

Qur'an:8:39

> "So fight them until there is no more Fitnah (disbelief [non-Muslims]) and all submit to the religion of Allah alone (in the whole world)." http://prophetofdoom.net/Islamic_Quotes.Islam

With social media we are hearing more and more reports of Christians martyred for their faith in most Muslim countries. Women raped, hung, burned, abused and murdered, houses and churches burned, great persecution in the Middle East and some parts of Africa too. Sadly, we have rarely gone to their defense. Here, we sit in our comfy cars or homes, with clean water, food in the fridge, electricity, hot showers, flushing toilets and too much stuff. We are fortunate there is not much persecution here, yet...just an increasing amount of rebellious young adults on stabbing and shooting rampages. Slowly, but systematically our rights as Christian believers in Judeo-Christian nations are vanishing...more ungodliness appears to be prevailing since the 60's with rampant exploitative pornography, demonic video games, and the same-sex agenda in school curriculums to name a few. Have we lost our light and saltiness?

It is good to know and be familiar with what people are taught as children, as it will have an impact on their future actions and perceptions.

Nonetheless, it is so exciting to hear about the conversions of Muslims to faith in Yeshua. God is LOVE, and He taught us to love our enemies. Have you ever noticed that every suicide bomber is a Muslim, but of course, not every Muslim is a suicide bomber? I pray that they will come to know the Shalom peace of God, through Yeshua.

Communist China & The One-Child Policy was initiated by the Communist Party in 1978. Although designated a "temporary measure," it continued for 37 long years. The policy limited couples to one child, two in some rural areas. Fines, pressures to abort a pregnancy, and even forced abortions and forced sterilizations accompanied second or subsequent pregnancies.

This brutal policy caused a shift culturally, in that boys are regarded more valuable to parents, then girls. Therefore, a disdain for female babies has resulted in millions of girls being killed, just because they are girls! Sex selected abortions, neglect, abandonment, and even infanticide are known to occur to girls there.

I think it was in 2013, when I submitted an official Complaint to the High Commissioner for Human Rights in Geneva, Switzerland regarding the barbaric One Child Policy in China. A coalition of prolife groups added their names to this complaint, and we never heard a word or got a response. Nevertheless, we were thrilled to learn that in 2015, China announced it has gone to a 'Two-Child' policy, which is a step in the right direction, however, sources report that women are still forced and coerced to abort their children.

Where is the feminist outrage for women's rights to have as many children as they want?

We know that several studies state that induced abortion causes depression, and women are six times more likely to attempt or commit suicide after having an abortion.

Therefore, it is not surprising to me that China, which does the most amount of abortions per capita in the world, also has the highest suicide rates for women, in the world.

According to the World Health Organization, (WHO) **Every year 1.5 MILLION Chinese women attempt suicide;** and 150,000 of them succeed in doing so. Consequently, every three minutes a Chinese woman is killing herself! No wonder. The communist regime is anti-God, and anti-Christ, it forces women to abort their babies, and forcibly sterilizes them also. Why aren't the feminists outraged about this? We all should be! Canada Silent No More, a non-profit organization I founded ten years ago, along with a handful of other NGO's, recently submitted a formal complaint To the High Commissioner on

Human Rights in Geneva against the People's Republic of China regarding forced abortions, and condemning the one child policy. We included testimonies and 36 cases of women who were forcibly taken into the family planning clinics to have their babies killed (several were late term abortions), and some of these women were forcibly sterilized. These women are suffering post-traumatic stress disorder and are devastated.

One Chinese woman told me that she felt like the government of China was raping her when she was forced to abort her children. Cancer rates are increasing and an epidemic is on the horizon.

The result of such draconian family planning has resulted in a huge shortage of women. Today there are over 37 million more males, then females under the age of 20. The ramifications of a male dominated population, with men unable to find a wife, opens the doors to more violence against women in the form of rapes, prostitution, human trafficking, homosexual trends and the like. This is just beginning to surface in China and India. I also wonder how so many children without siblings will fare in the long haul?

By a huge margin, China has the highest abortion rates in the world. We have testimonies from Chinese women who had abortions and sterilizations forced on them. Some women were 8 months pregnant!

In 2010, the Lord sent Melody and I to China. It was so polluted, my eyes burned the whole two weeks I was in Beijing and Shanghai. Funny, but there was not one protestor or environmentalist in sight. God opened doors for us to meet with a Pastor from an underground church. He asked me to pray for and minister to every person there. I just love them! As well during the trip, I met a young Chinese woman in the elevator, and began to share my testimony, and with tears welling up in her eyes, I could see she was touched, and probably had an abortion too. I asked if she would like to come to our room, so we could pray with her, and she did! Melody blessed her with a Bible, and yes, she had an abortion, and a 4-year-old son. She was so depressed about the abortion.

I was able to lead three Chinese women to the Lord, who were all post abortive. Almost every woman in China has had an abortion. The mission to minister to those women is gigantic. God's will be done. I would love to go and teach on abortion healing and recovery, what a huge impact that would make in China, once millions of women get saved there! Wow. God is moving, He has heard their cries.

Not so long ago, we watched in horror as a giant Tsunami washed away thousands of lives in Japan. I wondered why God allowed this to occur. As I began my research, I discovered these interesting facts. In 1948, Japan became one of the first nations to legalize abortion under the Eugenic Law. In Japan doctors executed over 350,000 abortions in 2001; they regularly do over 250,000 abortions a year. Some Japanese documents show records of induced abortion from as early as the 12th century.

The tsunami happened just days before their annual pagan Fertility Festival. In Japan, only 1% of the population is Christian, the rest are Buddhist or Shintoist. This tsunami greatly affected the nuclear reactors and they have been leaking into the ocean since then. Please pray that all of the nuclear reactors will stop leaking, and that abortions will cease in Japan too.

Chapter 14

The Bride, The Body of Christ

Millions of women and men around the world are suffering and tormented as parents of dead children, knowing that they were responsible for the execution of their own child or children.

Most pregnant women who succumbed to having legal abortions, believed the lies proclaiming it was a "safe" procedure. We were deceived and pressured to resort to going for abortions, especially since we were told by nurses and doctors that it was not really a "baby". We were told we could just forget about it, and have children later in life. Yet, many of my friends could NEVER have children after legal abortion! Once out of denial women and men have to live with the deep sorrow, remorse, guilt, grief and the fact that our child or children were killed…and can never be replaced.

Yes, we ultimately chose abortion, albeit, mostly in ignorance. It was a wrong, and not a right, and should be made unthinkable! I thank God for His amazing grace and that we can be forgiven because Jesus (Yeshua) paid the penalty for our sins, even the sin of abortion! God wants to take our mess, and turn it into a message! He wants us to "Have nothing to do with the fruitless deeds of darkness, but rather to expose them." Eph. 5:11. God wants us to be the salt and light of the earth, and to be a voice for the voiceless.

By faith, in May of 2004, around my kitchen table, with a few other former abortion patients, we prayed, and decided to start up a non-profit association called, "**Canada Silent No More**". We had all suffered years of pain after our abortions, and wanted to make a difference to reach out to women like us. The Holy Spirit led me to the Book of Revelation which reads, "We defeat Satan by the Blood of the Lamb and the word of our testimony, and did not love our lives even unto death." Rev. 12:11 This is the foundation of our work and mission.

To reach out to other women hurt and injured by legal abortion, to collect testimony/declarations as evidence that abortion damages women and took the lives of our children. To minister to the broken hearted with God's love and compassion. To reach, teach and encourage teenagers and young adults to hang on to their hormones, as we are not animals. To bring education and awareness to the forefront on the studies proving abortion causes breast cancer, pre-term births and mental health issues in the aftermath, as well as bring humanity to the children in the womb.

This is a huge evangelistic outreach to the millions of women in Canada and millions more around the world who have had abortions, and need to know about God's mercy and grace. His love, His forgiveness, healing and shalom, peace, is the good news.

The most difficult thing is to forgive ourselves, but we must.

Next year, in 2017, I will be going into my 30th year of being a voice for my children, who had no voice. God had called me out of darkness and into HIS light to expose the evil of abortion and declare His way, truth and life. He has sent me to Israel four times, sadly they do over 30,000 abortions a year. He has sent me with this message to teach in the Philippines, Ghana-Africa, Jamaica, twice to Moscow-Russia, Siberia, Holland, Belgium, Northern Ireland, Berlin-Germany, Spain, the USA, China, Delhi-India and twice to Australia as well as to the UN in New York for the last 10 years and to the WHO in Geneva, the last 5 years.

In 2005, the CBC-The National aired a documentary on my work, and in 2012 I received The Queen's Diamond Jubilee Medal. To God be the Glory!

However, the greatest honour and joy for me, is knowing that some children are alive today, because their mother's heard my testimony on radio or television. Last year I got an email from a single Mom, who declared that my Facebook posts on prolife information made her cancel her appointment for an abortion. Her son is alive, and she is so blessed.

Pathetically, the babies are legally murdered by paid assassins, it is premeditated, it is systematic, and they are exterminated at the hands of "doctors". The College of Physicians and Surgeons, and those Medical Associations are most accountable, because they know that from conception it is a little baby with all the DNA and potential in the world to live for 70 years and could accomplish much on this planet. The right to have one's child killed, no matter how young, should be inconceivable!

It is almost never a medical necessity. The politicians have a duty to legislate just laws into our society to protect the innocent, and the police are to enforce those laws. They have all fallen short, by allowing abortion to be legal, easily accessible and mostly unrestricted.

"What does Christianity look like in a culture that kills its children?"

The Church is the Body of Christ, we should be having the mind of Christ, and we are to be the doers of His word, and not hearers only. When we get "born again" we get the DNA from the Holy Spirit. We are the Bride of Christ.

From the prophets of old we read how the people used to sacrifice their children to the gods of Molech and Baal, Ashtoreth... Most of the prophets like Moses, Isaiah, Jeremiah, King David, Joel, Ezekiel and Micah share God's heart and Word on how the shedding of innocent blood is an abomination to Him, and how HE has, and will bring judgment on the people who practice and tolerate this great evil in the land.

> *"They angered the Lord also at the waters of Meribah, so that it went ill with Moses for their sakes; [Num. 20:3-13.] For they provoked [Moses'] spirit, so that he spoke unadvisedly with his lips. They did not destroy the [heathen] nations as the Lord commanded them, But mingled themselves with the [idolatrous] nations and learned their ways and works And served their idols, which were a snare to them.*
>
> ***Yes, they sacrificed their sons and their daughters to demons [II Kings 16:3.] And shed innocent blood, even the blood of their sons and of their daughters, whom they sacrificed to the idols of Canaan; and the land was polluted with their blood. Thus were they defiled by their own works, and they played the harlot and practiced idolatry with their own deeds*** *[of idolatrous rites]. Therefore, was the wrath of the Lord kindled against His people, insomuch that He abhorred and rejected His own heritage. [Deut. 32:17.] And He gave them into the hands of the [heathen] nations, and they that hated them ruled over them. Their enemies also oppressed them, and they were brought into subjection under the hand of their foes."*
> Psalm 106:32-42

> *"Thus says the Lord: Execute justice and righteousness, and deliver out of the hand of the oppressor him who has been robbed. And do no wrong; do no violence to the stranger or temporary resident, the fatherless, or the widow, nor shed innocent blood in this place."* Jer. 22:3, Jer. 7:5-8

> *"Egypt shall be a desolation and Edom shall be a desolate wilderness for their violence against the children of Judah, because they have shed innocent blood in their land."* Joel 3:19

Abortion is shedding innocent blood. It is human/child sacrifice! Jesus preached that we should repent, turn away from sin, be baptized, and preach God's way, truth and life. God is love, yes, but He is also a God of justice.

> *"Righteousness and justice are the foundation of Your throne; mercy and loving-kindness and truth go before Your face."* Psalm 89:14

We are to be the salt and light of the earth... Yeshua said, "**You are the salt of the earth, but if salt has lost its taste (its strength, its quality), how can its saltiness be restored? It is not good for anything any longer but to be thrown out and trodden underfoot by men. but IF we lose our saltiness, we are no good but to be trampled on by the foot of man**." Mathew 5:13

According to a study published by the popular pro-abortion Guttmacher Institute, who tragically have money and clout to supply their biased stats to the World Health Organization, agencies and governments. **"Almost three-quarters of women obtaining abortions in 2008 reported a religious**

affiliation. The largest proportion were Protestant (37 percent), and most of the rest said that they were Catholic (28 percent) or that they had no religious affiliation (27 percent). One in five abortion patients identified themselves as born-again, evangelical, charismatic or fundamentalist; 75 percent of these were Protestant."

Though the study suggests that attending religious services regularly indicates a lower-than-average rate of abortion, the fact remains: Professing Christians abort their children in large numbers. It is estimated that one in three adults in America today is the parent of an aborted child, and that rate is likely the same both inside and outside the church.

Christian teenagers and young adults don't want to deal with the shame a pregnancy brings. So they abort their baby, instead of telling their parents.

Not only is the Bride of Christ losing children through the sin of abortion, we are also losing children through chemical weapons of mass destruction via taking the Birth Control Pill, Patch, and Injections which can also cause abortions. This is true! We are destroying offspring because of Intrauterine Devices (IUD's) where again, conception can take place, but due to the toxic environment, the newly created child will die and/or be aborted and the mother may, or may not even realize it. However, many can survive to be healthy born children too, if she chooses LIFE for her child.

Hang on now, get ready, because I have to share this truth. I do not say this in a spirit of condemnation, for there is no condemnation to those who are IN CHRIST, but so that you may repent to God, if this applies to you.

We are killing our future children, our seed, perhaps the other one or two or three children that God had planned to bless us with. So sad that many Christians have gone the way of the world, the heathen, by permanently sterilizing themselves. On what scripture and verse do you base this on? How many Pastors and Believers have had a vasectomy? How many Christian women have had their fallopian tubes tied to prevent another pregnancy and child birth?

Oh, yes, I've heard it...but I thought, but I was afraid, but we...What about what GOD wants, what is HIS plan for you and your "family"...remember HE will never give you more than you can handle.

Is the Bride walking in fear, instead of walking in faith?

Jesus said, He is coming for a Bride without stain, wrinkle, fault or blame, according to the Greek. (Eph. 5:26, 27) Does the "Bride of Christ," have any faults? Yes, we sure do. Do we have stains on our hands, our clothes because we fall short? Yep. Do we tolerate and pay for the shedding of innocent blood with our tax dollars and silence? Selah…think about it. Yes… then it is time to repent, to stop it, and change our ways, while there is still time.

The Prophet Ezekiel gave notice to the people in chapter 3 and again in chapter 33 to warn the wicked of their wickedness, and IF they did not warn them, the blood would be on our hands.

So is the church warning the wicked of their wickedness today? Or is she more afraid to offend people, then to offend God? Is she more concerned about being "politically correct" or about losing her charitable tax status? Is she afraid to speak out and say, "no to homosexual marriages or no to abortion on demand"?

Does she more resemble the unfaithful bride willing to compromise herself, so as not to upset anyone; does she heap material goods and selfish desires to herself? Is she spending lots of money on the big, new elaborate million dollar buildings and plenty of Priests to do the temple work? Or is she determined at all costs to be true to her first love, obeying His commands, characterized by unselfish sacrificial love?

It is more important to care about what God thinks; then what people think.

"If ye love me, keep my commandments. *And I will pray the Father, and he shall give you another*

*Comforter, that he may abide with you forever;
Even the Spirit of truth; whom the world cannot
receive, because it sees him not, neither knows
him: but you know him; for he dwells with you,
and shall be in you." **John 14:15-17***

This may be strong meat, and I hope you are not offended, but the wayward bride, it seems, is every bit as accepting of a "final solution" (sterility) to the annoying impositions of "unwanted" children.

Does the church have on its hands the blood of millions of aborted people-created in the image of God? The ones God called, to be the future Apostles, Prophets, Teachers, Evangelists and Pastors? Perhaps, their destiny was to be that mother, or that father who would build an orphanage in Bhutan, or bring the gospel to Iran, Iraq and Indonesia in greater relevance and power?

Abortion blood that was shed with the church's unspoken permission, her implicit approval, or her effective complicity; needs to be repented of? Unbelievably, there is a group called, "Catholics for Choice" as well as several Protestant denominations who condone the shedding of innocent blood (abortion) in some cases. For example, the United Church is totally pro-abortion, and pro-homosexual, and some Anglican churches are very pro-abortion also. In the USA some of The Presbyterian Churches, the Episcopal Churches, the United Methodist Churches, the United Churches of Christ, the Unitarian Universalist Association of Congregations, and some Reform and Conservative Judaism synagogues along with the Salvation Army have some occasions to believe it is ok to take the innocent child's life, as in cases where there might be some disability in the child's physical or mental health, like Down's Syndrome, or if the mother was raped. How sad is that? Scripture and verses for those beliefs?

Did God allow that conception to take place? Does He have a purpose and plan for that child created in His image? Why should a child get the death sentence for the crime of the sperm donor, or being disabled in some way? **Adoption is the loving option**.

Think about this:

- Christians of this present generation could have spoken up...
- They could have regularly and passionately preached against this horrific evil…
- They could have prayed, marched, and held vigils day and night…
- They could have voted, lobbied, advocated and cried aloud without ceasing….
- They could have written letters and held signs and stood outside abortion clinics day in and day out…
- They could have made it clear to their Pastors, Priests, elected leaders, their neighbors, and to themselves, that here is an unspeakably great evil that cannot, that must not be tolerated... But they didn't. By and large they haven't so far.

And by not doing what we could have done about this great crime against humanity, we committed an even greater evil, because we know better than to let it happen, and we let it happen anyway. We give support it with our money and silence. As a direct result of us not doing what we could have done, and should have done, year after year for over 40 years. Over 59 million utterly helpless human beings (children) were murdered in cold blood across North America with virtually no opposition and scarcely a second thought.

How long will GOD put up with this injustice?

It is time for the Bride of Christ to ask God to forgive her, and repent for her apathy, complacency and silence. It is time to be brave and courageous, and do whatever it takes in prayer and fasting, in voice, in finances and in action to stop this great injustice of our day. How long will God withhold His wrath? How long until He returns to judge and condemn us with HIS vengeance? Many, many scriptures throughout the Bible talk about how God hates the evil and wickedness of man and promises to judge with His righteous judgments, for He is Holy and Justice is the Foundation of His throne.

Truly, I thank God for the remnant of brave men and women who sacrifice their lives on the frontlines to give pregnant women hope and alternatives to abortion before they walk into the death camps. I thank God for the Pastors and Priests and Body of Christ who are actively praying and fasting and supporting missionaries for life! God knows we need prayers and help as we war in the spirit, and in deed against the spirit of murder and human sacrifice.

Canada is among the seven most liberal countries in the world offering no protection for children in the womb. 140 countries have various restrictions. 59 countries have gestational limits, but only seven countries in the world allow abortions past the 20-week threshold, including the USA and Canada.

Canada, along with most developed nations around the world have very high abortion rates. Very few women were actually self-aborting when it was illegal. Now it has become a huge industry. After the abortion doors began to open in 1969, then again in 1973, then after the abortion law was struck down in Canada in 1988, women began going to hospitals and abortion clinics in the droves for this new form of birth control.

The abortion epidemic began, from a few dozens a year if that; to averaging over one hundred thousand abortions annually across Canada. Systematic, large-scale killing centers were established.

There is a huge cover-up of incomplete reporting on exactly how many abortions we are paying for now, how old these children are when they are executed, or what all the complications are for the women. We do know that in Canada hundreds are being aborted over 20 weeks' gestation. A time when babies can feel pain, and are viable. Some nurses in a Calgary, Alberta Hospital were complaining that some of these little babies actually survived the abortions, were struggling to live, and were just cast aside and left to die.

Healthy children are killed at more than 28 weeks' gestation! Gasp! That is a baby who is seven months old! Some at 8 months old...but more and later term pregnant women are going to Boulder, Colorado to see an assassin who will inject a lethal dose of potassium chloride into the child's heart and force the delivery of the baby for $12,500.00. Canadian dollars. I call this murder! Where is the outrage? Brings tears to my eyes.

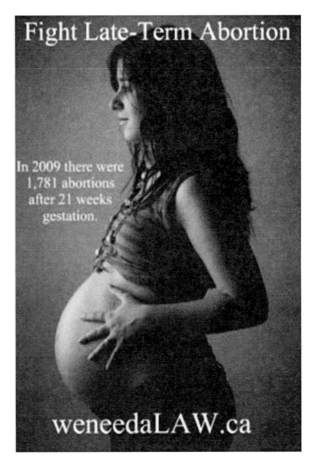

The only records available on complications after legally induced abortions comes from the hospitals, not the abortion clinics. Why is that? Out of 27,576 hospital abortions, 649 women suffered immediate complications following the abortion, or 2.3%. So if there are over 100,000 abortions annually, that would be over 2,300 women a year that we know of. How many women suffer mental or reproductive health problems on top of that, perhaps days, weeks, months or years after their induced abortions? Thousands of women are, and we are getting the phone calls. Women devastated and broken physically and psychologically. Right now we have over 5,000 signed testimony declarations from women across North America who say that legal abortion damaged them big time in several ways...we are starting to come out of the closet, so look out Goliath, your time is short. Let us start somewhere to slow the tide of bloodshed in our land.

MP Maurice Vellacott was shocked to the core and greatly saddened by information researcher Patricia Maloney provided at http://run-with-life.blogspot.ca/2012/10/late-term-abortions-statistics-born.html under the heading "Late term abortions statistics – born alive, but left to die."

Based on Section 223(2) of the Criminal Code, there should be hundreds of homicide investigations or prosecutions in connection with these deaths. Section 223(2) of the Criminal Code reads *"A person commits homicide when he causes injury to a child before or during its birth as a result of which the child dies after becoming a human being."*

Persecution & Discrimination against Christians in Canada

Some brave Canadians and others are paying a hefty price as salt and light, because they did not bow down to worldly sins and condone them. Since Canada enacted "hate crimes" legislation at the provincial and national levels, it has given special bubble status to homosexuals, and set up liberal secular human rights commissions and tribunals. So the persecution against Christians has grown steadily. Today in Canada, Christians are taken to court and fined thousands of dollars for speaking out or refusing to condone the sin of homosexuality and for renouncing homosexual marriages. Talk about discrimination and harassment against Christians...and it's getting worse. Where is the tolerance for Judeo-Christians? **Where is the JUSTICE for Christians?** Here are a few cases I am familiar with:

Chris Kempling, a teacher for 13 years, and counselor in the public school system in British Columbia, BC. was declared guilty of conduct unbecoming a member of the BC College of Teachers by the College (BCCT). Kempling was reprimanded for simply writing letters to the editor objecting to the promotion of the homosexual agenda in the public school system as well as for writing unpublished research essays, and private letters to his supervisors and elected officials.

My friend, another Christian and a grandmother **Linda Gibbons** has spent about 10+ years in jail. Her crime? Peacefully, walking on a public sidewalk, in front of an abortion clinic with a sign that says, "Why Mom?" She has spent more time in prison than Karla Homolka who was charged with murder! Also, Mary Wagner arrested and spending many months in jail. Her crime? Handing out roses and offering alternatives to abortion, to pregnant women. The list goes on…

> Toronto Christian printer, **Scott Brockie** was fined $5,000.00 by the Ontario Human Rights Commission because he refused to print materials for the Canadian Lesbian and Gay Archives.

> In January 2006, Catholic city councilman **JOHN DECICCO** of Kamloops, British Columbia, was fined $1,000 and required to apologize for saying that homosexuality is "not normal or natural".

> In June 2008, **Stephen Boisson**, an evangelical youth pastor, was banned from expressing opposition to homosexuality in any public forum and ordered to pay $7,000 to the homosexual activist who complained against him.

Do you realize that there are dozens of studies proving that homosexual acts lead to shorter life spans and many sexually transmitted diseases including HIV/AIDS? It is not a good thing. God calls it an abomination! Romans chapter one, talks about it. There is no evidence people are born that way, any more than people are born with a desire to have sex with children. Often it is due to molestation as children, or dysfunctional family life, too many hurts from the opposite sex, even abortion has turned some women to one another. However, God gives us a free will, and we have a choice to do things HIS way, or our way. We will all come before His judgment seat one day for what we did, and did not do. So glad Jesus died for all our sins, and in His mercy, we can be forgiven, if we change, and overcome.

As the majority of Christians remain silent and passive, the enemy becomes louder and pro-active, pulling down Godly foundations in nations and erecting secular humanist philosophies in the schools, the governments, the media and wherever else they can get away with it.

Have we lost our saltiness? Is our light only shining in church on Sundays? Today, I thank God for Ezra Levant, Monte, Brett and the few dedicated lawyers fighting for our rights.

The New School Prayer

Now I sit me down in school
Where praying is against the rule
For this great nation under God
Finds mention of Him very odd.
If Scripture now the class recites,

It violates the Bill of Rights.
And anytime my head I bow
Becomes a Federal matter now.
Our hair can be purple, tangled or green,
That's no offense: it's a freedom scene.
The law is specific; the law is precise.
Prayers spoken aloud are a serious vice.
For praying in a public hall
Might offend someone with no faith at all.
In silence alone we must meditate,
God's name is prohibited by the state.
We're allowed to cuss and dress like freaks,
And pierce our noses, tongues and cheeks.
They've outlawed guns, but FIRST the Bible.
To quote the Good Book makes me liable.
It's "inappropriate" to teach right from wrong,
We're taught that such 'judgments' do not belong…
We can get condoms, and birth controls,
Study witchcraft, vampires and totem poles.
But, the Ten Commandments are not allowed.
No word of God must reach this crowd.
It's scary here I must confess,
When chaos reigns, the school's a mess.

So, Lord, this silent plea I make:

Should I be shot; My Soul please take! Amen

Sound familiar? Our government run elementary, high schools and universities teach there is no God, and that the theory of evolution is truth. Since prayer to God has been taken out of the schools, and the promotion of evolution, homosexuality and tolerance of anything goes has taken over, there have been more divorces, more violence, more suicides and more gang wars to name a few of the fruits manifesting. Very sad, indeed. However, there is no tolerance for God, or Christian beliefs...more and more we are being condemned, ridiculed and discriminated against.

Originally, most, if not all schools in Canada and the USA were founded by churches. In the beginning class would begin with prayer, singing the national anthem and teaching the word of God. Over the years, more secular people took over, as Christians quit or stopped getting involved, and thus the spiritual enemy took their positions and changed education in schools.

The devil knows that if he can influence children while they are young, putting doubt and unbelief into their minds, he can mess them up as teenagers and adults. Teachers can use massive amounts of anti-religious propaganda in class and mock believers. We have the spirit of anti-Christ working in public television, institutions, discriminatory laws, and also a persecution campaign against Christian believers.

Some children in Grade One are being taught that lesbianism and homosexuality is okay, using books to desensitize them like: "Heather has two Mommies", and "Daddy's Roommate".

Who will stand up for God's way, truth and life? My Bible says that *"Righteousness exalts a nation, but sin is a reproach to any peoples."* Prov. 14:34 *"Thus says the Lord: Execute justice and righteousness, and deliver out of the hand of the oppressor him who has been robbed. And do no wrong; do no violence to the stranger or temporary resident, the fatherless, or the widow, nor shed innocent blood in this place."* Jer. 22:3

Jewish doctor breaks laws to change laws in Canada

Henry Morgentaler, was a Jewish man who survived the horrid conditions of Nazi concentration camps in Dachau and Auschwitz, then immigrated to Canada. He became a doctor who began doing illegal abortions in his office. He had such a determination to kill babies in the womb; despite the fact that it was a criminal act!

Morgentaler rebelliously defied the abortion laws, spent time in jail, and became a hero to the feminist, pro-abortion lobbyists. They pushed to legalize the killing of children in the womb and have taxpayers fund it. The strategy worked, as he broke the laws, to challenge the laws, to change the laws. Taking it to the Supreme Court of Canada, where liberal minded secular judges condoned the practice of abortion. He got all the money needed to pursue the ideology that women have the right to have their children killed, and that he could do the job better than them. He not only opened the doors to lawlessness, but insisted Canadians pay them for this shedding of innocent blood. In Canada we tragically have no laws or restrictions on abortion to this day.

There was little to no resistance or opposition from the church to stop abortions. It is mainly the Catholics who work to fight this onslaught of abortion in our land. I thank God they have pretty much been on the frontlines against abortion for the long haul. I learned that several Protestant mainline churches actually condone abortion in some way or completely; which is contrary to Biblical teachings, and pathetic in my view.

It is noteworthy that in 1968 Henry Morgentaler, Canada's notorious abortionist became the founder and president of the "Humanist Association of Canada" until 1999. Surprise? Please pray for them.

Morgentaler had this motto advertised on his website for years: "Every child a wanted child." Appealing to young vulnerable pregnant women, he was really saying, *if you don't want your child, come to us and we will get rid of that child for you.*

It is disheartening that our Governor General, actually gave Morgentaler the 'Order of Canada', the highest civilian award in July of 2008. Many secular humanists, feminists, liberal journalists and wealthy people supported and nominated him to this position. Although, he had terminated the lives of over 60,000 children in the sanctuary of their mother's womb; with his own two hands. Hardly a peep of revolt from the church. How long will God put up with this great crime against humanity in our generation?

I launched a petition online, in protest of him receiving this honour, as well flew to Ottawa, meeting with the Director of Honors to give her our petition. Vickie, a social worker, post abortion counselor and former abortion patient of Morgentaler's joined me in urging the Government not to give him this award, because of the damage he has caused thousands of women, along with all of the shedding of innocent blood he committed. We shared our testimonies on how abortion hurt us, and killed our children. She wanted to share how he lied to her about the fetal development and deceived her into believing the lie that this was not her baby. Well, 'If it is not a "baby" then you are not pregnant!'

Sadly, the church was far too silent, not enough uproar from Christians to prevent this reward going to the most notorious abortionist in Canada.

If we believe that God is the Creator of all life, and that according to His word, He knew us before we were born, then how can we say as the Body of Christ that it is okay to murder a baby in his or her mother's womb for any reason?

If there is an abnormality with the baby, can we say it's okay to have that child killed? *"And the Lord said to him, Who has made man's mouth? Or who makes the dumb, or the deaf, or the seeing, or the blind? Is it not I, the Lord?"* Exod. 4:11

I thank God for the courageous remnant, who are speaking out. People who know their God and are doing great exploits for His Kingdom; who are not afraid to take a stand and do something to defend the lives of children in the womb.

In January of 1987 I asked God to forgive me for all of my sins. I surrendered my life to Jesus Christ and He changed my life. I had a spiritual awakening. John 3. Soon I wanted to please God, more than myself. So I quit smoking, drinking, taking drugs and having sex until I got married in 1991 to my husband of 25 years now.

My favourite song is *Amazing Grace*. I began to read the Bible and learn about our creator and His purpose for our lives.

Pierre Trudeau our former Prime Minister, opened the doors to abortion in 1969. But, there were still restrictions. However,

I never had to go before any doctors, or committee before any of my abortions. I was also physically and mentally fine, before my abortions. The appointments were made, and no questions asked.

My abortions were done in 1973, 83 and 84. I will never forget the night of Jan. 28, 1988 while sitting alone on my couch, watching the evening news when abortionist Henry Morgentaler and his supporters were cheering and gloating on their victory that the Supreme Court of Canada struck down the abortion law. I was distraught and crying aloud, thinking, 'Oh my God, the gates of hell are opened wide now', I felt the anguish of women damaged like myself from legal abortion. This was horrible news!

Soon after, I was prompted by the Holy Spirit to go down to the abortion clinics and do sidewalk counseling. I became an activist, no longer could I just sit around and say and do nothing. Yes, prayer came first, I prayed about everything, prayed while on the frontlines, prayed for repentance, prayed in faith, and I keep on praying now.

Women were being led to the slaughter and their children were paying the price. I would tell them that I had abortions, and knew the pain of abortion. I would warn the pregnant women of the dangers of abortion to their body and mind. As well telling them that their baby had a beating heart by three weeks; and assuring them that right now their baby was still alive.

Reassuring them that we could help them with baby clothes and whatever they needed. I urged them to "please let your baby live". Most of these women wanted to stop and talk to me, to listen, but they were quickly pulled along by the arm by abortion clinic 'escorts' who were shouting to drown out our voices. They would order the pregnant girls to keep going, not to listen to us, and they were commanded not to talk to us.

Years later, one of those paid escorts, that we know about, who used to cuss me out, got cancer, but he cried out to God, for forgiveness and healing, he repented. He has become a powerful pro-life voice now.

Then there were several "Operation Rescues" that were held across the USA and Canada. In 1989 and 1990, I joined numbers of believers, (mostly Catholics) where we would show up in the early morning to do a peaceful, non-violent sit-in in front of, and at the back door steps of abortion mills. We would reverently sing songs like, "Jesus loves the Little Children... all the children in the womb...red and yellow, black and white, they are precious in His sight, Jesus Loves the Little children in the womb". Do you?

Clinic workers quickly called their cohorts who would yell, scream obscenities at us, kick us, spit on us, and chant their rhetorical slogans. The evil presence at these facilities are huge. I usually did the sidewalk counseling, offering alternatives and offering practical help to the pregnant women, as I shared my testimony on the damage legal abortion did to my body, spirit and soul.

One time, I felt the Holy Spirit telling me to go and join the others in sitting in front of the abortionist's front door; so I did. Then this handsome young police officer, came and picked me up in his strong arms, and carried me over to the paddy wagon and gently put me into it...I thought, "Wow, are you ever strong". Soon we were released and went home.

Then Morgentaler launched a lawsuit against me and four other people, in April of 1989 for one million dollars. It seems that we were bad for their abortion business. They made all kinds of false accusations against us. They used this tactic to get a "Temporary Injunction" which prohibited anyone to enter the bubble zone, even on public sidewalks around the abortion clinics. This lasted for over 10 years, then they made it into a permanent injunction. I had no support from the church. Sadly, it appeared like the 'fear of man' dominated the pastors and church boards.

Dreadfully, this case set a bad precedent against freedom of speech, religion and peaceful civil disobedience for believers. Yet, history shows that slavery stopped when real believers fought in a civil war for the rights of our black sisters and brothers for freedom. Segregation and racism was fought to a large scale when the Christians took to the streets and peacefully demonstrated against it. There are always martyrs paying a price for it. God has called us to be the salt and light of the earth.

Yeshua once said, *"You are the salt of the earth, but if salt has lost its taste (its strength, its quality), how can its saltiness be restored? It is not good for anything any longer but to be thrown out and trodden underfoot by men."* Mat. 5:13

Today we have so much godlessness and immorality in our streets, on TV, in our schools and in our homes because we tolerate that spirit of Jezebel. Now homosexuals are getting 'married' and adopting straight children. They are doing presentations in public schools, grades 8 and up, on how good it is to be gay, and how they believe there is nothing wrong with it, and so forth. Conversely, many studies prove it is a dangerous lifestyle. Homosexuals have a much shorter lifespan than heterosexual men. God loves the sinner, but hates the sin...as He said to the woman caught in adultery...'Now go and sin no more.' Amen.

More than ever, we have people calling good evil, and evil good. There will be huge consequences for not taking a stand against the shedding of innocent blood in our land, in this world. We want to tolerate everyone and everything, but not stand for anything. Yeshua preached, *"Repent, and be baptized for the remission of sins."*

> **"For we wrestle not against flesh and blood, but against principalities, against powers, against the rulers of the darkness of this world, against spiritual wickedness in high places."** *Eph. 6:12*

The history is clear...the connections obvious, the results disastrous. Believing there is no God, makes it a dog eat dog, world. The only purpose in life is to survive, just get rich, and get away with whatever you can. Morality is all relative, and crime abounds. If it is just survival of the fittest, and there is no God, no judgment, no absolutes and no rules, it brings in anarchy, communism and dictatorships. Most communist governments based their ideology on the fathers of communism like Karl Marx, Friedrich Engels and Vladimir Lenin. Communist countries like the former Soviet Union, the Eastern European Bloc, Nazi Germany and China promoted atheism in the schools. Much like they do in public schools around the world in developed countries today.

Thank God that the walls of Soviet Communism finally fell in 1989, and the Orthodox Church is being resurrected.

In 2007, the Lord sent me on a mission trip to Ghana, Africa with a small team of post abortive women from the USA. We had interviews on TV, and did many talks in schools and churches. We spoke to Aglow Women plus met with the President's wife, and the Minister of Women and Children's Health. I noticed that, although there was a lot of poverty in Ghana, but the people had families, joy, and led simple lives.

Then I travelled from Ghana to Moscow, Russia. Where a Russian Orthodox Priest had invited me to come and speak at his Pro-Life Conference. There were Priests attending from over 49 regions across Russia, including Siberia. I shared my testimony on the pain of legal abortion and how much it damages women physically, psychologically and spiritually. He also interviewed me on his broadcast and had it translated into Russian.

Russia reports over 1 million abortions annually. There are millions of women across Russia who are injured after abortion. There were hardly any children on the streets, or visible, while we were there. They too have far below population replacement levels of 2.15 children, necessary just to maintain a culture, a nation. Russian President Vladimir Putin; directed his nation's parliament to develop a plan to reduce the country's falling birthrate. In a speech to parliament on May 10, 2006, Putin called the problem of Russia's dramatically declining population, "The most acute problem of contemporary Russia."

Chapter 15

Advancing the Seed in the Kingdom of God

Life is in the SEED!

Human beings are created in the image and likeness of God. He created us and commanded us to multiply and be fruitful and to subdue the earth for HIS kingdom. He wants us to be the salt and light of the earth, to expose the lies and evil, to declare His Way, His Truth and Life. Would God the Father, creator of Heaven and Earth, the one who is and was and is to come, the one who knew us before we were born, want HIS seed, His children to be conceived, and then killed by doctors before they are born?

Yet, He does sometimes allow miscarriages and still births to happen. I had a miscarriage, after our son was born. Mostly, this is a natural occurrence. Sometimes they are caused because something is wrong with the baby, or it's genetic, or toxins in our body, or it can be a result of other complications, but for whatever reason, God permits those to occur.

However, the Muslim populations in Russia, are growing by leaps and bounds. By 2005, the census found there were over 20 million Muslims in Russia.

God willing, I would love to go back there and minister again. It is a huge mission field. The Russian president called on parliament to provide incentives for couples to have a second child to increase the birth rate in order to stop the country's plummeting population.

Russia's population peaked in the early 1990s (at the time of the end of the Soviet Union) with about 148 million people in the country. Today, Russia's population is approximately 143 million. The United States Census Bureau estimates that Russia's population will decline from the current 143 million to a mere 111 million by 2050, a loss of more than 30 million people and a decrease of more than 20%.

There is also a gigantic alcoholism problem in Russia. They have an aging/dying population like most developed countries. The primary causes of Russia's population decrease and loss of about 700,000 to 800,000 citizens each year are a high death rate, low birth rate, high rate of abortions, and a low level of immigration.

THE BIRTH CONTROL PILL, Patches, Injections etc. on the other hand, are our own doing. Besides causing abortions at times, it also increases the risk of heart attack, stroke, cardiovascular complications, and younger women have greater susceptibility to sexually transmitted diseases as well as breast, cervical and liver cancers!

Today, according to the Center of Disease Control statistics, 82% of all women of reproductive age are already taking these carcinogenic hormonal drugs. Breast cancer incidence, especially in young women, will continue to rise as more women are enticed to be sexually active before marriage, and to take "free" and carcinogenic birth control.

Besides, these man-made pills made from pregnant horse urine, can also result in breakthrough ovulation, whereas conception can take place. Then, due to the inhospitable effect of The Pill in the uterine wall, the newly conceived child cannot attach itself to the wall for nourishment, and will starve and die...often without the mother's knowledge. How many women actually know all this about the pill?

Intrauterine Devices (IUD's) can also cause infections and pregnancies can still happen.

Here are some tough, hard questions we need to ask ourselves as the Body and Bride of Christ; according to Word of God. Should the Body of Christ, have instruments like IUD's, or chemicals inserted into our bodies to prevent life from happening or developing? Should we be having surgeries to make us permanently sterile?

Have you ever taken Morning After Pills, had an IUD inserted, or taken other contraceptives or abortion chemicals? Or did you go the way of the world in sexual immorality or pornography or any other sins? Have you been ignorant and/or deceived by the father of lies? Did you ever get someone pregnant, and/or pressure someone to have an abortion? Or were you apathetic or complacent instead? Did you ever get pregnant and then have an abortion(s)? Did you get yourself permanently sterilized, so you could not have any more children? If you have done any of these things, ask God to forgive you, right now. Repeat this short prayer with sincerity: "Father God in heaven, right now I ask you to forgive me for ALL of my sins… (Be specific) I am so sorry. I believe that Yeshua/Jesus was born of the Virgin Mary, died on the cross for my sins, was raised from the dead and is alive. Come into my life God, and help me to read and understand Your Word, and truths in the Bible, help me to find a good church, and obey Your commands from this day forward, in Yeshua's Holy Name. Change your life, turn to God, and ask Him what He wants you to do for His Kingdom and Glory. Begin to share this book, and this message with others. Then get help, and learn to forgive yourself and save others.

"Speak up for those who cannot speak for themselves and for the rights of the needy." Prov. 31:8

The BIG PICTURE

There are approximately seven billion people on the planet now. There is enough food and water, resources and know how to support everyone. Yet, evil dictators, godless governments and selfish greed keep the rich-rich, and the poor-poor.

We have the technology to supply all their needs...but certain people would rather go in and take advantage of their ignorance, steal their valuable resources, exploiting them as cheap labour. Did you know that all seven billion people (using the city density of New York City), could all live in the space of the state of Texas? Now that is perspective!

WHAT is the FRUIT after ABORTING CHILDREN for 40+ years in our land?

Globally, corruption abounds in godless places...and the helpless are abandoned and controlled by their own governments and people.

It is now the year 2016, and we have had over 50 years of birth control pills, intrauterine devices (IUD's), injections, implants, cervical caps, diaphragms, spermicides, condoms, permanent sterilizations and now the morning after pills (MAP) to prevent and to stop babies from being conceived, staying alive, or even be born.

In the last 50+ years there have been frantic population control campaigns which have resulted in millions of children being slaughtered in the womb legally, and often paid for by governments, including most developed nations. This is where young children in the womb are meticulously and deliberately killed at the hands of abortionists, which often target the 'girl' child in India and China.

Over the next 20 years developed nations such as Canada, UK, Europe, Australia, Russia, etc. are headed for big economic troubles. There is a demographic time bomb emerging as baby boomers age and die off. Even with the influx of immigrants coming into our developed nations, we are not even replacing ourselves-the workforce is aging fast! Birth rates are still far below replacement levels, and at this rate are irreversible.

We now have aging, dying populations in all the developed nations where abortion is also used as birth control. Canada is aging, and fast! According to the 2006 Census report released by Statistics Canada, it stated that children will likely be outnumbered by those over 65 in about 10 years. When Canadians in the baby boomer generation begin turning 65 by about 2011, the senior population category is expected to soar. Canadians aged 55 to 64 make up the fastest growing section of the population, increasing by 25 percent since 2001 to 3.7 million people. Who will then die.

The economic impact of the global aging population is expected to be significant. Labour force population projections for the period from 2006 to 2031 anticipate a "sharp" decline in the number of Canadian workers. *The low fertility rate, along with the increased life expectancy rate and the influx of retiring baby boomers, together create an inevitable downward spiral of workforce participation.*

Canada's birth rate is one of the lowest in the world, even with the influx of immigrants and refugees, we have just 1.5 children per woman of fertility age, well below the replacement level rate of 2.15.

The number of children in the country has continued to fall— **just 17.7 per cent of the population is under the age of 15.** Canadian children declined by nearly 146,000 over the past five years, dropping 2.5 percent to only 5.6 million.

Children are the heritage of the Lord. They are the future workforce, future taxpayers, future caregivers, future police, doctors, military, farmers and residents in a dying world. When we have our babies killed before they are born, when we sterilize ourselves permanently and use birth control, we are wiping out future generations and cutting down the foundations of our culture and way of life. We are cursing ourselves when we tolerate the shedding of innocent blood, which pollutes our land.

*"So you shall not pollute the land in which you live; for **blood pollutes the land**, and no atonement can be made for the land for the blood shed in it, but by the blood of him who shed it." Numbers 35:33 "And shed innocent blood, even the blood of*

238

their sons and of their daughters, whom they sacrificed to the idols of Canaan; and the land was polluted with their blood." Psalm 106:38

Sadly, the spirit of BAAL and MOLECH has taken over many nations. Those under their influence are first of all very selfish, and self-centered, it is all about me, what can I get, how much more can I be blessed, people indulging in alcohol and drugs etc…secondly sexual immorality becomes rampant, and today pornography, fornication, homosexuality and adultery is widespread. These demons also feed off of human sacrifice, which is what abortion is, and it also includes cutting and suicides.

We should agonize at the thought of so many human lives being destroyed in countries that like to think of themselves as civilized. We should be disturbed at the thought of the silent –and forbidden – suffering of so many women and mothers of today and tomorrow as a result of legal abortion.

We must pay attention and support the brave women who, for a number of years now, have shared their post-abortion suffering with the world. We expose our shame and pain so others will live and know the truth about this horrific procedure. We do not care what people think of us. We care more about what God thinks, and what HE would have us say and do in this generation. We want to be a voice for our aborted children, who had no voice.

If we are to understand the aftermath, the physical effects (sterility, cancer of the cervix, miscarriages, ectopic pregnancy, pre-term births, suicides, breast cancer, etc.) and the devastating emotional impact that abortion on request has on many women, we must take heed.

It is interesting that the polls show that the majority of Canadians want restrictions on abortions, and do not want to pay for them, yet the killings go on, and on, and on...

I am so proud of my friends in the USA who are pressing on to get more and more laws and restrictions on abortion, including the Ban on Dismemberment Abortions, called D & E's where doctors go into the womb and with instruments forcibly pull off the arms and legs of the 18 to 24-week old baby who is fully human and alive and is cruel and inhumane torture. They have Parental Consent Laws, Waiting laws, Informed Consent laws and many other restrictions. Canadians, why don't we have any restrictions after decades?

In the face of so much suffering and destruction, the testimony of Mr. Stéphane Hessel, a hero of the French resistance against the Nazis during the Second World War, has something to teach us. He was born in Berlin, Germany and immigrated to France at the age of seven. During the Nazi occupation of France, Hessel joined the French resistance, was caught, tortured and deported to Buchenwald and Dora concentration camps where he escaped hanging. After the war, he helped to draft the Universal Declaration of Human Rights and later became a diplomat.

A message of resistance to evil: He said, "I would like everyone – every one of us – to find his or her own reason to cry out. That is a precious gift. When something makes you want to cry out, as I cried out against Nazism, you become militant, tough and committed. You become part of the great stream of history … and this stream leads us towards more justice and more freedom but not the uncontrolled freedom of the fox in the hen-house."

*   "The worst of all attitudes is indifference…" Apathy, complacency...

William Burke once wrote: "All that is necessary for the triumph of evil, is that good men do nothing."

Will you inherit eternal life?

> *"Therefore, you will fully know them by their fruits. Not everyone who says to Me, Lord, Lord, will enter the kingdom of heaven, but he who does the will of My Father Who is in heaven. Many will say to Me on that day, Lord, Lord, have we not*

prophesied in Your name and driven out demons in Your name and done many mighty works in Your name? And then I will say to them openly (publicly), I never knew you; depart from Me, you who act wickedly [disregarding My commands]."
Mat 7:20-23

The Holy Spirit revealed to me that whenever a man, or woman, or doctor, or politician, teacher or pastor, government or a nation… comes into an agreement with abortion…we are coming into an agreement/covenant with a spirit of death/murder and human sacrifice.

Only a few brave men and women in government have not bowed down to the pressure to tolerate abortion in the land, and some of them have presented bills and policies to either reduce the number of abortions or provide some legislation to slow it down with some restrictions, or stop it, but to no avail in Canada...so far. This abortion/human sacrifice daily at the tune of about 300 children per day in Canada, becomes not only a sin for the woman, doctors and all those involved, it also becomes a National SIN!

One day I cried out to the Lord, saying, I need a New Testament scripture for the church on this issue. Please show me what I can use, and the Holy Spirit led me to the Book of Luke, chapter 10:25-37; *"And then a certain lawyer arose to try (test, tempt) Him, saying, Teacher, what am I to do to inherit everlasting life [that is, to partake of eternal salvation in the Messiah's kingdom]? Jesus said to him, What is written in the Law? How do you read it?*

And he replied, You must love the Lord your God with all your heart and with all your soul and with all your strength and with all your mind; and your neighbor as yourself. [Lev. 19:18; Deut. 6:5.] And Jesus said to him, You have answered correctly; do this, and you will live [enjoy active, blessed, endless life in the kingdom of God]. And he, determined to acquit himself of reproach, said to Jesus, And who is my neighbor?

Jesus, taking him up, replied, A certain man was going from Jerusalem down to Jericho, and he fell among robbers, who stripped him of his clothes and belongings and beat him and went their way, [unconcernedly] leaving him half dead, as it happened.

Now by coincidence a certain priest was going down along that road, and when he saw him, he passed by on the other side.

A Levite likewise came down to the place and saw him, and passed by on the other side [of the road].

But a certain Samaritan, as he traveled along, came down to where he was; and when he saw him, he was moved with pity and sympathy [for him], And went to him and dressed his wounds, pouring on [them] oil and wine. Then he set him on his own beast and brought him to an inn and took care of him.

And the next day he took out two denarii [two day's wages] and gave [them] to the innkeeper, saying, Take care of him; and whatever more you spend, I [myself] will repay you when I return. Which of these three do you think proved himself a neighbor to him who fell among the robbers? He answered, The one who showed pity and mercy to him. And Jesus said to him, Go and do likewise."

Did you notice that He is talking about how to get "eternal" life here? Yeshua did not say our neighbor is the person next door. Do you see that we must RESCUE those being beaten and robbed, and left to die on the streets?

How much more important is it to rescue the least of them, tiny defenseless babies created in the image of God?

Also, Prov. 24:11, 12 declares,

> **"Deliver (rescue) those who are drawn away to death, and those who totter to the slaughter, hold them back [from their doom]. If you [profess ignorance and] say, Behold, we did not know this, does not He Who weighs and ponders the heart perceive and consider it? And He Who guards your life, does not He know**

**it? And shall not He render to [you and] every
man according to his works?"**

Can you imagine going up to a doctor and telling him you
want your right leg cut off? Why? Well, just because it is your
body, and besides it is your choice, and it's your right to have
it cut off, if you want to. Well, do you think any doctor would
amputate a perfectly fine leg, and disable a person? No way,
because they would fear getting sued later; especially once
the girl realizes how difficult life is without her leg. Many post
abortive women and men, are living in deep sorrow, regret and
pain in the aftermath of abortion. It is not a medical necessity,
and it is not just a hunk of flesh, it is a child.

Please DECREE *this prayer out loud:*

Psalm 94
*O LORD God, You to Whom vengeance belongs, O God, You
to Whom vengeance belongs, shine forth!*
*Rise up, O Judge of the earth; render to the proud a fit
compensation!*
*Lord, how long shall the wicked, how long shall the wicked tri-
umph and exult?*
*They pour out arrogant words, speaking hard things; all the
evildoers boast loftily. [Jude 14, 15.]*
They crush Your people, O Lord, and afflict Your heritage.
*They slay the widow and the transient stranger and murder the
unprotected orphan.*
*Yet they say, The Lord does not see, neither does the God of
Jacob notice it.*
Consider and understand, you stupid ones among the people!
And you [self-confident] fools, when will you become wise?
*He Who planted the ear, shall He not hear? He Who formed
the eye, shall He not see?*
*He Who disciplines and instructs the nations, shall He not
punish, He Who teaches man knowledge?*

The Lord knows the thoughts of man, that they are vain (empty and futile—only a breath). [I Cor. 3:20.]
Blessed (happy, fortunate, to be envied) is the man whom You discipline and instruct, O Lord, and teach out of Your law,
That You may give him power to keep himself calm in the days of adversity, until the [inevitable] pit of corruption is dug for the wicked.
For the Lord will not cast off nor spurn His people, neither will He abandon His heritage.
For justice will return to the [uncompromisingly] righteous, and all the upright in heart will follow it.

Who will rise up for me against the evildoers? Who will stand up for me against the workers of iniquity?

Unless the Lord had been my help, I would soon have dwelt in [the land where there is] silence.
When I said, My foot is slipping, Your mercy and loving-kindness, O Lord, held me up.
In the multitude of my [anxious] thoughts within me, Your comforts cheer and delight my soul!
Shall the throne of iniquity have fellowship with You—they who frame and hide their unrighteous doings under [the sacred name of] law?
They band themselves together against the life of the [consistently] righteous and condemn the innocent to death.
But the Lord has become my High Tower and Defense, and my God the Rock of my refuge.
And He will turn back upon them their own iniquity and will wipe them out by means of their own wickedness; the Lord our God will wipe them out.

"So let us not grow weary in well doing, for in due season, we shall reap a harvest, if we faint not." Gal. 6:9,10

Spiritually

He revealed to me that when a woman has an "illegal" abortion, it is between her, the abortionist and God. However, when a woman has a "legal" abortion, it is sanctioned by our elected Government leaders, placing the blood on our hands; as well we are paying for it with our tax dollars and silence. By faith, we all need to break that agreement with abortion (death) over us, our families, our cities and nations!

Whenever a man, woman, doctor, nurse, parent, friend, government or society comes into an agreement with abortion, (by condoning/legalizing it) we are really coming into a covenant with a spirit of murder and death. When we know that abortion is happening in our city, province, state or nation and we do nothing to stop it, we are lining up with that iniquity. Iniquity means injustice, immorality, immoral act, wickedness, evil, sin, and crime. With our apathy and complacency, we tolerate that spirit of human sacrifice.

If you are a former abortion patient, I want to encourage you to contact me, and to speak out. I learned long ago that Jesus Christ/Yeshua took ALL of my guilt, and shame on the cross when I asked God to forgive me, repented of sins, and come into my life. That woman who ignorantly had those abortions was the old me, when I was young, foolish and stupid. I was pressured and lied to, this is how I made the biggest mistakes of my life! Now I am born again, a new creature in Christ...I do not care what people think of me, or how they might judge me. I only care about what GOD thinks of me, and I only want to obey HIS commands while I am on this planet we call Earth.

God has commanded us to WARN the wicked of their wickedness...and if we do not, the blood is on our hands. Ezek. 3:18, 33:8

If you read the early church fathers, they had a fair bit to say about abortion as well. It was a common Greek and Roman practice that they stood firmly against.

There is almost 2000 years of church history backing up the sanctity of human life....and very specifically about abortion.

The church has fought abortion for centuries, and now seems to have fallen asleep. The early church fathers in the first 100-300 years of the church viewed abortion as murder. A document that was discovered in Istanbul in the 1880's called the Didache, or the TEACHING OF THE 12 APOSTLES (TO THE GENTILES) is profound. It is a manuscript copied between 1000-1100 AD that comes from a text that has been placed between about 70 and 150 AD at a time of relative silence in the early church. The Didache is roughly in the same age bracket as the Book of James, which is one of the oldest books in the New Testament. James was written to a Jewish audience; while the Didache was written to new Greek or Gentile converts as they were discipled. It was like an early Christian training reader-primer. You have to remember at this time there was no Bible as we know it today....no definitive New Testament.

What is substantial is what it says in the first part of this short book:

"And the second rule of training is this: you will not murder offspring by means of abortion..."

As I was working on this book back in September of 2014, there was a $140+ million-dollar complex opening in Winnipeg, Manitoba. It is the 'Canadian Human Rights Museum'. When we think of Human Rights, don't you think about the rights of Africans who were forced into slavery, or the rights of First Nations peoples, or the rights of Jews and other ethnic races and injustices to mankind?

I had been corresponding with the staff there, and learned that they have an Exhibit on 'Women's Reproductive Rights' including the Morgentaler Case which opened the floodgates of abortion on demand in our nation. They are showcasing the RIGHT to KILL children before birth! Yet, they do not have anything on the basic Human Right to Life for children in the womb. I have requested to also be able to have an Exhibit on the

RIGHT TO LIFE in there according to Declaration on Human Rights and the Convention on the Rights of the Child, with no response! I felt God wanted me to attend the opening and together with a few others we had a demonstration showing graphic images of aborted children massacred at the hands of abortionists. Where is the RIGHT to LIFE in our nation?

SOME THINGS YOU CAN DO

PRAY, PRAY, PRAY... lay down your life for the least of these...

Go visit your government leaders with the truth on fetal development, showing them the humanity of children in the womb. Tell them that it is a "child with potential," not a potential child. Science confirms this.

Show them the facts on the mental and physical damage to women after abortion by visiting www.afterabortion.org, www.abortionbreastcancer.com **and** www.bcpinstitute.org

Get a copy of the new documentary, "HUSH" and show it wherever you can as it is well done and exposes the Breast Cancer, Cervical Damage and Mental Health issues in the aftermath of abortion. www.hushfilm.com

Write letters to editors...& ask God for wisdom and courage

Go to every PROLIFE March, and event you can...

Go to one of our healing and equipping conferences...

Lay down your life for the least of them; Go in front of the abortion clinics and hospitals who are doing this evil deed, and offer help and alternatives to pregnant women...

Buy lots of copies of this book for libraries, schools, friends and family...

Support prolife apostles and missionaries financially, like me. (I get no salary or wage, walking by faith, as God opens doors)

It is a matter of life and death, remember that.

The Holy Spirit led me to read Jeremiah chapters 2, 18, and 26 then Isaiah 38 while writing this book. Basically, He was showing me that IF we do not turn away from our sins, and the sins of our nation, that God's judgments will come. BUT IF we repent, and turn from these things, He will also repent. The

Lion of the Tribe of JUDAH (the Bride) must ROAR to protect her young... the innocent, to protect our nations, to protect our sons and daughters and future generations from being swallowed up by this dragon, this beast.

As I wrap up this book, I am preparing to bring a case before God, the judge of all things. I want to proceed with expert witnesses joining me. First, we will repent of all judgements we have made about others. We will read scriptures on how Yeshua, paid the penalty for our sins, then we repent again, knowing that His mercy endures forever. Justice is the foundation of His throne. We must begin to enter into the Courts of Heaven, by faith. My charge is against the enemy doing abortions across Canada and globally. First degree murder and the shedding of innocent blood, through induced abortion is the charge. I will ask God for His judgments to come, to stop these heinous crimes against children created in God's image. We will continue to pray for exposure to this diabolical practice, that it would be outlawed once again, and that women, the second victims would be forgiven and healed.

Recently, I met a lawyer who actually wants to challenge the Supreme Court of Canada on the right to Life! I am so excited that finally someone has the courage to do this, and I am assisting him in this effort as a witness and expert on this issue so prevalent in our generation. My hope and prayer is that after 30 years of being a voice for the voiceless, our labour was not in vain, and together we shall see truth and justice prevail, as it is a matter of life and death.

Life on earth is short for us. God loves you, He is merciful, turn from your own ways, and do things His way. Read the Bible daily! He has a purpose and plan for your life. By faith, hear His voice, obey Him and accomplish His will on earth. It will line up with His Word. We are only on this journey for so many years. Will your name be written in the book of Life? Will your record show you laid up more treasures for yourself in the worldly kingdom; or did you lay up more eternal treasures in the heavenly realms for the Kingdom of God?

We need to PRAY big time for more followers and disciples of Christ to get into Law, Media, becoming journalists, Judges, TV and Radio Hosts, Producers, Politicians and Teachers etc. Pray that the Body of Christ would wake up, rise up and take her positions in places of authority for the advancement of the Kingdom of God on earth.

Please pray as we follow Christ in this special assignment as Ambassadors for the King of Kings. Hoping we will make awesome music videos, documentaries and movies to expose the evil and harm of legal abortion and be a strong voice for our aborted children.

Mother Theresa once said, *"Any country that accepts abortion is not teaching its people to love, but to use violence to get what they want. That is why the greatest destroyer of love and peace, is abortion"*

My prayer is that the Body of Christ, His Bride, the Church would begin to roar for the protection of the young, that she will be brave and courageous to take a stand against abortions now, as a united VOICE for the voiceless. Soon the Lord will return to judge the inhabitants of the earth for all this slaughter! Read the Book of Revelation; only those who overcome, shall inherit eternal life in heaven.

"We defeat Satan by the Blood of the Lamb and the word of our testimony and did not love our lives even unto death." Rev. 12:11

"I call heaven and earth as witnesses today against you, that I have set before you life and death, blessing and cursing; therefore choose life, that both you and your children may live;" Deut. 30:19

Thanks for listening!

Endnotes

i   Blackburn, ST. Maternal, Fetal, and Neonatal Physiology. 2nd (2003, page 573, Vanhatalo, S & van Niewuwenhuizen, O. "fetal Pain?" Brain Development.22 (2000)

ii   Moore, K. and Persaud, T. the Developing Human, Clinically Oriented Embryology, 6th Edition, Philadelphia:W.B. Sanders, 1998, p. 333. Valman, H. and Pearson, J. "What the foetus feels," British Medical Journal, January 26, 1980.

iii Mika Gissler, et al., "Pregnancy Associated Deaths in Finland 1987–1994," Acta Obstetrica Gynecal. Scandi 76, 1997, p. 651-657

iv 1 Saccone G, Perriera L, Berghella V. Prior uterine perforation of pregnancy as independent risk factor for preterm birth: a systematic review and meta-analysis. Amer J Obstetrics Gynecology May 2016;214(5):572-591

http://www.ajog.org/article/S0002-9378(15)02596-X/ abstract 2 Shah PS, Zao J. Induced termination of pregnancy and low birthweight and preterm birth: a systematic review and meta-analysis. British J Obstetrics Gynaecology 2009;116:1425-1442. [URL:http://onlinelibrary.wiley.com/ doi/10.1111/j.1471-0528.2009.02278.x/pdf]

Swingle HM, Colaizy TT, Zimmerman MB, et al Abortion and the risk of subsequent preterm birth: a systematic review and meta-analysis. J Reprod Med 2009;54:95-108. [URL: http://johnrodgerssmith.com/MedicalObservations/ Swingle/JRM%20Swingle%20paper%202009.pdf]

Lemmers M, Vershoor MA, Hooker AB, Opmeer BC, Limpens J, Huirne JA, Ankum WM, Mol BW. Dilation and curettage increase the risk of preterm birth in subsequent pregnancies. A systematic review and meta-analysis. Human Reprod. Advanced Access

2015;0(0):1-12 Abstract URL: http://humrep.oxfordjournals. org/content/early/2015/11/02/humrep.dev274.abstrac

v   Citations for *Psychological Risks of Abortion* Fact Sheet

1.   Gissler, Hemminki & Lonnqvist, "Suicides after pregnancy in Finland, 1987-94: register linkage study," *British Journal of Medicine* 313:1431-4,1996; and M. Gissler, "Injury deaths, suicides and homicides associated with pregnancy, Finland 1987-2000," *European J. Public Health* 15(5):459-63,2005.

2.   D. Reardon, *Aborted Women, Silent No More* (Springfield, IL: Acorn Books, 2002).

3.   DC Reardon et. al., "Deaths Associated With Pregnancy Outcome: A Record Linkage Study of Low Income Women," *Southern Medical Journal* 95(8):834-41, Aug. 2002.

4.   B. Garfinkel, et al., "Stress, Depression and Suicide: A Study of Adolescents in Minnesota," *Responding to High Risk Youth* (University of Minnesota: Minnesota Extension Service, 1986); M. Gissler, et. al., "Suicides After Pregnancy in Finland: 1987-94: register linkage study," *British Medical Journal*, 313: 1431-1434, 1996; and N. Campbell, et. al., "Abortion in Adolescence," *Adolescence*, 23:813-823, 1988. See the "Teen Abortion Risks" Fact Sheet at www. theunchoice.com/resources.htm for more information.

5. JR Cougle, DC Reardon & PK Coleman, "Depression Associated With Abortion and Childbirth: A Long-Term Analysis of the NLSY Cohort," *Medical Science Monitor* 9(4):CR105-112, 2003.

6. DC Reardon, JR Cougle, "Depression and unintended pregnancy in the National Longitudinal Study of Youth: a cohort study," *British Medical Journal* 324:151-2, 2002.

7. VM Rue et. al., "Induced abortion and traumatic stress: A preliminary comparison of American and Russian women," *Medical Science Monitor* 10(10): SR5-16, 2004.

8. DC Reardon et. al., "Psychiatric admissions of low-income women following abortions and childbirth," *Canadian Medical Association Journal* 168(10): May 13, 2003.

9. PK Coleman et. al., "State-Funded Abortions Versus Deliveries: A Comparison of Outpatient Mental Health Claims Over Four Years," *American Journal of Orthopsychiatry* 72(1):141-152, 2002.

10. Ashton,"The Psychosocial Outcome of Induced Abortion", *British Journal of Ob & Gyn.* 87:1115-1122, 1980.

11. JR Cougle, DC Reardon, PK Coleman, "Generalized Anxiety Following Unintended Pregnancies Resolved Through Childbirth and Abortion: A Cohort Study of the 1995 National Survey of Family Growth," *Journal of Anxiety Disorders* 19:137-142 (2005).

12. DC Reardon and PK Coleman, "Relative Treatment Rates for Sleep Disorders and Sleep Disturbances Following Abortion and Childbirth: A Prospective Record Based-Study," *Sleep* 29(1):105-106, 2006.

13. DM Fergusson et. al., "Abortion in young women and subsequent mental health," *Journal of Child Psychology and Psychiatry* 47(1): 16-24, 2006.

14. T. Burke with D. Reardon, *Forbidden Grief: The Unspoken Pain of Abortion* (Springfield, IL: Acorn Books, 2002) 189, 293

15. DC Reardon, PG Ney, "Abortion and Subsequent Substance Abuse," *American Journal of Drug and Alcohol Abuse* 26(1):61-75, 2000.

16. PK Coleman et. al., "A history of induced abortion in relation to substance abuse during subsequent pregnancies carried to term," *American Journal of Obstetrics and Gynecology* 1673-8, Dec. 2002.

17. Benedict, et al., "Maternal Perinatal Risk Factors and Child Abuse," *Child Abuse and Neglect* 9:217-224, 1985; P.G. Ney, "Relationship between Abortion and Child Abuse," *Canadian Journal of Psychiatry*, 24:610-620, 1979; Shepard, et al., "Contraceptive Practice and Repeat Induced Abortion: An Epidemiological Investigation," *J. Biosocial Science* 11:289-302, 1979; M. Bracken, "First and Repeated Abortions: A Study of Decision-Making and Delay," *J. Biosocial Science* 7:473-491, 1975; S. Henshaw, "The Characteristics and Prior Contraceptive Use of U.S. Abortion Patients," *Family Planning Perspectives*, 20(4):158-168, 1988; D. Sherman, et al., "The Abortion Experience in Private Practice," *Women and Loss: Psychobiological Perspectives*, ed. W.F. Finn, et al., (New York: Praeger Publishers, 1985) 98-107; E.M. Belsey, et al., "Predictive Factors in Emotional Response to Abortion: King's Termination Study–IV," *Social Science and Medicine* 11:71-82, 1977; E. Freeman, et al., "Emotional Distress Patterns Among Women Having First or Repeat Abortions," *Obstetrics and Gynecology* 55(5):630-636, 1980; C. Berger, et al., "Repeat Abortion: Is it a Problem?" *Family Planning Perspectives* 16(2):70-75 (1984).

18. George Skelton, "Many in Survey Who Had Abortion Cite Guilt Feelings," *Los Angeles Times,* March 19, 1989, p.

28 (question 76). See also Mary K. Zimmerman, *Passage Through Abortion* (New York, Prager Publishers, 1977).

19. David C. Reardon, "The Duty to Screen: Clinical, Legal, and Ethical Implications of Predictive Risk Factors of Post-Abortion Maladjustment," *The Journal of Contemporary Health Law and Policy* 20(2):33-114, Spring 2004.

20. For more on this topic, see T. Burke, *Forbidden Grief: The Unspoken Pain of Abortion* (Springfield, IL: Acorn Books, 2002).

21. Shepard, et al., "Contraceptive Practice and Repeat Induced Abortion: An Epidemiological Investigation," *J. Biosocial Science* 11:289-302, 1979; M. Bracken, "First and Repeated Abortions: A Study of Decision-Making and Delay," *J. Biosocial Science* 7:473-491, 1975; S. Henshaw, "The Characteristics and Prior Contraceptive Use of U.S. Abortion Patients," *Family Planning Perspectives*, 20(4):158-168, 1988; D. Sherman, et al., "The Abortion Experience in Private Practice," *Women and Loss: Psychobiological Perspectives*, ed. W.F. Finn, et al., (New York: Praeger Publishers, 1985) 98-107; E.M. Belsey, et al., "Predictive Factors in Emotional Response to Abortion: King's Termination Study–IV," *Social Science and Medicine* 11:71-82, 1977; E. Freeman, et al., "Emotional Distress Patterns Among Women Having First or Repeat Abortions," *Obstetrics and Gynecology* 55(5):630-636, 1980; C. Berger, et al., "Repeat Abortion: Is it a Problem?" *Family Planning Perspectives* 16(2):70-75 (1984).

22. "Facts in Brief: Induced Abortion," The Alan Guttmacher Institute (www.agi-usa.org), 2002.

23. Speckhard, *Psycho-social Stress Following Abortion*, (Kansas City, MO: Sheed & Ward, 1987); and Belsey, et al., "Predictive Factors in Emotional Response to Abortion: King's Termination Study–IV," *Social Science & Medicine* 11:71-82, 1977. See also P.K. Coleman, V.M. Rue, C.T.

Coyle, "Induced abortion and intimate relationship quality in the Chicago Health and Social Life Survey," Public Health (2009), doi:10, 1016/j.puhe.2009.01.005.

24. Priscilla K. Coleman, et. al., "Associations between voluntary and involuntary forms of perinatal loss and child maltreatment among low income mothers," *Acta Paediatrica* 94, 2005.

25. Benedict, et al., "Maternal Perinatal Risk Factors and Child Abuse," *Child Abuse and Neglect* 9:217-224, 1985; P.G. Ney, "Relationship between Abortion and Child Abuse," *Canadian Journal of Psychiatry*, 24:610-620, 1979. See also Reardon, *Aborted Women, Silent No More* (Springfield, IL: Acorn Books, 2002) 129-30, which describes a case of woman who beat her three year old son to death shortly after an abortion which triggered a "psychotic episode" of grief, guilt, and misplaced anger.

26. Leach, "The Repeat Abortion Patient," *Family Planning Perspectives* 9(1):37-39, 1977; S. Fischer, "Reflection on Repeated Abortions: The meanings and motivations," *Journal of Social Work Practice* 2(2):70-87, 1986; B. Howe, et al., "Repeat Abortion, Blaming the Victims," *Am. J. of Public Health* 69(12):1242-1246, 1979.21. David C. Reardon, "The Duty to Screen: Clinical, Legal, and Ethical Implications of Predictive Risk Factors of Post-Abortion Maladjustment," *The Journal of Contemporary Health Law and Policy* 20(2):33-114, Spring 2004.3. DC Reardon et. al., "Deaths Associated With Pregnancy Outcome: A Record Linkage Study of Low Income Women," *Southern Medical Journal* 95(8):834-41, Aug. 2002.